WordStar for DOS
Made Easy

WordStar for DOS
Made Easy

Walter A. Ettlin

Osborne McGraw-Hill

Berkeley New York St. Louis San Francisco
Auckland Bogotá Hamburg London Madrid
Mexico City Milan Montreal New Delhi Panama City
Paris São Paulo Singapore Sydney
Tokyo Toronto

Osborne **McGraw-Hill**
2600 Tenth Street
Berkeley, California 94710
U.S.A.

For information on translations or book distributors outside of the U.S.A.,
please write to Osborne **McGraw-Hill** at the above address.

WordStar for DOS Made Easy

1234567890 DOC 998765432

ISBN 0-07-881772-2

This is dedicated to my family

Publisher

Kenna S. Wood

Acquisitions Editor

Elizabeth Fisher

Associate Editor

Scott Rogers

Technical Editor

Harriet Serenkin

Copy Editor

Carl Wikander

Proofreaders

Jeff Barash
Emily Ross

Indexer

Valerie Robbins

Computer Designer

Michelle Salinaro

Cover Design

Mason Fong

Contents

Acknowledgments

Thanks to the following people for their time, enthusiasm, and expertise:

- Liz Fisher, Acquisitions Editor
- Scott Rogers, Associate Editor
- Harriet Serenkin, Technical Reviewer
- Madhu Prasher, Project Editor
- Hannah Raiden, Editorial Assistant
- Barry Bergin, Production Supervisor
- Michelle Salinaro, Designer

Thanks, also, to Ann Pharr for always being charming on the phone.
Finally, but most especially, my deepest thanks to my wife, Cynthia, for countless hours of typing, testing, and retyping the manuscript.

Introduction

WordStar is a very flexible word processing program published by WordStar International Corporation. The latest update of WordStar, Version 7.0, has several new features, in addition to various enhancements to earlier additions, such as an improved pull-down menu system that includes virtually all edit commands, mouse support, and an easy-to-use system for designing your own macros.

About This Book

WordStar for DOS Made Easy, Version 7.0, is designed both to help new users become proficient with WordStar and to make it easy for experienced users to familiarize themselves with WordStar for DOS's new features as well as those modified from earlier versions. This book will give you the skills required for most types of general word processing assignments.

WordStar comes with a variety of supplementary programs. Three of these—MailList, Inset, and ProFinder—are discussed in this book. If you maintain a mailing list, you will find MailList a powerful companion program to use with Merge Print. Inset allows you to create, edit, and incorporate graphic images in a WordStar file. ProFinder is for anyone working with a hard disk. If you work with a variety of files—whether just WordStar files or files from database, spreadsheet, or other commercial applications—the sooner you become familiar with ProFinder, the easier your work will be.

This book is not intended to replace the WordStar documentation published by WordStar International. The WordStar manual supplements the command descriptions presented here and introduces other WordStar commands and options not covered in this book. In the back of this book you will find a WordStar command card that summarizes the most commonly used commands in the WordStar manual. You will find it a useful aid whenever you work with WordStar. You may want to remove the card and keep it and this book near your computer for quick reference.

How This Book Is Organized

This book is divided into 20 chapters. Each chapter contains a set of instructions, exercises, and, in many cases, example text to be used in the chapter. If you follow all the instructions, the text displayed on your screen or printed by your printer should match the illustrations in this book.

The appendices will make life easier for both new and experienced users. Appendix A lists WordStar 7.0's new and modified commands, and the chapter where each is discussed. This appendix also contains a summary of mouse commands and shortcuts. Appendix B lists the various reference codes and indicators you'll see on your screen when you use WordStar, plus a list of the ASCII and extended character sets used with personal computers. Appendix C shows you, with examples, how to create a personalized version of WordStar. Appendix D presents the DOS commands that you need to become an efficient WordStar user.

If you are experienced with WordStar, you are already familiar with much of the material in this book. To take quick advantage of version 7.0's new and modified material, you'll want to look first at Appendix A, which lists these enhancements along with references to the chapters that discuss them.

Conventions Used in This Book

WordStar for DOS default values and screens are used in the illustrations throughout this book. Experienced users may wish to modify these values. New users probably will find it advantageous to become familiar with WordStar before customizing it. Keeping the default values means your screens and printouts will match the illustrations in this book as you proceed. (Appendix C tells you how to modify WordStar.)

Here are the typesetting conventions used in this book:

- The Control key, displayed on the keyboard as CTRL, is represented in this book by a caret (^) symbol.

- Text presented in boldface indicates entries you make via the keyboard.

- Words or phrases are italicized when first introduced and defined.

- When the symbol ^ precedes a letter, this tells you to press and hold down the CTRL key while you press the letter key indicated. For example, **^QD** means hold down the CTRL (^) key and press the Q (upper- or lowercase) key; then you can release the CTRL and Q keys before you press the **D** key.

Note to New Users

The code sent by the CTRL (^) key does not register on the screen. It commands WordStar to perform some editing or formatting function, such as setting margins, underlining, or saving a document on the disk. You will use the CTRL key quite frequently when working with WordStar.

Notes to Experienced Users

Even though you are probably very comfortable with the way you are currently using WordStar, try the new commands and the new screens. You may find some easier and more efficient ways to accomplish the word processing tasks that you perform daily. The essence and feel of the original WordStar are available, but the default opening screen (since Version 5.0) offers pull-down menus and the option of selecting commands from these menus using the arrow keys. The traditional menus and commands may be implemented easily by changing the Help level from 4 to 3 or lower.

In general, files created by earlier WordStar releases can be used with Version 7.0 without modification.

Since Version 5.0 of WordStar, the Spell Checking feature is automatically loaded each time you load WordStar. A dictionary that provides definitions as well as allowing you to check spelling is also included now as a part of WordStar.

1

Getting Started

This book makes two assumptions. The first assumption is that you are working with a computer that will run WordStar 7.0, which now means a computer with a hard disk. To run WordStar on a floppy disk system, you must use WordStar version 6.0 or earlier. The second assumption is that you have used WINSTALL to install WordStar on your hard disk.

The way WordStar for DOS works does not vary greatly from one DOS computer to another, but the way printers work with WordStar does. One of the major improvements of WordStar since version 6.0 is its ability to take advantage of the latest printer enhancements, such as selecting from a variety of fonts and font sizes, and printing the complete range of the graphics characters that come with many of the newer printers. Because of the wide variety of printers available, you will probably find it worth while to read your printer manual so that you can use WordStar to take advantage of its full range of printing abilities.

If you are new to WordStar, you will find that WordStar's pull-down menus provide an easy, user-friendly atmosphere for learning word processing. Full mouse support is included for selecting menu options and a variety of Edit screen applications. WordStar's expanded and easy-to-use macro system allows you to accomplish complex operations, such as entering a letterhead that includes your name, address, telephone number, and current date, by pressing a single key.

As always with WordStar, what you see is what you get—which means you see the same formatting on the screen that will appear on paper when your document is printed. By using the Preview command (Chapter 9), you can even see a graphical screen that includes different font sizes, and full-page portrait and landscape formatting.

If you are an experienced WordStar user, you will find all the traditional menus and commands that you expect. Enhancements such as expanded macro capabilities will make using the program even easier. And new features, such as fax support, give you even more flexibility. The fax feature lets you prepare your files for immediate fax transmission directly from your computer—provided, of course, that you have the proper hardware installed.

WordStar Terminology and Features

Before getting into the details of creating and editing a document in WordStar, it will be helpful to go through some of the terminology and features of WordStar.

Default Values

Default values are the settings WordStar uses unless you change them. In the case of line spacing, for instance, WordStar uses the default value 1 for single spacing. WordStar also supplies default values for margins, tabs, and other layout characteristics. You can accept these default values or change them to suit your needs. Default values will be discussed under the appropriate topics as you work through this book.

Commands

WordStar uses two general categories of commands for entering text into a file: *Edit commands* and *dot commands*. In general, Edit commands take effect instantly and you can see their effects on the screen—for example, when you reformat a paragraph. Dot commands, on the other hand, generally affect your work when it is printed, such as the command that sets page margins.

Edit Commands

The following are a few things you should know about Edit commands:

- You enter Edit commands from the keyboard. You can also enter most of them from the pull-down menus. Many commonly used Edit commands are executed by using the keypad arrows or function keys.

- To enter commands from the keyboard, you frequently use the CTRL key, pressing it and holding it down while pressing one or two other keys. When you do this, the caret symbol (^) will appear on the screen preceding the letter keys you have pressed. For example, if you press CTRL followed by **Q** and **Y**, ^QY appears on the screen. That is also how those keystrokes are expressed in this book. Other examples are ^Q-DEL and ^QT ENTER.

- Most Edit commands begin as soon as you give the command. If additional information is needed, a dialog box is displayed where you can enter the required information.

Dot Commands

Dot commands perform a variety of functions generally related to printing and formatting a document. All dot commands begin with a period (hence the name, dot command) and are immediately followed by two letters—for example, .op or .LS. The general requirements for dot commands are as follows:

- The period must be in column 1 of the page.
- The two letters can be uppercase or lowercase.
- Only text that is part of the dot command can be on the line with the command.
- After each completed dot command, press ENTER.

Windows/Menus/Dialog Boxes

Since version 5.0, WordStar has used pull-down menus, windows, and dialog boxes. A *window* includes both menus and dialog boxes. A *menu* is a window from which you make a selection. A *dialog box* is a window that both provides information to you and lets you provide information to WordStar.

In version 7.0 you can select virtually all of WordStar's edit and dot commands from menus. In some cases, when you select a command from a menu, something happens immediately. For example, if you press **X** from the File menu, you immediately exit WordStar and return to DOS. In other cases, the command produces a dialog box that may give you some information and will always ask you for additional information. The dialog box may offer a suggested response you can accept or replace, or it may ask you to type a response. An example of a dialog box is the Document box you get when you press **D** from the File menu as shown in Figure 1-1. This dialog box asks for one item of information: the name of the file you wish to open.

When you are in a dialog box you can do the following:

- Use WordStar's editing commands to enter or edit information, just as if you were editing a file.

- Make selections from a directory using the keypad arrow keys to highlight the filenames, and then press ENTER to select the file.

- Press TAB or the DOWN ARROW to move the cursor to the next field, or, if the cursor is in the last field, to accept the displayed entries.

Figure 1-1.   *Window displayed when Open Document is selected*

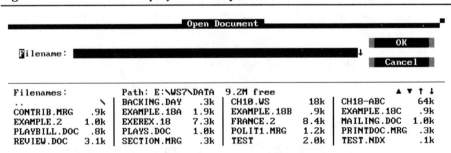

1

- Press SHIFT-TAB or the UP ARROW to move the cursor to the previous field.

- Press F10 to accept the entries in the fields and to carry out the command.

Note

When you press the ENTER *key, the cursor moves from field to field through a dialog box. The function of the* ENTER *key can, however, be changed to do what the* F10 *key does—accept the displayed values and return to the Edit screen. The command to make this change is* ^O-ENTER. *Press* ^O-ENTER *again to return the* ENTER *key to its original use.*

- Press ESC to return to the previous screen or to the file being edited without accepting any changes made in the window.

- Use ^R to replace values that were accidentally deleted from a field.

Whether dialog boxes are opened using traditional commands (explained below) or commands selected from pull-down menus, they look and work the same.

Selecting Commands

Since WordStar 5.0 you have been able to select a command from a menu by highlighting the command and pressing ENTER, or by using traditional WordStar commands such as ^KO. With WordStar 7.0 you have two additional options: You can select a command using an *accelerator key* or using a mouse.

Accelerator keys are single keys, displayed on pull-down menus in reverse video, or in a different color on a color monitor. You can press them to select a command, display a second command window, or display a dialog box. Figure 1-2 shows the WordStar Edit screen with the File menu displayed. The letters in reverse video or color (for example, S for Save) are accelerator keys.

Note

The accelerator keys are not always uppercase. In the Change Printer option, the lowercase h is the accelerator key.

A command followed by three dots will open a dialog box or window. You will also see on many of the pull-down menus the symbol ▶. Selecting

Figure 1-2.   *File menu from the Edit screen*

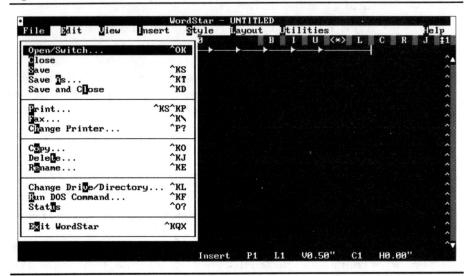

an option with this symbol produces a second menu. Along the right edge of the menu are WordStar's traditional commands. You can use these keys to select a command whether or not the pull-down menus are displayed.

Traditional Command Menus

Traditionally, the edit commands have been organized on four menus. The commands to display these menus and the menu title are shown below. Once you begin entering text into WordStar, you can display and examine these menus by pressing the commands listed below.

Command	Menu Title
CTRL-O	Onscreen Format
CTRL-Q	Quick
CTRL-K	Block and Save
CTRL-P	Print Controls

The traditional menus of WordStar for DOS are in the same style as those in earlier versions of WordStar. The pull-down menus organize the commands differently, but the commands themselves are still the same.

Throughout this book you will be asked to "select" a command to perform a function. You can use whichever option you wish to select a command. For example, to mark the beginning of a block, you can enter **^KB**, or use a function key (SHIFT-F9), or open the Edit menu and use the arrow keys to select ^KB, or use a mouse to mark the block directly.

Note

As you work through this book, you will note that section headings for commands show the key(s) you press to select the commands. Since there is more than one way to select most commands, the section heading shows the most efficient method. For example, to delete a word you can press one key, F6 (which is shown in the heading), or press the traditional two-key command ^T. A complete list of traditional commands is on the command card at the back of the book. Most of the traditional commands are also on the pull-down menus.

Changes and Enhancements to WordStar

A variety of changes and enhancements have been made in WordStar for DOS. They are listed in Table 1-1 and discussed throughout the book.

Table 1-1. *New and Enhanced WordStar Features*

New Feature	Chapter
Expanded pull-down menus	1
Mouse support	1
EMS support	1
Operation of lists	3
Hide dot commands and screen settings	3
Write ASCII File	4
Unmark Block	7
Mark Previous Block	7
Write Block to ASCII	7
Copy to/from Clipboard	11
Go To Style	12
Insert graphics	19

Mouse Support

You can use a mouse with WordStar 7.0. If you have a mouse installed and WordStar is loaded, you will see a small rectangular pointer on the screen. The mouse works with WordStar in standard edit mode and with Preview, but not with the other companion programs. Preview is the WordStar feature that allows you to view multiple pages, enlarged or smaller prints, and other special WordStar functions. Preview is discussed in detail in Chapter 9. Note, however, that Inset has its own mouse support feature. Inset is the WordStar companion program that lets you create or capture graphic images to enhance your WordStar documents. Inset is discussed in Chapter 19. If you are experienced working with a mouse, you won't have difficulties using it with WordStar. If you are new to the mouse, take a few minutes to practice; you'll soon feel quite comfortable with it.

When each WordStar feature is discussed, you will be told how to use the mouse with that feature. In addition, a summary of mouse commands is on the command card. Here are the terms used when describing how to use the mouse:

Click	Place the cursor on an item and press the left mouse button.
Double-click	Place the cursor on an item and press the left mouse button quickly twice.
Drag	Hold down the left mouse button and move the mouse.
Shift-click	Hold down the SHIFT key while pressing the left mouse button.
Ctrl-click	Hold down the CTRL key while pressing the left mouse button.

Memory Support

WordStar now takes advantage of expanded memory specification (EMS). It automatically detects whether or not your computer has expanded memory and uses it, when appropriate, with any of WordStar's features. For example, if more than 80K of expanded memory is available, Preview will use it. You can have Preview run with two windows open, as explained in Chapter 9.

Loading WordStar

Turn on your computer system and make sure you are on the right drive. Then type **WS**. (In the instructions in this book, characters you type on the keyboard are expressed in boldface.) You will see the copyright message. Then you will see WordStar's Opening screen as shown in Figure 1-3. The filenames displayed on your screen will, of course, be different.

Tip

Before loading WordStar, make a directory on your hard disk where you will keep the files you enter while working with this book. Appendix D has a brief discussion on how to use the DOS MKDIR (make directory) command.

The opening screen has four pull-down menus—File, Utility, Additional, and Help. To select a pull-down menu, you can use the LEFT ARROW and RIGHT ARROW keys, or press a highlighted letter (in uppercase or lowercase)—**F, U, A,** or **H.** For example, to select the File menu, type **F** and press ENTER. A discussion of some basic features on the menus follows. Later chapters discuss other features.

Figure 1-3.   *WordStar's Opening screen*

```
                                  WordStar
 File      Utilities    Additional                                        Help




 Filenames:              Path: F:\WS7\DATA    295k free
    ..            \  | ARROW.HP      .3k | CHEX.HP       .5k | DATA          .3k
 EXAMPLE.11B   2.9k | EXAMPLE.2    1.2k | EXAMPLE.3     .6k | EXAMPLE.6A   1.4k
 EXAMPLE.9     2.3k | EXAMPLE.BAK  1.0k | EXAMPLE.Z    4.5k | FRANCE.2     8.2k
 FRANCE.BAK    9.6k | ILLUS6.2      .4k | MAILING.DOC  1.0k | OUTLINE.WS7  8.3k
 PLAYBILL.DOC   .8k | PLAYS.DOC    1.0k | PLEAD.HP      .1k | README.BAT    .0k
 README.TXT     37k | REVIEW.DOC   3.1k | SHADE.HP      .0k |
```

Using the File Menu

To open the File menu, you can select **F** from the menu bar, or you can use a simpler way of selecting this most commonly used menu—just press ENTER. The screen is like that in Figure 1-4. The File menu has five sections, each of which contains commands that are related.

When you select a command from a menu, it executes as soon as you press the letter—either by performing its function or by displaying the dialog box where you enter the necessary additional information. The following discussion describes the File options as they appear on the menu.

Figure 1-4.   *File menu from the Opening screen*

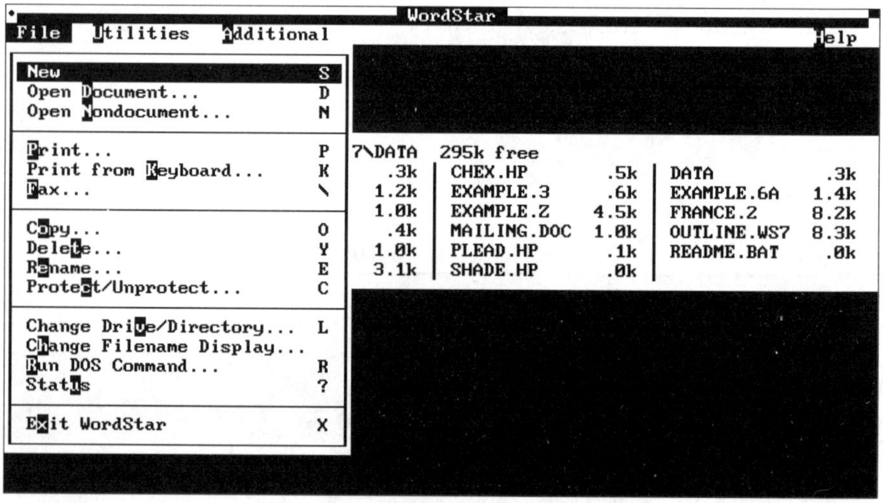

1

Open a Document (S, D, N)

S
New. Select **S** to open a file and begin entering text. You enter the name of the file when you select one of the save commands.

D
Open Document. Select **D** to edit an existing file or open a new file. For a new file, you will have to enter a filename before you can begin entering text.

N
Open Nondocument. Select **N** for nondocument file when you want to create a data file for merge printing, or write or edit a program using a computer language such as BASIC. You will have to enter a filename.

Print and Fax Commands (P, K, \)

P
Print. Select **P** to print the files you create.

K
Print from keyboard. Select **K** to print directly to your printer just as if you were using a typewriter. This is useful for addressing envelopes or writing short memos.

\
Fax. Select \ to prepare a document to be sent by facsimile. Of course, you must have the necessary hardware and software installed in your computer to use the fax feature.

Note

Print is discussed in detail in Chapter 4. Fax is discussed in Chapter 9.

File Commands (O, Y, E, C, L, h, R, ?)

The File commands are included in the next two sections of the File menu. The first three file commands, Copy (O), Delete (Y), and Rename (E), are DOS commands you can access through WordStar. Again, this book will provide more detail on these commands when you are actually working with files.

C   Protect/Unprotect. Select **C** to place a file in protected status to avoid accidental changes to it.

L   Change Drive/Directory. Select **L** to change the drive or directory. Remember to use directories to indicate the path. See Appendix D for a discussion of paths and directories.

Note

When you installed WordStar, you had the option of indicating the available disk drives. Your entry with the L command must be one of those listed drives, or a window will open stating "Not a valid directory path."

h   Change Filename Display. Select **h** to change the filename display. You will see a window like the one shown here:

```
████████████ Change File Listings ████████████                    ■

Change file listings to include only filenames that match:      ▓▓▓ OK ▓▓▓

                    ????????.???                                ▓ Cancel ▓

        Wildcard characters * and ? may be used.
```

Note

*Use standard DOS filename conventions for the filename. See Appendix D for a discussion on using the wildcards ? and * in naming files.*

R   Run DOS Command. Select **R** to leave WordStar and run other commands or programs from DOS. When you are finished, press any key to return to WordStar.

?   Status. Select **?** for information about the computer's memory. An example of the screen display is shown in Figure 1-5.

Figure 1-5. *WordStar statistics available on the Status window*

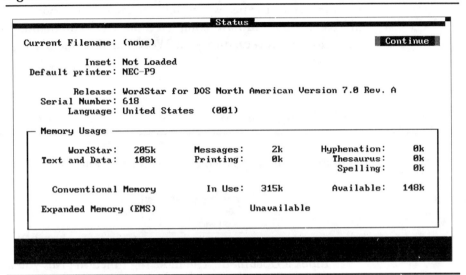

Exiting WordStar

There are two ways to exit WordStar and return to DOS. One takes you back to the DOS prompt, and the other allows you to use a DOS command within WordStar.

- To leave WordStar and return to the DOS prompt, press **X**. If you use this command and then wish to reenter WordStar, you must type **WS** at the prompt and press ENTER. You must then load a document before you can begin working. The best use of this command is when you are finished with your WordStar session and want to work with another program or turn your computer off.

- If you need to enter a DOS command but you still want to work on your WordStar document, press **R**. This will allow you to temporarily leave your WordStar document and enter DOS. For example, if you are in the process of creating a WordStar document and you realize you did not create a directory or subdirectory to put it in, pressing **R** lets you enter the necessary DOS command to create the needed directory. After you have completed the DOS command, you can press any key to return to your WordStar document and resume work on it.

Using the Utilities Menu

Select **U** in the menu bar to display the Utilities menu shown below.

I   Index a Document. The indexing function gives you a fast
               method to index the documents you write. Indexing is
               covered in Chapter 15.

T   Table of Contents. This command lets you build the table
               of contents as you enter a document and easily print the
               results. This option is covered in Chapter 15.

M   A macro is a way to create your own commands. This topic
               is covered in Chapter 14. Note the symbol ▶ following
               Macros. When this symbol is shown on any menu, it
               indicates the selection will open a second menu.

Using the Additional Menu

Select **A** in the menu bar to display the Additional menu. You will then have access to three supplementary programs provided with WordStar 7.0: MailList, TelMerge, and Star Exchange. MailList is discussed in Chapter 18. TelMerge and Star Exchange are not described in this book. You can read about them in *WordStar Professional: The Complete Reference,* by Carole Boggs

1

Matthews and Martin S. Matthews (Berkeley, CA: Osborne/McGraw-Hill, 1989).

Help Menu

Select **H** to see the Help menu shown here:

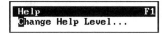

Help (F1)

When you are entering or editing a WordStar file, pressing F1 provides help on the topic you are currently working with. For example, to receive help on a particular command, highlight that command on a pull-down menu and press F1. As you go through the topics in this book, select Help to review the information supplied. Keep in mind help is available by pressing F1 regardless of whether you are in the Edit screen, a pull-down menu, or a dialog box.

Change Help Level

WordStar's screen display is determined by the *help level* in effect. The default screen is help level 4, which offers command selections from the new pull-down menus. Help levels 3 through 0 offer the traditional WordStar screens. As you decrease the help level from 3 to 0, you get progressively less on-screen help and a greater portion of the screen available for text. The help available by pressing F1 does not change.

To change the help level, press **H** for help and then **C** for Change Help Level. The dialog box shown in Figure 1-6 is displayed. You can explore these levels at your convenience.

Figure 1-6.   *Help Level dialog box*

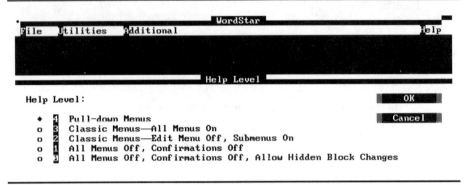

As you become more proficient with WordStar, you may wish to reduce the help level on your screen. Note the selection procedure on Figure 1-6, which is standard on all windows. When you must select one of several options, a diamond is next to the one that is already selected. Open circles are next to options not currently selected.

The screens in this book were produced with commands selected from help level 4, the pull-down menus. You will therefore most likely find it convenient to use level 4 while working with this book.

Working with the Edit Screen

In Chapter 2 you will enter a document. Here you will look at the features you will use as you enter or edit a file in WordStar. To begin, select New from the File menu, and press ENTER.

Default Screen

Figure 1-7 shows the WordStar screen after you open a file but before you enter any text. It provides a name for each item of information. The idea is to give you an overview of the cryptic information available on WordStar's

1

Figure 1-7.   *WordStar's Edit screen*

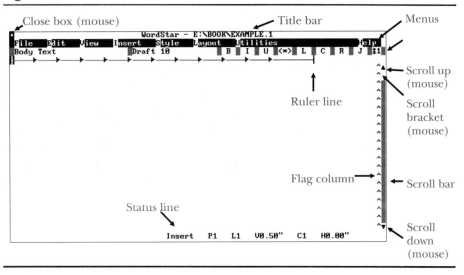

Edit screen while you are entering or editing a document. The information will become more meaningful as you become aware of and use the command options available to control the presentation of the documents you create.

Each line of the document has a variety of basic information. As you enter a document into WordStar, some of this information (such as cursor position, font, and so on) will change to reflect the current state of your data entry.

Note

Figure 1-7 shows the WordStar screen with a mouse installed. There are a few features in this figure that do not appear on the screen if a mouse is not installed. These are noted where the word mouse *is enclosed in parentheses.*

Title Bar

The *title bar* has the name of the file you are entering or editing, along with the name of the disk drive and directory containing the file. The display of the drive letter and the directory name before the filename is called the *path*. In this case the path is E:/BOOK; the filename is EXAMPLE1. On the far left is the *close box*. Double-clicking on the close box saves your file and returns you to the Opening screen.

Menu Bar

The *menu bar* shows the menus you can open to select WordStar commands. All of these menus give you access to additional menus so that, in WordStar 7.0, virtually every WordStar Edit and dot command is accessible from here. Notice there is a File menu on the Edit screen, just as there was on the Opening screen; these two File menus contain different options.

To access a menu from this Edit screen, hold down the ALT key while you press the highlighted letter of the desired menu. Try this now to display the File menu. Press ALT-F, and you will have a screen like that in Figure 1-8. Compare it to the File menu from the Opening screen in Figure 1-4.

Style Bar

The *style bar* serves two functions. One, it tells you that style features such as the font, left or right justification, underlining, and so on, are in effect in

Figure 1-8.   *File menu from the Edit screen*

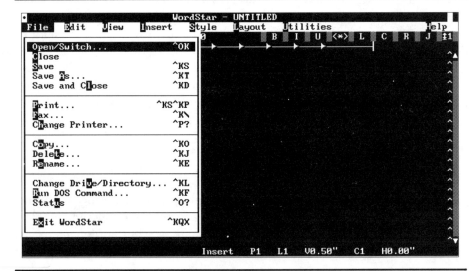

1

your document at the position of the cursor. Two, if you use a mouse, it lets you select a feature on the style bar with a click of the mouse.

The left end of the style bar in Figure 1-7 shows the paragraph style being used, Body Text, which is WordStar's default. Next is the font, Draft 10 (the font is determined by the printer you have installed). The next portion displays B, I, and U. These three options allow you to select from WordStar's most commonly used print features—Bold, Italic, and Underline. The intensity of the next item, *, indicates whether style features on the screen are turned on or off: Bold means on; regular intensity means off. The next group of options, L, C, R, and J, tell you which alignment feature is in effect. L, C, and R stand for Left, Center, and Right justification. J stands for Justified, meaning text on both the left and right margins is aligned—as the text on this page, for example. The default value L (for Left justified) means all lines are aligned on the left. The last item, the 1 on the far right, shows that single spacing is in effect.

Status Line

At the bottom of the screen is the *status line*. It indicates the position of the cursor in the file, along with some other basic information. Starting on the right, it tells you if insert is on or off. When you see "Insert," it means you are in insert mode. Press the Insert key (INS); the status line changes to "Ins-Off," and you are in overtype mode.

The next five items are page number (P1), line number (L1), vertical distance from the top of the page (V0.50"), column number (C1), and the horizontal distance from the left margin (H0.00"). All of these items will change continually as you enter text.

When certain WordStar commands are in use, a few other items are shown on the status line. Your attention will be drawn to these when the commands are discussed.

The ruler line sets the position of the left and right edges for the text you enter. The default values give you a 6 1/2-inch width for text entry. The ▶ symbols on the ruler line show the default tab settings. Chapter 5 is devoted to the ruler line; there you will see how to change these default values, as well as how to use many other commands that affect the ruler line.

Scroll Bar

Two columns along the right side of the screen have useful information. The bracket on the *scroll bar* gives you a quick indication of where you are in the file relative to the top or bottom. Since no file is currently loaded, the bracket in Figure 1-7 is at the top of the scroll bar. The usefulness of this feature will be more apparent when you work with a file. Also notice the up pointer at the top of the scroll bar and the down pointer at the bottom of the scroll bar. Clicking on these will scroll the screen up or down one line at a time through the file you are editing.

Flag Column

The *flag column* shows which lines contain dot commands, carriage returns, page breaks, and other information pertaining to your file. The details of all the features pertaining to the flag column, scroll bar, and other items of information will be discussed when the edit and dot commands that affect them are introduced.

All of the lines shown in Figure 1-7 are displayed on the Edit screen by default. But any combination or all of them may be eliminated from the screen to allow more room for the text you are entering. If you are new to WordStar, you will find these lines useful until you become familiar with WordStar's commands. Even if you are an experienced WordStar user, you may wish to retain these lines until you become familiar with the information they contain.

With the background presented in this chapter, you are now ready to begin entering and editing a WordStar 7.0 document.

Exercises

1. Examine the pull-down menus on both the Opening screen and the Edit screen. Note the differences. Press ESC to close a menu.

2. If you have a mouse installed, use the mouse to display and close menus.

1

3. From the pull-down menus, select some of the commands that are followed by an ellipsis (three periods). Examine the dialog boxes that appear.

4. From any menu, select a command that is followed by a ▶. Note the differences between selecting a command followed by a ▶ and one followed by an ellipsis.

2

Document Entry and Cursor Movement

In Chapter 1, "Getting Started," you opened the WordStar Edit screen and were introduced to selecting a menu. You also examined all the elements and information lines of the default screen, help level 4. Now you will take the next step: opening a document file and entering text into it.

Experienced users will remember that in all earlier versions of WordStar text was aligned vertically at both the left and right margins. In WordStar 7.0 the default text entry format is left justified only.

Note

Creating a Document File

At the Opening screen, display the File menu and, with New highlighted, press ENTER; the Edit screen appears. In the title bar following "WordStar" is the filename, UNTITLED. You will give the file a name when you finish the text entry and save the file. Using the text in Example 2 at the end of this chapter, just start typing. Don't press ENTER at the end of a line as you would on a typewriter—only press ENTER at the end of each paragraph. WordStar's word wrap feature, which is on when you load WordStar, causes text that would extend past the right margin to automatically wrap around to the left margin of the next line. To skip a line between paragraphs, simply press ENTER again. For now, don't worry about any mistakes; you'll take care of those shortly.

As you are typing, notice the following:

- WordStar automatically hyphenates words to avoid having too much space at the end of a line. Hyphenation is discussed in Chapter 6.
- The < character is displayed in the flag column each time you press ENTER. This symbol indicates that ENTER was pressed on that line. It identifies, or flags, the end of any paragraph, the insertion of a blank line, or short lines of text, such as lines in a table of data.

When you have finished entering Example 2, your screen will be similar to Figure 2-1.

Moving the Cursor Around the Screen

Now that you've entered some material into WordStar, you will next prepare for another major function of word processing: editing. To edit the text you see on the screen, you want to be able to quickly move your cursor to any position on the screen. You can do this using the keypad or other key combinations discussed in this chapter. If you are using a standard keyboard, the numeric keypad doubles as the cursor movement keypad. If you are using an extended keyboard, you have a set of cursor movement keys in addition to a numeric keypad. Both types of cursor movement keys are illustrated in Figure 2-2.

Also, if you have a mouse installed on the computer, you can use that to quickly place the cursor at any position on the screen. As each cursor movement operation is discussed, try it by moving the cursor within the material you just entered.

2

Figure 2-1. *The Example 2 text on the screen*

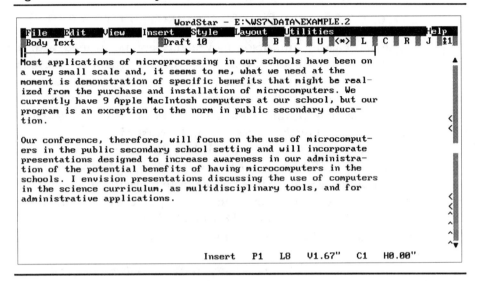

Figure 2-2. *The standard keyboard and extended keyboard pads*

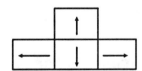

Cursor movement keys
Standard keyboard

Cursor movement keys
Extended keyboard

Moving with the Arrow Keys
(RIGHT ARROW, LEFT ARROW, UP ARROW, DOWN ARROW)

The most common cursor movements are performed with a single keystroke using the cursor movement keys on the right of your keyboard. For example, to move the cursor up, down, left, or right, press the arrow key that points in that direction; the cursor will move line by line or letter by letter. Holding down one of the arrow keys moves the cursor repeatedly in the direction indicated by the arrow. When the cursor is at the extreme right of a line and you press the RIGHT ARROW key, the cursor moves to the left end of the line below. If the next line below a text line is a blank line, pressing the DOWN ARROW key will also cause the cursor to move to the left end of the line below. Finally, notice that you cannot move past the end of the text you are entering. In Figure 2-1 you see the symbol ^ in the flag column; this symbol indicates the end of the document.

Note

If you use a standard keyboard, loading WordStar automatically sets the numeric keypad to perform these cursor movements. If you should accidentally press the NUM LOCK *(number lock) key, pressing the arrow keys will cause the number on each key to be inserted in the document. Should this happen, press* NUM LOCK *again to toggle the keypad's cursor-movement function back into operation.*

Moving to Top or Bottom of Screen (HOME, END)

Press the HOME key and then the END key. As you see, in addition to moving the cursor a single character or line at a time, you can move it directly to the top-left corner of the screen by pressing HOME and to the bottom of the screen (or file if the file does not extend to the bottom of the screen) by pressing the END key.

Moving Left or Right One Word
(^LEFT ARROW, ^RIGHT ARROW)

Now place the cursor at the left end of any line of text. Press ^RIGHT ARROW four or five times and notice how the cursor jumps to the first letter of the word to the right. Now place the cursor at the right end of any line and press ^LEFT ARROW several times. Notice how the cursor moves to the first letter of the word to the left.

Moving to Left or Right End of Line (^F9, ^F10)

Press ^F9 to move the cursor to the left end of the line. Then press ^F10 to move the cursor to the right end of a line. Practice by moving the cursor to any position in a paragraph and then trying these two commands.

Note

When you press a function key, either alone or simultaneously with the CTRL, SHIFT, *or* ALT *key, you are using a macro. The use of macros is a major added feature of WordStar for DOS. Chapter 14 describes how you can edit existing macros and how to write your own macros.*

Moving to Beginning or End of File (^HOME, ^END)

In addition to moving the cursor short distances, you can move it quickly to the beginning or end of a file. With the cursor in any position in a file, move directly to the beginning of the file by pressing ^HOME. To move to the end of the file, press ^END. You will find these commands useful when you are working with long files. Another cursor movement command, moving forward or backward to a specific page of the file, will be discussed in Chapter 6.

Moving to a Specific Character (^QG, ^QH)

You can also move the cursor to any character in your file. To try this, move the cursor to the beginning of the first word of the second paragraph. Hold down the CTRL key and press **Q**. Now press **G**. (^QG is the command for a forward search.) The top few lines on the screen clear, and the following dialog box appears:

```
Go to Character: █
    Esc to Cancel
```

If you pause between pressing ^Q and pressing G, the Quick menu is displayed. If this happens, you can still press G to complete the command. This is true for any of WordStar's traditional commands–those that start with ^K, ^O, ^P, or ^Q.

Type a lowercase **w**. The cursor immediately moves to the first *w* it finds—in this example, the first letter of the word *will*. This WordStar option is referred to as *case sensitive*. Here it does make a difference if the letter you ask WordStar to find is uppercase or lowercase. If you asked WordStar to find a capital *W*, the entire paragraph would be searched, the cursor would go to the end of the paragraph, and the following message would be displayed:

```
Can't find: W                          Continue
```

Following the same procedure, use **^QH** to search backward to a specified character. Note that if you quickly enter a character after you press **^QG** or **^QH**, the cursor movement will occur without the Go to Character dialog box being displayed.

You can use the menus to arrive at the same dialog box. Press ALT-E to display the Edit menu as shown in Figure 2-3. About halfway down the menu is the Go to Character command. The ellipsis (...) after the command tells you that a dialog box will be opened. Pressing G displays the same dialog box you saw when you pressed **^QG**.

Moving to Punctuation Marks and Numbers

The following cursor movement options are extensions of the previous options. In addition to moving to letters, you can move to punctuation marks, numbers, or any character displayed on the screen. For example, entering **^QG** and a period in response to the "Go to Character:" prompt moves the cursor directly to the next period character. Usually the next period is at the end of the sentence in which the cursor rests, but it may come earlier or later, depending on how the sentence is punctuated. Pressing ENTER in response to the prompt causes the cursor to move to the end of the paragraph (if **^QG**

2

Figure 2-3.   *The Edit menu*

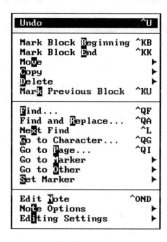

```
 Undo                     ^U

 Mark Block Beginning  ^KB
 Mark Block End        ^KK
 Move                    ►
 Copy                    ►
 Delete                  ►
 Mark Previous Block   ^KU

 Find...               ^QF
 Find and Replace...   ^QA
 Next Find             ^L
 Go to Character...    ^QG
 Go to Page...         ^QI
 Go to Marker            ►
 Go to Other             ►
 Set Marker              ►

 Edit Note             ^OND
 Note Options            ►
 Editing Settings        ►
```

was pressed), or to the line above the beginning of the paragraph (if **^QH** was pressed).

Note

If you ask WordStar to find the character the cursor is on, the cursor will not move in response to ^QG (forward search), but it will move in response to ^QH (backward search).

Using the Mouse to Position the Edit Cursor

To use the mouse to move the Edit cursor, just move the mouse so that its cursor moves to the position you want on the screen. Click the mouse, and the blinking cursor (your Edit cursor) is now under the letter at that position. Try this a few times by moving the cursor to the beginning and end of a paragraph. Then move the mouse cursor to any position you like on the screen. Click the mouse, and you see the Edit cursor stays at that position.

Figure 2-4.   *The Save As window*

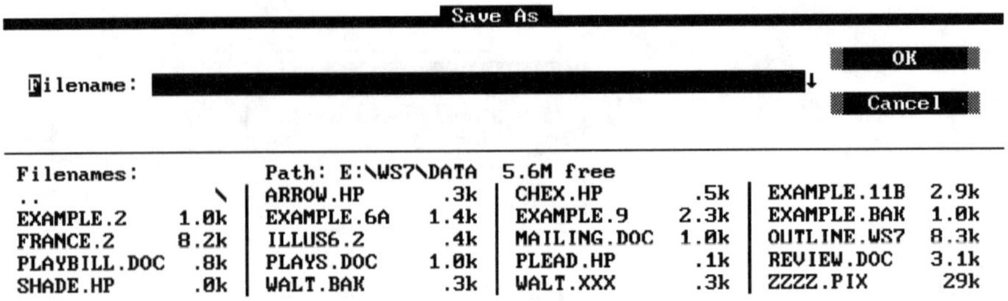

```
                                  Save As
 ┌──────────────────────────────────────────────────┐  ╔════════╗
 │ilename:                                         ↓  ║   OK   ║
                                                       ╚════════╝
                                                       ╔════════╗
                                                       ║ Cancel ║
                                                       ╚════════╝

 Filenames:              Path: E:\WS7\DATA  5.6M free
 ..              \   ARROW.HP       .3k │ CHEX.HP       .5k │ EXAMPLE.11B  2.9k
 EXAMPLE.2    1.0k   EXAMPLE.6A    1.4k │ EXAMPLE.9    2.3k │ EXAMPLE.BAK  1.0k
 FRANCE.2     8.2k   ILLUS6.2       .4k │ MAILING.DOC  1.0k │ OUTLINE.WS7  8.3k
 PLAYBILL.DOC  .8k   PLAYS.DOC     1.0k │ PLEAD.HP      .1k │ REVIEW.DOC   3.1k
 SHADE.HP      .0k   WALT.BAK       .3k │ WALT.XXX      .3k │ ZZZZ.PIX      29k
```

Saving a File

When you have finished working with Example 2 and are ready to save the file, press ALT-F to display the File menu. Select Save As, and the Save As window, shown in Figure 2-4, is displayed.

In the space for Filename, type **Example.2** and press ENTER. The material you have just typed will be saved on the directory shown by the path on your screen. In Figure 2-4 the path is E:\WS7\DATA. The path shows the directory you are logged into. If you want a file saved on a directory other than the logged directory, you must precede the filename with the complete path, starting with the letter designating the disk drive. When the save is complete, you will return to the Opening screen. Open the File menu next and select **X** to return to DOS. (Saving documents will be discussed further in Chapter 4.)

Now that you have entered a document and can move easily around the screen, you're ready to begin the next step: editing. That's the topic covered in Chapter 3, where you will use this example text again.

Exercises

1. Using the file EXAMPLE.2, practice moving the cursor to a predetermined position, using as few keystrokes as possible.

2. Practice using the mouse to move the cursor quickly on the Edit screen. Also, use the mouse to display various menus and make selections from the menus.

Example 2

Most applications of microprocessing in our schools have been on a very small scale and, it seems to me, what we need at the moment is demonstration of specific benefits that might be realized from the purchase and installation of microcomputers. We currently have 9 Apple MacIntosh computers at our school, but our program is an exception to the norm in public secondary education.

Our conference, therefore, will focus on the use of microcomputers in the public secondary school setting and will incorporate presentations designed to increase awareness in our administration of the potential benefits of having microcomputers in the schools. I envision presentations discussing the use of computers in the science curriculum, as multidisciplinary tools, and for administrative applications.

3

Editing a Document

Changing or editing an existing document is probably the single most useful function of word processing. You will use a wide range of functions during this editing process. The full extent of WordStar's edit functions will be introduced here and in the next few chapters. In this chapter, you will concentrate on inserting and deleting data, reformatting paragraphs, and changing the line spacing. Also covered in this chapter are screen settings, which allow you to control what information lines—menu bar, style bar, and so on—display on the screen.

Begin by loading WordStar (if necessary). When the Opening screen appears, press ENTER or **F** to display the File menu. If you are not logged into the directory that contains your file, press the accelerator key (**v**) to display the Change Drive\Directory window. Enter the appropriate path to the drive and subdirectory that contains the EXAMPLE.2 file. (If *path* and *subdirectory* are unfamiliar terms to you, check Appendix D. It has a brief explanation of several DOS commands that are useful with WordStar.)

When you have displayed the directory containing the file you wish to load, you are ready to select the file by one of the two methods discussed in the following section.

Selecting a File to Edit

Remember

Use the following procedure whenever you have entered and saved a document and then want to reload it so you can edit it.

First select your file using the File menu. To do this, press the letter **F** to display the File menu; then select the option **D**. As soon as you press **D**, the Open Document dialog box shown in Figure 3-1 is displayed.

Now type the name of the Example.2 file as it appears in the directory. (Although filenames always appear in uppercase in the directory, you may use either upper- or lowercase letters when you enter the filename in WordStar dialog boxes.) Press ENTER, and the text that you previously entered as Example 2 will be displayed on your screen.

To try the second method of selecting a file, return to WordStar's Opening screen. To do this, press ALT-F to display the File menu and select Close.

Note

If you typed anything in the file while it was open, the Close File window will appear and give you the option to Save, Abandon, or Cancel. Save will be in bold, the selected option; press ENTER to save. To change the selected option, press A for Abandon or C for Cancel; the new selection will be highlighted. Press ENTER to process your selection. Save keeps the file with whatever changes you made. Abandon keeps the file as it was before it was opened. Cancel returns you to the Edit screen for further editing.

Figure 3-1.   *The Open Document dialog box*

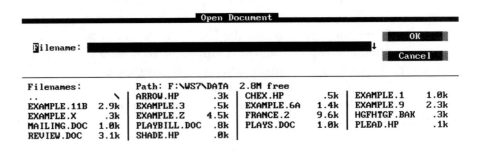

At the Opening screen, press DOWN ARROW to move the cursor into the directory portion of the Open Document window; your screen should look similar to the one shown in Figure 3-2. Now press the first letter of the name of the file you wish to load. For EXAMPLE.2, press E. The highlight moves immediately to the first file that starts with *E* (in Figure 3-2, EXAMPLE.11B). If the file you want is not first in this part of the list, use the arrow keys to move the highlight to it. With the file highlighted, press ENTER. Your file is immediately loaded.

Note

By default this method loads a document file. Nondocument files are discussed in Chapter 18. This procedure for selecting from a list is most commonly used to select a file from a directory, but the same method is used to select from any list. Other lists—of fonts, paragraph styles, and printer drivers—are all discussed in later chapters.

Automatic Alignment (^OA)

The next two sections explain deleting and entering text. As you try these commands, you will notice that the text of the file you are working with is automatically realigned within the margins. This is because WordStar's default setting is with the Auto Align feature turned on. You can, if you wish, toggle Auto Align on and off by pressing **^OA**. (The setting can also be controlled from the Edit menu by selecting Editing Settings, then Auto Align.)

Figure 3-2. *Selecting a file from a directory*

```
                              WordStar
 File     Utilities   Additional                                    Help



 Filenames:          Path: E:\WS7\DATA  5.6M free
 ..              ↘   ARROW.HP      .3k | BACKING.DAY  .3k | CHEX.HP       .5k
 EXAMPLE.11B  2.9k   EXAMPLE.2    1.0k | EXAMPLE.6A  1.4k | EXAMPLE.9    2.3k
 FRANCE.2     8.2k   ILLUS6.2      .4k | MAILING.DOC 1.0k | OUTLINE.WS7 8.3k
 PLAYBILL.DOC  .8k   PLAYS.DOC    1.0k | PLEAD.HP     .1k | REVIEW.DOC  3.1k
 SHADE.HP      .0k
```

3

If you toggle Auto Align off, you can use the Paragraph Reformat command (presented later in this chapter) to align your text.

Deleting Text (DEL, BACKSPACE, F5, F6,^QY, ^Q-DEL, ^QT)

When you enter or edit a document, you may make errors or want to change your work. Frequently you will want to delete text. You can easily delete anything—from one letter to an entire document. Here you will learn several ways to delete small amounts of text. Before you try these delete operations, however, look over the list below and note the keys that perform the operations. Then read the section that follows, "Restoring Deleted Text (F2)." Once you know how to restore any text that you delete, try each of the delete commands, followed by F2 (Undo) where applicable.

Command	Action
DEL	Deletes the character above the cursor.
BACKSPACE	Deletes the character to the left of the cursor.
F5	Deletes an entire line. The cursor may be anywhere in the line. The text below moves up to replace the deleted text.
F6	Deletes from the cursor position to the end of the word. Deletes an entire word if the cursor is on the first letter. Deletes a portion if the cursor is within the word.
^QY	Deletes everything on the line from the position of the cursor to the right end of the line.
^Q-DEL	Deletes text on the line to the left of the cursor (similar to ^QY).
^QT	Deletes from the cursor to the designated character. ^QT . deletes from the cursor to the next period, usually the end of the sentence. ^QT ENTER deletes from the cursor to the end of a paragraph.

Note

If ^QY is entered at the beginning of a line and Auto Align (discussed in the previous section) is off, then ^QY deletes the text and leaves a blank line.

Remember

As you delete and insert text, your paragraphs will be automatically reformatted, unless you press ^OA to disable Auto Align).

3

The next section discusses how to undelete, or undo, a deletion. Try each of the preceding commands in conjunction with the Undo command.

Restoring Deleted Text (F2)

It can be very frustrating to press F5 instead of F6 and delete a whole line of text when you intended to delete a single word. The Undo command lets you restore material that has been deleted with the commands F5, F6, ^QY, ^Q-DEL, and ^QT. Undo does not, however, restore single characters you deleted using the DEL or BACKSPACE key. These letters must simply be reentered.

To restore text, press F2, the Undo command. The deleted text will be inserted starting at the position of the cursor.

Tip

You can use Undo to move or copy a small portion of text. To move text: Use the appropriate command to delete a word, line, or paragraph you want to move. Place the cursor at the position where you want the text inserted and press F2. To copy text: Delete the text you wish to copy and, without moving the cursor, press F2 to restore it. Move the cursor to the new position and again press F2; the text reappears. Text can be restored in this way any number of times, as long as you do not issue another delete command. The deleted text is stored by WordStar until it is replaced by text deleted with another delete command. Procedures for moving or copying larger amounts of text are described in Chapter 7.

Inserting Text (INS)

Insert mode is on by default. You can toggle insert mode off by pressing the INSERT key (marked INS or INSERT). The status line shows "Insert" when the insert mode is on and "Ins-off" when it is off.

If you notice that some text has been left out of your document, you can move the cursor to that position and type it in. You can insert a single letter or as much text as you like. As you insert text, everything to the right is pushed further to the right. WordStar reformats the material as you type.

You can insert characters, TAB spaces, and entire lines. To insert a blank line, place the cursor at the left margin of the line that should follow the blank line, and press ENTER.

To add words to a paragraph, move the cursor to where you want the word to start, and type it. Try adding a couple of words to your text from Example 2.

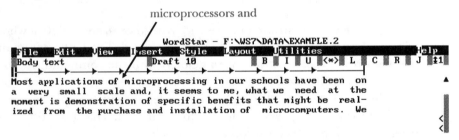

Move the cursor to the beginning of the word *microprocessing*, press INS (if the insert mode is not on), and then type **microprocessors and**. As you type, notice that text to the right automatically moves further to the right and that the paragraph is automatically realigned.

Determining Line Spacing

When you enter text, line spacing is set by default to single spacing. With WordStar, you can set the spacing of the material you type to double spacing, or even one line of text after every nine blank lines. You can also easily change the spacing of material that is already entered in a file. You can set the line spacing either by using a dot command, or you can enter the desired spacing in the Alignment and Spacing window, as described in the following sections.

Set Line Spacing Using the Dot Command (.ls *n*)

To set the line spacing using the dot command, place the cursor on line 1 and in column 1 of your example. Enter **.ls** *n*, replacing the *n* following the **.ls** with a value from 1 to 9 to represent the desired line spacing. The *n* in the command represents a value from 1 to 9. For this example use **2** for double spacing. Remember to press ENTER at the end of the command. Using this method or others discussed shortly, you can include as many line spacing settings in your file as you like. Regardless of how they are set, the line space settings are saved with your file and are in effect the next time it is opened.

Keep in mind these characteristics about dot commands:

- The period (dot) must be in column 1.

- Lines containing dot commands do not affect the line count because they do not print. They appear on the screen simply so you can be aware of the command. To see this, watch the line count in the status line as you move the cursor past the dot commands.

- Always press ENTER after a dot command unless you intentionally wish to delete a line when the file is printed.

Now move the cursor to the line preceding the next paragraph and enter the dot command **.ls 3**. Next you will reformat these two paragraphs so the screen display is in the double and triple spacing you just entered.

Reformatting

While deleting and inserting text, you have seen that automatic alignment or paragraph reformat is on by default. You can also reformat an individual paragraph or an entire document with a single command. Here you will reformat the paragraphs individually. In a later chapter, you will reformat more complex files.

Reformatting Paragraphs (^B, F7)

Pressing ^B starts the paragraph reformatting from the line where the cursor is currently positioned and will reformat text until WordStar reaches an Enter flag (<), usually at the end of a paragraph. Move the cursor to the beginning of the first paragraph and press ^B to reformat the paragraph. Notice that the cursor is now at the blank line between paragraphs. Press ^B twice to reformat the second paragraph. (The first ^B advances over the blank line.) This process can be repeated to reformat all the material in any document, regardless of length. Now go back to the beginning of the first paragraph.

A similar reformat function is accomplished by pressing F7. When you press F7 the paragraph is reformatted, but the cursor returns to its original position. You will find each of these reformat commands has an advantage, depending on the type of editing you are doing.

Tip

If you find you have an unwanted Enter flag, here is one way to delete it. Use ^QD to place the cursor at the right end of the line. Press the DEL key until the line below jumps up to the end of the current line. Then press F7 to reformat the paragraph (if Auto Align is off).

Reformatting an Entire Document (^QU)

The process just described requires you to reformat each paragraph individually. The command ^QU allows you to reformat more than one paragraph, even an entire document, with one Edit command. Try this by returning to the dot commands and changing the line spacing to 1. With the cursor at the beginning of the first paragraph, press ^QU. Both paragraphs are quickly reformatted. This command is most useful with long documents.

Set Line Spacing Using Alignment and Spacing Window (^OS)

You previously changed the line spacing by entering dot commands directly. This time you will change the spacing using the Alignment and Spacing window to enter the dot commands. First delete the existing .ls commands and reformat the paragraphs to single spacing, if you haven't already done so. Place the cursor at the top of the screen and press ^OS. The window shown in Figure 3-3 is displayed.

Figure 3-3.   *Alignment and Spacing window*

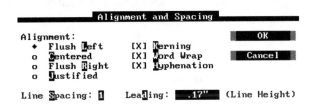

The cursor is in the box after Line Spacing, ready for you to enter a line spacing value from 1 to 9. To double-space, type **2**. Press ENTER to return to the file.

There are two screen indicators to show line spacing: On the far right of the status line is the number 2, and above the cursor is the dot command .ls 2. Both are illustrated here:

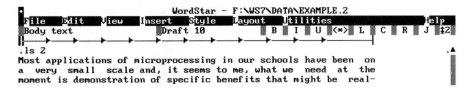

Note

The options of either selecting WordStar commands from a dialog window or entering a dot command will be offered to you throughout WordStar. When a window is displayed, you may select an individual command or any combination of the commands displayed in the window. When the Alignment and Spacing window first appeared, the cursor was in the field, ready for you to enter the spacing value; this is true throughout WordStar. When an Edit command requires additional information, the cursor is placed in the proper field to enter the information. If the Edit command is a simple toggle, such as the ^QU used in the previous section, the command is executed immediately.

At the beginning of this section you displayed the Alignment and Spacing window by pressing **^OS**. You can also display this window by clicking the line spacing indicator in the status line or by selecting Alignment and Spacing

3

from the Layout menu. The window will be the same as that shown in Figure 3-3. Notice that if you use the spacing indicator ^OS to open the window, the cursor is in the Spacing field waiting for your entry. If you use the menu, the cursor is in the Alignment options.

Controlling Screen Settings (^OB)

As you become more familiar with WordStar's commands, you will find less need for the information lines, such as the status line, scroll bar, and so on, that are displayed on the screen. These can be eliminated from the screen by using the Screen Settings window. To display this window, press **^OB**, or select the View menu and then choose Screen Settings. Your screen display is similar to Figure 3-4.

Under the heading Display On Screen are five options. You can remove any or all of them from the screen. To remove an item, press the reverse-video accelerator key associated with that item. The *X* is removed from the box, indicating that item will no longer display. To return to your document display, press F10.

Figure 3-4.   *Screen Settings window*

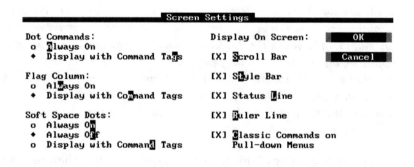

If you turn off all of the Display On Screen items, your screen display will be like that in Figure 3-5.

To see the effect of removing the last Display On Screen item, Classic Commands, press ALT-V to display the View pull-down menu. Notice that the Classic Commands normally on the right side of the View menu are no longer displayed.

Each of the five screen display items shown in Figure 3-4 is a toggle. If you return to the Screen Settings window and press the accelerator key again for each item, it displays again on the Edit screen.

Note

Using the Screen Settings window to turn display items off does so only for the current editing session. If you exit to DOS and return to WordStar, the screen settings will again be the default values. The default values may be changed using WSCHANGE. Customizing WordStar is discussed in Appendix C.

Try the various settings to see the effect on your screen display. Even experienced users will probably want to keep the information lines on their

Figure 3-5.   *Screen without information lines and columns*

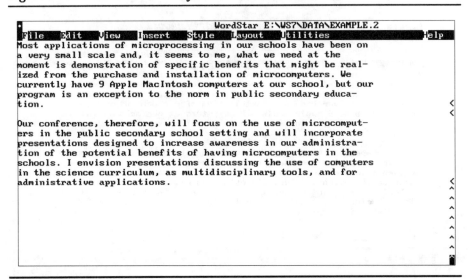

screens until they are familiar with the features of WordStar 7.0. New users will find it helpful to have their screen match the displays in this book, as well as to have all of the information available to help in learning the WordStar traditional commands.

Command Tags (SHIFT-F1)

The other Screen Settings options that may be toggled on and off are the *command tags*. Command tags include dot commands, the flag column, and soft space dots. These may all be hidden by pressing SHIFT-F1. Try this command to toggle the display of these three items on or off. You can also execute this command from the View menu by selecting Command Tags. With all Screen Settings items removed from the screen, it looks like Figure 3-6.

The combination of which three items will be turned on or off by the View menu's Command Tags option is determined in the Screen Settings window. On the left of the Screen Settings window, Figure 3-4, are the controls for the dot commands, flag column, and soft space dots. Notice each item has

Figure 3-6.   *Screen with command tags removed*

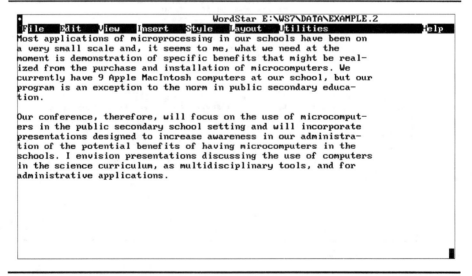

an option called Display with Command Tags. You select whether each option should remain on or off when Command Tag Off is selected.

Now that you have learned the fundamentals of editing a file, you are ready to go on to Chapter 4, which covers saving and printing a file.

Exercises

3

1. Enter Example 3. Set the line spacing to 3 and reformat the paragraph.

2. Set the line spacing back to 1, and reformat the paragraph using a single command.

3. Practice using the delete and Undo commands on Example 3.

4. Practice using the delete and Undo commands with Auto Align turned off. Press F7 to reformat the paragraph.

Example 3

Computer-Assisted Instruction (CAI)An example of a CAI program is the Milliken Math sequence. It consists of a comprehensive mathematics curriculum for grades one through six. The advantage of this sequence is that instruction is completely individualized according to each student's needs and abilities. CAI programs are success oriented and provide structured drills with immediate feedback and reinforcement. Students work at their own pace toward mastering specific skills. The time-consuming chores of grading and record keeping are done automatically, providing the teacher with more time for other instructional activities. Perhaps the greatest benefit of CAI programs is the motivational power of the computer.

4

Saving, Printing, and Other File Operations

All of the material named and saved on a disk is referred to as a file, whether it is something you type into the computer and save, or a complicated commercial program like WordStar (which is really a group of files). WordStar has five commands that let you save and print files. These commands are on the File menu.

To begin, let's examine the Save commands. Open a file, and at WordStar's Edit screen, press ALT-F. You will see the File menu shown in Figure 4-1.

Note

With each of these file commands you may, of course, precede your filename specification with a disk drive letter (as in B:EXAMPLE.2), or a subdirectory (as in \WS\EXAMPLE.2).

Figure 4-1.   *WordStar's File menu*

```
Open/Switch...                    ^OK
Close
Save                              ^KS
Save As...                        ^KT
Save and Close                    ^KD

Print...                       ^KS^KP
Fax...                            ^K\
Change Printer...                 ^P?

Copy...                           ^KO
Delete...                         ^KJ
Rename...                         ^KE

Change Drive/Directory...         ^KL
Run DOS Command...                ^KF
Status                            ^O?

Exit WordStar                    ^KQX
```

Saving Files (File Menu)

Before you look at the individual Save commands, note these general features:

- When you save a file that already has a name, the saving begins as soon as you give the Save command.
- When you save a new file, you will see the Save As dialog box shown in Figure 4-2. Name the file using the standard DOS naming convention (a maximum of eight letters for the filename and three letters for the extension).

Now take a look at the Save commands.

Close

The Close command is most useful when you have displayed a file to examine it and then want to return directly to the Opening screen. If you

Figure 4-2.   *The Save As window display when saving a file*

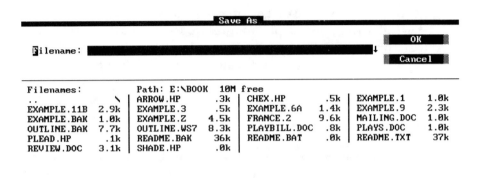

enter or edit any text in the file, selecting Close will display this Close File window:

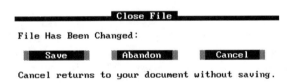

Save is the default selection; to select it, press ENTER. The other two options are Abandon and Cancel. To select one of these, press **A** or **C**, then press ENTER.

Save (F9)

The Save command saves what you have entered on a disk, and then returns you to the Edit screen so you can continue working.

Tip

It is a good idea to save your work every 15 to 20 minutes so you will not lose too much data if there is a power failure or other mishap.

Save As... (^KT)

Save As lets you save an existing document with a new name. This feature is useful when, for example, you wish to write a letter or create a document based on an existing document. Your original file will be unchanged and keep its name. Pressing **^KT** gives you the same Save As dialog box shown in Figure 4-2.

Save and Close (^KD)

When you have finished working with one file and are ready to open another file or start a new one, select **^KD**, Save and Close. This saves the opened file using the existing name and returns you to the Opening screen. You can then open an existing file to edit or begin a new document.

Exit WordStar (^KQX)

When you are finished working on a file and want to leave WordStar, select Exit WordStar at the bottom of the File menu. If you made any changes, you will see the same window as when you select Close. The choices and selection procedures are the same. The difference is if you select Save or Abandon, you leave WordStar and return to DOS.

Printing Files (File Menu)

You can print a file from either the Opening screen or the Edit screen. In either case, you open the File menu and select Print. The options and procedures are then identical.

Print Options (P)

From the Opening screen or Edit screen, open the File menu and select **P** (Print). WordStar will show you a Print dialog box similar to the one in

Figure 4-3. (If you were working on a file, its name will be in the Filename field.)

Note that you have several choices in this dialog box. Normally, you will enter a filename in the Filename field, or accept the one displayed, and press F10 to accept the default values for the remaining fields.

At times you may wish to change one or more of the default values. To do so, after you insert the name of the file to print, press the highlighted letter associated with the option you wish to change. Take a look now at each option, described in the following paragraphs. (The default values, if any, are shown here in parentheses.)

Tip

To review how to move around dialog boxes, see Chapter 1.

Filename

Type the name of the file you wish to print. You can also use the arrow keys to move to the directory, highlight your selection, and press ENTER.

Figure 4-3.   *WordStar's Print dialog box*

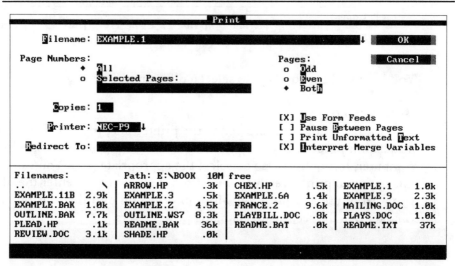

Page Numbers (All)

You can print an entire file or selected pages. To print selected pages, press **S** and then type the page numbers you want to print. Separate non-consecutive page numbers with commas and consecutive pages with a hyphen. For example, entering 1,4,7-9 will print pages 1, 4, 7, 8, and 9.

Pages (Both)

You can print odd-numbered pages, even-numbered pages, or all pages (Both). Make your choice by pressing **O**, **E**, or **h** (the default).

Copies (1)

The default is one copy. If you want more than one, just enter the number, up to 999, and press ENTER.

Printer (Default Driver)

The name in the Printer field is the one you chose when you installed WordStar. When the cursor is in this field, you will see a list of other available print drivers at the bottom of the screen. This example shows WordStar's built-in drivers, ASC256, ASCII, DRAFT, FAX, WS4, plus two installed drivers, HP-III and NEC-P9:

```
Printers:
ASC256   | ASCII    | DRAFT    | FAX      | HP-III   | NEC-P9   | WS4
```

You can use the arrow keys to select a different driver.

Redirect To

Printing is normally directed to the printer port you selected during the installation process. If you have more than one printer connected to your computer, this option lets you select the appropriate port. You can also use this option to print directly to the hard disk. In that case, enter the filename you wish to use and press F10. More information on using this option is in Chapter 8 in the section on changing print drivers.

Use Form Feeds [X]

If you are using continuous-form paper and your printer has a top-of-form setting, printing will be faster and more accurate if you turn on the Use Form Feeds option (the default). If you are using single sheets of paper or if your printer does not have a top-of-form setting, do *not* use form feeds; in this case press **U** to remove the *X*.

Pause Between Pages [ ]

The default is not to pause while printing. If, however, you use single sheets of paper in a tractor-feed printer, enter an **X** to enable this option. The printer will pause to allow you to insert a new sheet of paper for each page.

Print Unformatted Text [ ]

Select this option to print dot commands as they appear on the screen instead of interpreting them. Always select this option when printing non-document files. Nondocument files are discussed in Chapter 18.

Interpret Merge Variables [X]

By default, WordStar interprets Merge Print commands. If you change the default and turn this option off, names will be printed in your document rather than the variables that represent the names. Also, all Merge Print commands will be ignored. Merge Print is discussed in Chapter 18.

Print While Editing (^KP)

When you finish editing a document, you can save it to a disk and then print it. To do this, from the Edit window open the File menu and select **P**. The file will be saved and you will see the same Print dialog box shown in Figure 4-3. Press F10 to accept the defaults and print the document, or change the options as described above. In either case you will return to the Edit screen while the document is being printed. You can wait until the printing is finished and exit WordStar, continue editing the document, or edit another document.

4

Note

If you opened the current file using the New option, when you select Print you will see the Save As dialog box. After you save the file, you will be at the Opening screen.

To print a document other than the one you are editing on the screen, select Print (^KP) from the File menu. Again, the Print dialog box is presented. Select the file you wish to print and follow the print procedure described in the foregoing paragraph. While the document is printing, you can continue to edit the current one.

Now let's use some of the print options just discussed. Suppose you just printed a four-page document and discovered something on page 3 that must be corrected. You return to WordStar, load your document, and make the necessary corrections. You select Print from the File menu. Your file is saved, and the Print dialog box is presented. Press TAB at the Filename field to get to the Page Numbers field; press **S** to choose Selected Pages and enter **3**. Press F10 to accept the default settings for the remaining options.

Interrupting Printing

You can interrupt printing that is in progress. To do this while you are printing one file and editing another file, press **^KP**. If you are printing from the Opening menu, press **F** to display the File menu, and then press **P** for Print. In either case the dialog box shown here is displayed:

You can now continue by pressing **C**, or you can pause at the next page by pressing **P**.

How quickly the printing stops depends on your printer. These options stop the flow of data to the printer, but the data stored in the printer will continue to print until it is exhausted.

The Print dialog box shown in the preceding illustration is only displayed if there is material remaining in the computer waiting to be sent to the printer.

File Operations

Four other file commands you can access from the File window are Copy (O), Delete (Y), Rename (E), and Protect/Unprotect (C). When you select any of these commands you are given a dialog box. You can then type a filename or use the arrow keys to select the desired file.

Copy (O)

The Copy option lets you copy a file from one disk to another or from one directory to another. It also lets you copy a file to the same disk under another filename. To use the Copy option, press **O**. The Copy dialog box shown here is displayed:

Figure 4-4. *WordStar's Copy dialog box*

```
                                 Copy
  Existing Filename: EXAMPLE.1                          ↓    OK

        New Filename:                                   ↓    Cancel

  Filenames:             Path: E:\BOOK   10M free
    ..                 \ ARROW.HP     .3k │ CHEX.HP      .5k │ EXAMPLE.1    1.0k
  EXAMPLE.11B   2.9k │ EXAMPLE.3     .5k │ EXAMPLE.6A   1.4k │ EXAMPLE.9    2.3k
  EXAMPLE.BAK   1.0k │ EXAMPLE.Z    4.5k │ FRANCE.2     9.6k │ MAILING.DOC  1.0k
  OUTLINE.BAK   7.7k │ OUTLINE.WS7  8.3k │ PLAYBILL.DOC  .8k │ PLAYS.DOC    1.0k
  PLEAD.HP       .1k │ README.BAK    36k │ README.BAT    .0k │ README.TXT    37k
  REVIEW.DOC    3.1k │ SHADE.HP      .0k │
```

Select or type filenames for the Existing Filename and the New Filename. Then press ENTER and the file will be copied. If for the new filename you enter an existing filename, a window will open telling you the file already exists. You then have the option to overwrite the existing file or cancel the copy operation. If you select Overwrite, the existing file is deleted. If you select Cancel, you return to the New Filename field where you can enter a new name.

Delete (Y)

To delete a file, press **Y**. The Delete dialog box is displayed. Type the name of the file and press ENTER. Then choose OK. Use this option to delete any file on your disk. You can use this command to rid your disk of files you no longer need.

Rename (E)

Use the Rename option to change the name of a file. From the File menu press **E**. The screen displays a dialog box similar to the one used with Copy. As an example, let's rename the file EXAMPLE.2. In the Current Filename field, enter **EXAMPLE.2**. In the New Filename field, enter **EXAMPLE.X**. Press ENTER. Notice that the name in the directory has changed. Now, using the same procedure, change the filename back to EXAMPLE.2, because this file will be referred to in later chapters.

Protect/Unprotect (C)

The Protect option lets you lock a file. You can examine a locked file, but you cannot change it in any way. This option will prevent other WordStar users from accidentally changing your file.

To access the Protect option from the File menu, press **C**. A dialog box similar to the one for Delete is shown. Try this: From the File menu, press **C**. In the Filename field, enter **EXAMPLE.2** and press ENTER. A window opens telling you the status of the selected file (protected or unprotected) and asking, in this case, to confirm that you want to protect it. Enter **Y**. The file becomes protected and you return to the Opening menu. When you next open the file, the status line will display "Protect" to indicate it is a protected file.

Exercises

1. Use the New option from the Opening screen File menu, and enter Example 4. Type the entire example; then use Save As (^KT) from the Edit screen File menu to name the file EXAMPLE.4.

2. Print the EXAMPLE.4 file from WordStar's Opening screen and then from the Edit screen.

3. Print one file while you are editing another. Open EXAMPLE.4 and make any changes you like. At the same time, print EXAMPLE.2.

4

Example 4

March 23, 1992

Mr. Larry Gangi
1313 Valencia Street
Santa Ana, CA 92699

Dear Mr. Gangi:

Enclosed is a flyer with a brief description of CSAS,
our Continuation School Administrative System. Also
included is a price schedule for this software. In
addition to the continuation school software, we have
also developed an administration package for comprehensive schools. I believe you reviewed this
software while you were associated with Apex.

This fall I plan to set up a couple of demonstrations
of our continuation school software at computer
centers in Southern California. If it works out, I
will inform you of the dates and locations.

Sincerely,

Mike Verila

5

The Ruler Line

In Chapter 1 you were briefly introduced to the *ruler line*. There you saw that when you begin editing a document, its left and right margins are set to WordStar's default values—column 1 for the left margin and column 65 for the right margin. Tab stops are also set. In this chapter you will learn how to use WordStar's ruler line to change the document's margins, paragraph indents, and tabs.

To begin, load the EXAMPLE.2 file you created in Chapter 2. Next, from the Layout menu select Ruler Line. You will see the Ruler Line dialog box shown below. Note the default values in the ruler line displayed on your screen.

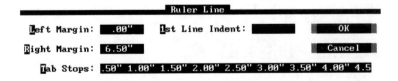

The following table shows the dot commands affected by changes in the Ruler Line window:

Ruler Line Dialog Box Item	Dot Command Affected
Left Margin	.lm
1st Line Indent	.pm
Right Margin	.rm
Tab Stops	.tb

Ruler Line Symbols

Seven symbols can appear on the ruler line; you will read about these symbols as you work through this chapter. The following table shows the symbols and what they represent:

Ruler Line Symbol	Represents
⊢	Left margin
⊣	Right margin
–	Columns between margins
•	Decimal tab column
]	Temporary indent
▶	Tab column
¶	Paragraph margin

If you do not wish to have the ruler line show, you can turn it off from the Screen Settings window (^OB).

Remember

The Ruler Line Dialog Box

In the Ruler Line dialog box you can change the left and right margins, paragraph indents, and tab settings. Keep in mind the following as you work with the Ruler Line dialog box:

- All entries are in decimal fractions of an inch (for example, .80 equals 8/10, or 4/5 of an inch).

Note

Generally, distances from the left or right side of the paper are measured to the nearest tenth of an inch because, most commonly, each screen column represents 1/10 of an inch.

- The values you first see in the Ruler Line dialog box are the WordStar defaults.
- To enter a new value, just type it in.
- To move the cursor to the next field, press TAB or DOWN ARROW.
- To move the cursor to the previous field, press SHIFT-TAB or UP ARROW.
- When you move the cursor to a field, press the SPACEBAR to clear the field. When you move the cursor within a field, press the SPACEBAR to insert a space.
- If you delete the contents of a field by mistake, you can reenter it by pressing ^R.
- Press ENTER or F10 to accept the values in the dialog box and return to the file.
- Press ESC to cancel changes you made in the dialog box and return to the file.
- Any changes you make to these default values will show up in your file as dot commands. (You'll see an example of this shortly.)
- When you return to a file after changing a left or right margin, a dot command will be on a line above the first blank line before the cursor. If the cursor is in the middle of a paragraph, the dot command may be several lines above the cursor.

    You can also display the Ruler Line dialog box by pressing ^OL, ^OR, or ^OI. Each of these commands will show the Ruler Line dialog box with the cursor in a particular field. ^OL puts it in the Left Margin field, ^OR in Right Margin, and ^OI in Tab Stops.

    You can change the left and right margins in as many places in a file as you like. The values that are in effect and displayed on the ruler line (and in

5

the Ruler Line dialog box if it is displayed) are the ones that affect the file at the position of the cursor.

Setting Margins from the Ruler Line Window

To change the left and right margins, make sure the cursor is in the top-left corner of the screen. Then press ^OL to display the Ruler Line dialog box. Note that the cursor is in the Left Margin field. Change the left margin setting by entering .5; then press the TAB key twice to move to the Right Margin field. Enter 5; you do not have to enter the inch (") symbol. Press F10 to save your changes and return to the file. Notice these three changes in the screen:

1. The left and right ends of the ruler line have shifted.
2. The top of the screen shows the two dot commands, .lm .50" and .rm 5.00", indicating the changes you made to the left and right margins.
3. Dots appear in the flag column on the lines containing the dot commands.

Note

Dot commands will cause symbols to appear in the flag column, although they will not always be dots. A complete list of the flag column characters is in Appendix B.

Your screen should look like this:

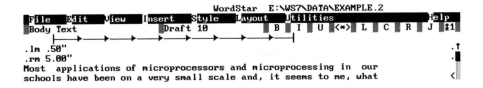

To see what happens to the text after you set new margins, move the cursor to column 1, line 1, so it is on the *M* in the word *Most*. Press ENTER to move the text down and produce a blank line. Notice that the paragraph is reformatted to the margins you just set. Next, use the arrow keys to move the cursor to column 1 of the blank line. Type your name. Notice that as soon as you press the first letter, it appears on the screen under the left edge of the ruler line. If you move the cursor to the first letter of your name, you'll see that the ruler line indicates the cursor is in column 6. If you continue typing, the text will wrap at column 50 instead of column 65, as it did when you originally entered Example 2.

If you do any editing in either paragraph of Example 2, the paragraph will automatically reformat to fit the new ruler line. Also, just as you did in Chapter 3, you can press HOME to place the cursor at the beginning of the first paragraph and then press F7 to reformat. The paragraph will quickly conform to the new margins. As you proceed through this chapter, use the F7 key to change the file to the margins that are set.

To return the left and right margins to their default values, move the cursor to column 1 of the line containing the .lm .50" dot command, and press ^Y to delete the line. Do the same for the line with .rm 5.00". If you look at the Ruler Line dialog box, you will see the default values 0 and 6.5 inches for the left and right margins, respectively. Before you continue with the next section, use F7 to reformat the paragraphs to their original settings.

Setting Margins with Dot Commands (.lm, .rm)

Another way to set margins is to enter the dot commands .lm and .rm directly into a file. In the Ruler Line dialog box, the default unit of measurement is inches or decimal fractions of an inch. With dot commands, however, the default measurement is number of columns. If you wish to use inches, just type the inch symbol (") after the value. Note that even if you enter a value in columns, the Ruler Line dialog box will show it in inches (each column represents 1/10 inch).

To try this method of setting margins, move the cursor to the beginning of the second paragraph of Example 2 and press ENTER to insert a blank line. Enter **.lm 3** and press ENTER. Then enter **.rm 70** and press ENTER. (Make sure the dots are in column 1.)

Consider what happened: First, the left and right ends of the ruler line have shifted to column 3 and column 70, respectively. Move the cursor above the .lm 3 and you'll see the ruler line display the default margins. Move the cursor below the dot commands, and the new left and right margin values are displayed.

Now try another example. Move the cursor so that it is after the 3 on the
.lm 3 line, and enter the inch symbol ("). Notice how the left margin indicator
in the ruler line moves when you enter or delete this symbol. The inch symbol
changes the meaning of the 3 for the left margin, from column 3 (3/10 of an
inch) to 3 inches (column 30).

*In addition to entering the left and right margins in columns and inches, you can
enter them in centimeters or points. Use the following designations; you can use these
measurement symbols either in the Ruler Line dialog box or with the dot commands.*

Note

Symbol	Measurement	Example
" or in	inches	5in or 5" = 5 inches
r	columns	5r = 5 columns
c	centimeters	5c = 5 centimeters
p	points (1 p = 1/72 inch)	5p = 5 points

Setting Relative Margins (.lm +, .lm -)

In addition to setting specific left and right margins, you can also set left
and right margins relative to existing margins. For example, in the previous
section you set a left margin at column 3 and a right margin at column 70. If
later in the file you entered the command .lm +7, the left margin would then
be 10 (3 + 7). You can change the left and right margins in this manner as
often as you like.

You can increase a margin by entering a + value or decrease it by using a
– value. The change is always relative to the current margin. The values can
be in columns or inches and can be mixed. The advantage of using relative
margins is that if you change the initial, specific left or right margin, all relative
margins (before any new specific margins) change automatically.

Tab Stops

Now that you've examined the margins, the next step is to examine tabs.
To advance the cursor to the next tab stop, press the TAB key. If there is no

text on the line, the cursor will move ahead one tab stop. If there is text to the right of the cursor and insert is on (which it is by default), the text will move to the right the same number of spaces the cursor moves.

Setting Tabs (.tb)

As you saw when you looked at the Ruler Line dialog box, the default tab settings are .5, or 1/2 inch. You can change the tab settings in a variety of ways. The most comprehensive is with the Ruler Line dialog box, so start there. Move the cursor to the Tab Stops field and press the SPACEBAR to clear the field. Now enter **1.5** and **4.0** (between the numbers, enter either a comma or a space). Press ENTER, and you will see the following:

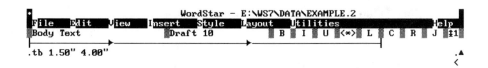

Note the tab symbols on the ruler line at 1.5 inches and 4.0 inches to indicate tab stops. A file may contain as many different tab dot commands as you like.

While you are editing, as the cursor moves toward the end of the file, the last tab dot command that the cursor passed is the one in effect. If the cursor is moving from the end of the file toward the beginning of the file, the tab command it is approaching is the one in effect. If there are no tab commands between the cursor and the beginning of the file, the ruler line displays the default tabs.

Note

If you are accustomed to using a version of WordStar earlier than 5.0, be aware that ^ON is no longer used with tabs. That command is now used to display the Notes (footnotes and endnotes) menu. This menu will be discussed in Chapter 15.

Using Decimal Tabs

To set *decimal tabs*, follow the same procedure you used to set standard tab stops. To try it, return to the Ruler Line dialog box and move the cursor to the Tab Stops field. Then move the cursor after the 4.00" and enter **#6.0** (# is the number sign). Press F10. On the ruler line you now have a • at the point representing 6 inches, as shown here:

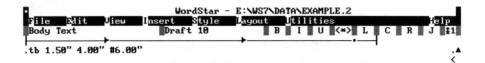

To see how decimal tabs work, make sure the cursor is in the line below the tab dot command and press TAB three times. Now watch the screen as you type $1,240.49. First type **$1,240**; as you type each number, the cursor stays in the same position, and each character you enter forces the previously entered characters to move left. Now enter **.**, the decimal point. It takes the position of the cursor, which moves to the right. Finally, type **49**; the numbers are entered at the right in the normal manner.

Before you begin the next section, return the tabs to their default settings by deleting the decimal tab dot commands.

Using Temporary Indent (^OG)

The *paragraph tab* (^OG) is a special tab—it allows you to reset your left margin temporarily. When you press **^OG**, it sets the left margin to the first tab on the ruler line. Each time you press **^OG**, it moves the left margin of the ruler line one additional tab stop to the right. The position of the temporary left margin is shown on the ruler line with a], the close bracket symbol. The following illustration shows the ruler line after **^OG** has been pressed twice:

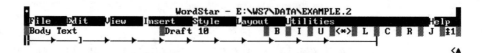

A common use of the paragraph tab is to format indented lists or paragraphs. The ruler line automatically returns to the original left margin after you press ENTER or reformat a paragraph.

Embedding a Ruler Line (^OO)

After you have changed the margins and/or tabs on the ruler line, you can save the ruler settings with your document. That way, the next time you open the document, that ruler line will be in effect from the point at which it was embedded.

To try this, place the cursor in column 1 of a blank line and enter **^OO**. A copy of the ruler line in effect at that point is inserted in your document.

Note two things about the embedded ruler line:

- Ruler lines you insert will not print when the document is printed.

- The .rr symbol is on the left of the line. It is the dot command used to establish a new ruler line. As with all dot commands, the ruler line command will work only if the dot is in column 1.

In preparation for the next section, close the current file and abandon your changes. Then open EXAMPLE.2 again.

The Paragraph Margin Command (.pm)

Another dot command that's useful with the ruler line is the Paragraph Margin command (.pm). Just as with the left and right margin commands (.lm and .rm), you can set a .pm command using either the Ruler Line dialog box or the dot commands. Also, just as with the margin commands, the unit of measurement for .pm can be columns, inches, centimeters, or points. If you set the command directly into the file and want the value in inches, enter the inch symbol (") after the value.

5

When you place a .pm command in a file, the first line following a carriage return will be indented the number of spaces you specify. For example, to indent the first line of each following paragraph by seven columns, type **.pm 7**. Notice that your .pm 7 entry causes a ¶ to appear in the ruler line in column 7. Also, you would normally remove any tabs between the left margin and the paragraph margin. The following illustration shows an example of this:

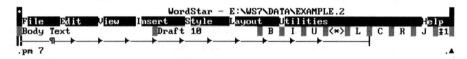

With the .pm command you can quickly place paragraph indentations in a file. To see how this works, move the cursor to the beginning of the file, insert a blank line, and with the cursor in column 1 of the blank line, type **.pm** followed by a space and the desired value. Then press **^QU**. All the paragraphs will be reformatted with the selected indentations. You can use this procedure with documents of any length. You can also use .pm commands to insert different indentations throughout your document. Note that the .pm command will not eliminate indentations placed in the file with the TAB key. Now close EXAMPLE.2 and open a new file.

Setting Hanging Indents

Another application of the Paragraph Margin command is to use it for a *hanging indent*. With a hanging indent, the first line of a paragraph extends to the left. Commonly used with numbered lists, a hanging indent is the opposite of a standard indent.

An example of a hanging indent is shown in the numbered list of requirements in Example 5A at the end of this chapter. Here is the procedure to create the hanging indent in this example, as shown in the following illustration:

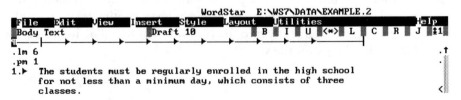

Use the Left Margin command **.lm 6** to set the margin for the start of the text of the numbered requirements in the example. Use the Paragraph Margin command **.pm 1** to set column 1 as the place where the requirement numbers will print.

After entering the dot commands, on the next line enter number **1** and a period. Press TAB to move the cursor to the left margin at column 6. Enter the text of the requirement. As you type, it will automatically reformat within the left and right margins. Press ENTER at the end of requirement 1, and follow the same procedure to enter number **2** and the next requirement.

Setting Relative Paragraph Margins (.pm)

Just as you set relative left or right margins earlier in this chapter, you can also set a *relative paragraph margin*, using the .pm command. For example, if you type .pm +3 while a .pm 7 is in effect, your new paragraph margin will be 10. This has the following advantage: changing the initial .pm command in the file changes all subsequent .pm commands.

You now have learned a variety of methods to set margins, tabs, and indentations. Become familiar with all of them so that you can use the one best suited to a particular situation. Also, be sure to embed a nonprinting ruler line in your file wherever the ruler line changes. This saves a great deal of time on subsequent edits.

Using Margin Release (^OX)

You can use the Margin Release command, ^OX, to enter data outside the ruler line margins. To try using Margin Release, set your left margin to 10 by entering the dot command **.lm 10**. With the cursor in column 1, press **^OX**. You can now enter information at the position of the cursor—outside the margins. Press **^OX** again to turn Margin Release off; the next character you type will print at the left margin.

Preformatted Ruler Lines (.rr 0 through 9)

WordStar comes with four preformatted ruler lines: .rr 0, .rr 1, .rr 2, and .rr 3. The default ruler line is .rr 0. To look at a preformatted ruler line, move the cursor to the end of a file and place it in column 1. Type **.rr 1**. Notice how the ruler line changes when you enter the **1**.

You can have up to 10 preformatted ruler lines in WordStar (.rr 0 through .rr 9). To create your own ruler lines 4 through 9, use WSCHANGE (see Appendix C). In addition to creating these ruler lines, WSCHANGE can be used to change ruler lines 0 through 3 that come with WordStar.

Tip

Generally, it is a good idea to place the ruler line in a file. At times you will move rapidly through a file while editing. To be aware of tab or margin changes in the ruler line, it is useful to display a copy of the ruler line in your file–this is considerably more eye-catching than just a .rr dot command in the file. To place the ruler line in the file, move the cursor below the dot command .rr 1 and press ^OO. The following illustration shows how the screen will look:

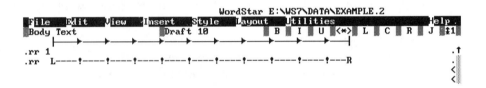

You have now covered the fundamentals of word processing in WordStar. In Chapter 6 you will work with text justification, along with page layout and numbering commands.

Exercises

1. Enter Example 5A, setting the appropriate ruler line prior to each change in format. Be sure to use the paragraph margin command, .pm, to include a hanging indent.

2. Example 5B is in Block style, where all lines are flush with the left margin. Open a file named EXAMPLE.5B and type in the text of the example in the Block style shown. Then change the format of the letter to the Indent style by using the .pm command. Set a tab command to center the complimentary close.

3. Open a file and call it EXAMPLE.5C. Set up a ruler line with tabs at 25 and 50 and with a right margin at 75. Enter the nine names and addresses shown in Example 5C. Practice deleting text. Be sure you can quickly delete names in the left, right, and middle columns without deleting those names you wish to keep.

4. You now know the basic commands necessary to edit a document. Proofread and correct any errors in all the examples you have previously entered and saved.

5. Using the examples you have created, practice changing margins. Be sure to try relative margins, and use the different measurement units—columns, inches, and so forth.

5

Example 5A

```
                       STRAND HIGH SCHOOL
                        415 Green Street
                       Concord, CA 94520
                         (415) 798-5209


Dear Student Employer:

Please be advised that one of our students who has
been employed by you has applied for credit in the
Outside Work Experience Program.

We would like to acquaint you with the basic
requirements of this program so that there is no
misunderstanding at a later date.

Requirements

1.  The student must be regularly enrolled in the high
    school for no less than a minimum day, which
    consists of three classes.

2.  Absence from school automatically is considered
    absence from the Outside Work Experience job
    station. It is generally considered that if a
    student cannot attend school, he or she cannot go
    to work.

3.  A student cannot be employed in excess of eight
    hours per day, including school time.

For example:
```

Example 5A (*continued*)

If a student has four classes in the morning, and works four hours after school, he or she is within the requirements. However, if a student has a full class schedule, he or she will be entitled to work four hours after school.

4. All students under the age of eighteen must have a duly issued work permit.

I hope this letter is informative and that you and your employee will be able to comply. We would like to express our appreciation for your cooperation. If you have any questions, please call me at 666-1111.

Yours very truly,

JOHN SMITH

5

Example 5B

```
                    STRAND HIGH SCHOOL
                     415 Green Street
                    Concord, CA 94520
                      (415) 798-5209

March 23, 1992
Mr. William Price
Alhambra High School
211 C Street
Martinez, CA 94553

Dear Mr. Price:

The high school data base is being tested at
Martinez High School. Testing of the report genera-
tor for these programs will also begin this week
at Martinez High School.

Any suggestions for additional information or func-
tions to be incorporated in the data base should
be given now. It is more cost-effective to incorpo-
rate changes now than to wait until the project is
complete. All high school principals and their sec-
retaries and the high school nurses should review
the program and make suggestions.

Any information that needs to be prepared for
transfer to the district office computers should
be outlined by the appropriate district administra-
tor.

I am available to demonstrate the software at any
time. Please have those reviewing the software re-
turn any suggestions, comments, criticisms, etc.,
to me by December 19.

Sincerely,

Walt Elison
```

Example 5C

```
Veronica Lopez         Mark Jones          Lisa Maxwell
570 Ridgeville Drive   872 Olivet Road     956 Bristol Road
San Jose, CA 94395     Alma, IL 62807      Lyman, WA 98263


Mary Lewis             Sam Parker          Julie Rogers
120 Colgate Road       754 Alameda Drive   504 Sucrest Lane
Steele, MI 49888       Downey, ID 83234    Alto, TX 75925


Susie Waldo            Johnny O'Brien      Greg Saunders
2321 Brisbon Lane      483 Virginia Street 384 Sunset Road
Shook, MI 49087        Chula, GA 31733     Lott, TX 76656
```

5

6

Page Alignment, Layout, and Numbering

In this chapter you will work with page alignment, page layout, and page numbering. You had a brief introduction to the Alignment and Spacing dialog box in Chapter 3, where line spacing was introduced. Now you'll work with the other options in that window.

Page Alignment

WordStar makes it very easy to change the way your document appears on the screen and in printed form. The various alignment options are discussed in this section. To display the Alignment and Spacing dialog box, at the Layout menu press **A**.

```
╔═══════════════ Alignment and Spacing ═══════════════╗

Alignment:                                    ▐  OK  ▌
   ◆  Flush Left      [X] Kerning
   o  Centered        [X] Word Wrap           ▐ Cancel ▌
   o  Flush Right     [X] Hyphenation
   o  Justified

Line Spacing: 1     Leading: ▐ .17" ▌ (Line Height)
```

77

To select an Alignment option in the Alignment and Spacing dialog box, use one of the following three methods:

- Use the UP ARROW or DOWN ARROW to place the selection diamond next to your choice, and press F10.
- Enter one of the dot commands shown in Table 6-1 directly into your document at the appropriate spot.

Only text that is part of the dot command can be on the same line with the dot command.

Remember

- Using the mouse, click one of the alignment options L, C, R, or J in the style bar.

Whichever method you use to change the alignment, your choice is indicated by the highlighted alignment letter in the style bar.

Table 6-1 lists the dot commands you can use in your files for alignment and spacing, and the commands are described in the paragraphs that follow.

Table 6-1.   *Alignment and Spacing Dot Commands*

Function	Dot Command
Alignment Commands:	
Flush Left	.oj off
Centered	.oj c
Flush Right	.oj r
Justified	.oj on
Kerning	.kr on/off
Word Wrap	.aw on/off
Hyphenation	.hy on/off
Spacing Commands:	
Line Spacing	.ls n
Leading (line height)	.lh, lh a

Flush Left (.oj off)

As shown in Table 6-1, you can align your text in four ways. Flush Left is the default selection, as indicated by the diamond to its left in the Alignment and Spacing dialog box. As you have seen with the examples you've entered, flush left means that text is flush with the left margin.

Centered (SHIFT-F2, .oj c)

To center a single line of text, position the cursor on the line and press SHIFT-F2. The material will be centered.

Practice centering text using Example 6A. To enter the heading at the top of the page, move the cursor to column 1, line 1 of a blank screen, and type **STRAND HIGH SCHOOL**. Now press SHIFT-F2, and the text you typed will be centered within the ruler line. Press ENTER to end the line, then type the next three lines, using SHIFT-F2 to center one.

If the material you are centering involves more than one line, as in the previous example, you may find it more convenient to enter the command **.oj c** directly into your file, or to select Centered from the Alignment and Spacing dialog box. To try this, type the dot command **.oj c** on the next line to turn centering on, and press ENTER. Then type the heading from Example 6A again. This time each line is automatically centered as you type it. When the section you want centered is complete, place the cursor in column 1 on the next line down and type **.oj off**. This turns centering off and returns you to the default alignment, flush left.

Whether you choose the .oj c command or the Centered option in the dialog box, the centering stays in effect until you turn it off. Should some information in the heading change at a later time, just reenter or edit it, and the new text will automatically be centered.

Flush Right (^O], .oj r)

At times you may want to print a heading or other text flush with the right margin. To cause one line of text to be flush right, enter the text and press ^O]. The text will automatically be aligned flush right.

6

As with centering text, if you want to align several lines flush right, you can select Flush Right from the Alignment and Spacing dialog box or enter the dot command, **.oj r,** directly preceding the text. When you finish, enter **.oj off** to return to the default flush left alignment.

Justified (^OJ, .oj on)

In all earlier versions of WordStar, Justified was the default alignment option. Justified means that all the lines are the same length and the right margin is even. To accomplish this, WordStar distributes excess space throughout the line rather than placing it at the end of the line. To justify text, use one of the three methods described previously for page alignment: Select a command from the Alignment and Spacing dialog box, use the dot command, or select from the style bar. Justification can also be toggled on or off using the command ^OJ. If justification is off, pressing **^OJ** toggles it on; if it is on, **^OJ** toggles it off. Figure 6-1 shows the text in Example 2 justified.

Figure 6-1.   *Example 2 printed with Justification on*

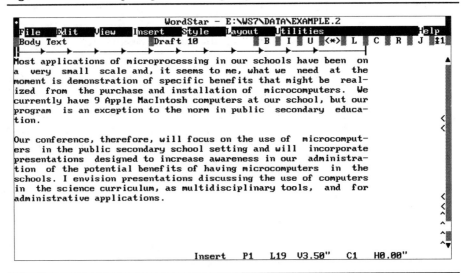

Note

If you want to make Justified the default alignment, use ^OFD to display the Define Paragraph Style dialog box, change the alignment to Justified, and be sure to select Update Style Library. For new WordStar users, Paragraph Styles are discussed in Chapter 12.

Kerning (.kr)

Kerning is the process of adjusting the space between certain pairs of letters that have too much space between them. This makes the printing appear more professional. Examples of letter pairs that typically appear together and look better when kerning is available are shown here:

| Kerning on | TA Ta Tc Td Te To T LT |
| | LV LW LY Ly WA Wa W. |

```
Kerning off    TA    Ta    Tc    Td    Te    To    T    LT
               LV    LW    LY    Ly    WA    Wa    W.
```

WordStar supports kerning in fonts that contain the necessary information. Currently, kerning is only available for fonts printed on the newer laser printers, such as the HP LaserJet III. To turn kerning on, select **R** in the Alignment and Spacing dialog box or use the dot command .kr; to turn it off, use .kr off. WordStar's default setting is kerning on.

Word Wrap (^OW, .aw on/off)

Word Wrap is the command that causes the cursor when it reaches the end of one line to automatically move to the next line. Occasionally when you enter tables or other special material, you may wish to turn Word Wrap off. You can turn Word Wrap off by using the toggle ^OW or by unmarking the Word Wrap check box in the Alignment and Spacing dialog box. You can also insert the dot command **.aw off** before the section where Word Wrap is to be turned off. To turn Word Wrap back on, enter **.aw**.

6

Automatic Hyphenation On/Off (^OH, .hy on/off)

Since WordStar 5, *automatic hyphenation* is on when you open a document file. With automatic hyphenation, when you enter data or reformat a paragraph, hyphens are inserted in words that extend past the right margin. You can turn hyphenation off (or on—it's a toggle) using one of the following methods:

- Unmark the Hyphenation check box in the Alignment and Spacing dialog box.
- Use the edit command ^OH.
- Enter the dot command **.hy off/on.**

Soft Hyphens (^OE)

If you wish, you can specify where hyphens will be placed, using the command ^OE. To try this, put the cursor on a character immediately before where hyphenation should occur. Press **^OE.** An equal sign appears to show you where the hyphen will occur if paragraph reformatting places the word in a location where hyphenation is necessary. An equal sign also appears at the beginning of the word. The equal signs do not appear, of course, when you print the file. If the word needs to be hyphenated during reformatting, the equal sign within the word becomes a hyphen on the screen and when the document is printed.

Leading, or Line Height (.lh)

The distance between lines of print is called *leading*. In WordStar, the space from the base of one printer line to the base of the next is a fixed distance. This is called *absolute leading* and is WordStar's default setting. Another kind of leading, automatic leading, lets WordStar adjust the distance between printed lines depending on the size of the font being used. Automatic leading is discussed next.

In WordStar, leading is set to a specific value using the Line Height command, .lh. This command allows you to specify how many lines per inch are printed on a page (not all printers can be controlled this way; you'll want to find out whether yours can). Line height is specified in units of 1/48 inch. The default value is 8, which is 8/48 or 1/6 inch; that is, six lines per inch. (In the Alignment and Spacing dialog box this displays as .17".) All of the examples you have printed so far have been printed using this default value. Line height can also be specified in centimeters or points.

When you set the line height to something other than six lines per inch, WordStar automatically adjusts the page breaks accordingly. The line height on the screen does not change, but you can see how it will appear when it is printed by using Preview (Chapter 9).

To experiment with changing the line height, load EXAMPLE.4 from Chapter 4, and print it at eight lines per inch (if your printer has this capability). On a blank line at the beginning of the file, type **.lh 6**. This tells WordStar to make the printer scroll down 6/48, or 1/8, inch after each line is printed. Check the status line to be sure the dot in the .lh command is in column 1. Select Print from the File menu to save the file and display the Print dialog box. Press F10 to print the file and observe the results.

Automatic Leading (.lh a)

Since version 5.5, WordStar also offers *automatic leading*. Automatic leading is invoked by entering the dot command **.lh a**. With automatic leading in effect, the distance between the printed lines will be determined by the largest type size used on that line. When you use different sizes of type that differ from the default type size, insert **.lh a** before the text that uses the varying type size. This command adjusts the line height for fonts both larger and smaller than the normal font. After completing the section of text with the varying type size, set the leading back to the default value by entering the command **.lh 8** (for six lines per inch).

When graphics are inserted in a WordStar file, leading must be set to absolute.

Note

The remaining item in the Alignment and Spacing dialog box, Line Spacing, was discussed in Chapter 3.

Note

Figure 6-2.   *Page Layout dialog box*

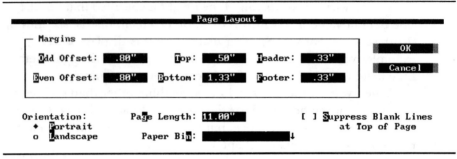

Page Layout

This section discusses the Page Layout options, available by choosing Page on the Layout pull-down menu. You will see the Page Layout dialog box shown in Figure 6-2.

Table 6-2 lists the dot commands.

Table 6-2.   *Page Layout Dot Commands*

Function	Dot Command
Margins:	
Page Offset	.po
Odd Offset	.poo
Even Offset	.poe
Top	.mt
Bottom	.mb
Header	.he
Footer	.fo
Orientation:	
Portrait	.pr or=p
Landscape	.pr or=l
Page Length	.pl
Paper Bin	.bn *n*
Suppress Blank Lines at Top of Page	.sb on/off

Before reading about the options on the Page Layout dialog box, examine Figure 6-3. It shows the default page offsets and margins you can change using the dialog box or dot commands.

Page Offset (.po)

The Page Offset (.po) command determines the width of the left margin; it has a default value of 8 (8/10 or 4/5 inch). The default is appropriate when you are using a 10-pitch font and the default ruler line with a length of 6.50 inches. If your line width is particularly short or long, or if you are using a 12-pitch font, you may need to change the Page Offset value.

Figure 6-3. *Page layout diagram showing offset, headers, footers, and margins*

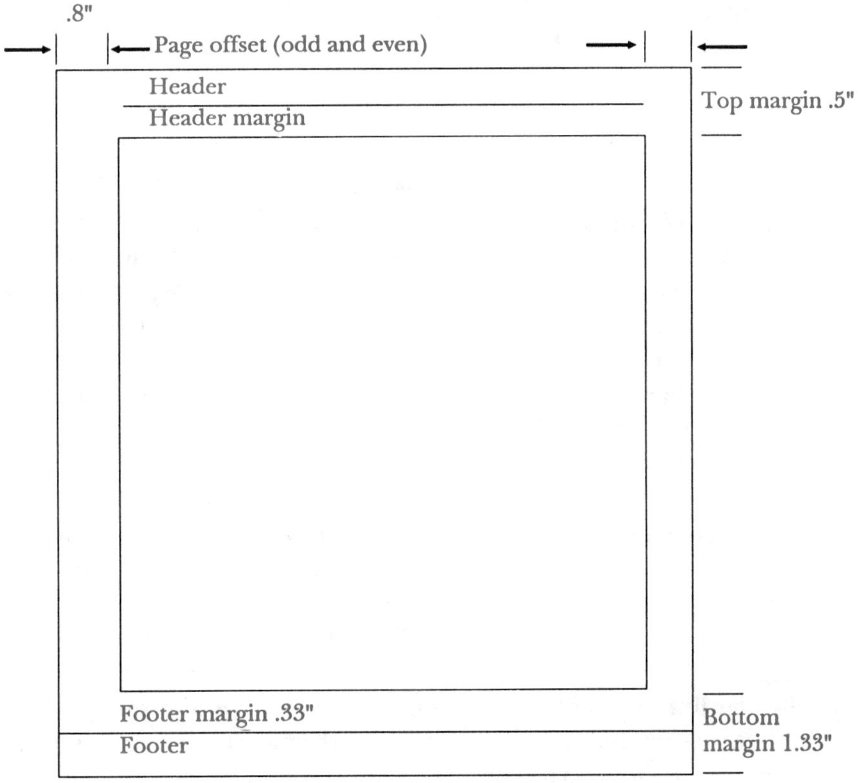

.8"

Page offset (odd and even)

Header

Header margin

Top margin .5"

6

Footer margin .33"

Footer

Bottom margin 1.33"

Note

Always use the .po command to control where text prints on a sheet of paper, rather than changing the position of continuous-feed paper in the printer. If you forget to return the paper to its original position, it's aggravating to the next user.

Page Offset on Odd/Even Pages (.poo, .poe)

If you are preparing a document that will be bound or placed in a folder and the pages will be printed on both sides of the paper, you may want to use different offset values for the odd and even pages. An example of this application is this book—the the even-numbered pages have a smaller page offset (a narrower left margin) than the odd-numbered pages to allow for the book's binding on the left.

To set the offset separately for odd and even pages, use the **.poo** (odd) or **.poe** (even) Page Offset commands. Do not put a space between the .po and the third letter. For example, the command **.poe .5"** will set the left margin on even pages to .5 inch, and **.poo .8"** will set the odd pages to .8 inch. Note that **.po 12** will set the offset for both even and odd pages to 12 columns.

Margin Top (.mt)

The .mt command that sets the margin at the top of the paper has a default value of 3 (three lines). This command may be set directly by using the .mt command or by entering the appropriate value in the top field of the Page Layout window. Normally, your printer is set at the top of the paper and, on screen, your text begins on line 1. When printing a file, the printer scrolls the paper up three lines before it begins to print. If this distance is not satisfactory, you can change it by entering **.mt** followed by the number of lines you want the printer to scroll. This value can be either more or less than the default value. Another way to control the top margin, particularly for single-page documents, is to insert blank lines at the top of the file.

Keep in mind that the value you specify for the top margin (.mt) must be large enough to contain the header margin (.hm) and all the header lines. For example, the default value for the top margin is 3 (lines) and the default value for the header margin is 2. The difference between these values (3 minus 2) is 1; this is the number of lines available to print the header. To use all five header lines available, .h1 through .h5, you can enter **.mt 8** and **.hm 3**.

As we continue our examination of the page layout elements, we will work our way down the page.

Header Margin (.hm)

A *header* appears in the space between the top of the page and the header margin; headers are discussed in the section just below. The .hm command lets you control the header margin—the space between a header and the beginning of the main text. This command may also be set in the Page Layout dialog box by entering the distance in the Header field.

The space for the header margin must be included in the value for the top margin.

Headers (.h1 through .h5)

Note

The procedures for creating headers also apply to creating footers, discussed later in this chapter.

Use header commands to place text at the top of each page of a printed document. Any text you type on the same line as a header command will be printed at the top of all pages in the document. You can use up to five header lines.

To create headers you can enter the dot commands **.h1** through **.h5** directly, or you can make selections in the Header dialog box. To display this dialog box, from the Layout menu select **H**, then **H** again, and you'll see this window:

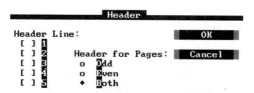

Select the number of header lines you wish and press ENTER. When you return to your document, you will see the dot commands in place and the cursor positioned for your first entry.

For example, entering the dot commands shown below at the top of your file will allow you to print five header lines and retain the default header margin of two blank lines (1/3 inch).

Note

The example below includes the header text on the same line as the dot command since the header is actually part of the dot command. The same concept is true for footers, discussed shortly.

.mt 8
.h1 *(header line 1 text)*
.h2 *(header line 2 text)*
.h3 *(header line 3 text)*
.h4 *(header line 4 text)*
.h5 *(header line 5 text)*

Refer to Figure 6-3 for a diagram showing the position of header and footer margins.

Headers on Odd/Even Pages (.hee, .heo)

You may want to use alternating headers on odd-numbered and even-numbered pages, as is done in this book. To do this, select the appropriate odd or even designation for the header lines you select from the Header dialog box. As an example, the commands in the following illustration would produce the headers for a manuscript of a chapter from this book.

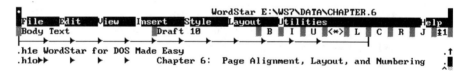

Margin Bottom (.mb)

The .mb command allows you to specify the number of lines for the bottom margin. The default value is 8 (lines), or 1 1/3 inches. Occasionally you will want to reduce this value so that you can fit another line or two of text on a page. You place this command, as well as the other commands affecting the bottom margin, at the beginning of your file.

As described previously for the .mt command, the value of the bottom margin must be large enough to contain the space for the footer lines and footer margin.

Footer Margin (.fm)

A *footer* appears in the space between the bottom margin and the last line of text; footers are discussed in the section just below. The Footer Margin command determines the space between the body of text and the page number or footer text. As with the header margin, the space for the footer margin and the footer lines must be included in the bottom margin value. The footer margin can be set by entering the dot command **.fm** directly into the file or in the Page Layout dialog box using the Bottom field.

Footers (.f1 through .f5)

The document page number is printed on the line controlled by .f1, but you can use the Footer (*.fn*) commands to print any information you like at the foot of each page of your file. As with headers, you have five lines available for footers. Again, the space available for footers is the difference between the bottom margin (.mb) value and the footer margin (.fm) value. Using the default values, the difference between the bottom margin (8) and footer margin (2) is 6, so you don't need to adjust the standard settings to take advantage of all five footer text lines.

The Footer dialog box is similar in appearance and operation to the Header dialog box; to open the Footer dialog box, from the Layout menu select **H** and then **F**.

Entering footers is a process similar to that of entering headers using the Header commands. However, there is one difference. When you use the Footer commands, you must use the # symbol (explained just below) to print and show the placement of the page number. This applies whether you use one or more of the footer lines. The page number symbol can be placed with any of the Footer commands. An example of the Footer commands placed at the top of your document is shown below; notice the # page number symbol for footer line 2:

.f1 *(footer line 1 text)*
.f2 *(footer line 2 text)*   #
.f3 *(footer line 3 text)*
.f4 *(footer line 4 text)*
.f5 *(footer line 5 text)*

Remember

It is not necessary to enter a Margin Bottom command, .mb, unless you wish to increase the space between the document text and the footer text.

Working with Headers and Footers

When using headers and footers, keep in mind the following:

- To stop the printing of a header or a footer, enter, at the top of the page where you want the printing stopped, the corresponding dot command without any text.

- You can enter a blank line between the lines of a header by entering a Header command followed by two spaces and then pressing ENTER. For example, **.h2** followed by two spaces and ENTER leaves a blank line between the first and third header lines. Follow the same procedure to enter a blank footer.

- Spaces entered between the Header or Footer commands and the start of the document text will be retained in printing.

- You can use bold, underline, and other print enhancements with headers and footers, just as you would in the text of a document. With headers and footers, the commands for the enhancements, rather than the enhancements themselves, will be displayed on the screen. Nevertheless, the enhancements will appear on the printed copy.

- A maximum of 100 characters is allowed in a header or footer. You can change this value by using WSCHANGE (see Appendix C).

- Headers and footers are not checked for spelling errors during a WordStar spell-check. See Chapter 13 for the command to check the spelling in headers and footers.

Special Header/Footer Format Commands (#, \)

Two special format characters can be used with the five Header (.h1 through .h5) and Footer (.f1 through .f5) commands. They are

Current Page Number (#)   The # symbol prints the current page number in place of the # symbol. In a document of two or more pages, WordStar automatically increments the page number and prints it in the position of the # symbol. You can include other text in the footer line with the page number. For example,

```
.fl Chapter 6 - #
```

will print *Chapter 6* followed by a hyphen and the appropriate page number in the footer of each page. The spaces between .fl and Chapter 6 will be retained. For example, if ten spaces are entered between the .fl and Chapter 6, Chapter 6 will print ten spaces to the right of the left margin. If you have more than one chapter in the same file, you can enter a similar footer command at the beginning of each chapter, so the footer text will reflect the correct chapter number.

Print Special Character (\)   The \ symbol prints the character following the \. For example, \# in a footer line will print the # character instead of the page number; \\ will print the \ character.

Page Length (.pl)

Because the standard paper length is 11 inches and printers normally print 6 lines per inch, the default page length value is 66 lines. When you are using paper of a nonstandard length, or if you have changed the line height, you can change the number of lines that will print on a page. To do this, change the Page Length value on the Page Layout dialog box, or enter the **.pl** dot command and a number of lines. (You can also use inches or centimeters for the Page Length value.) When you use .pl to change the page length, in the Print dialog box you must change the response to "Use form feeds?" from Y to N.

Note

Some laser printers use a default setting of 62 lines per page. Check your printer manual for more information.

Suppress Blank Lines (.sb on/off)

When you print a multipage document, occasionally a blank line (the blank line between paragraphs) will fall at the top of a page. To keep these

lines from printing, in the Page Layout dialog box mark the check box for
Suppress Blank Lines at Top of Page. You will see the dot command .sb on
appear in the document. You can also enter the dot command directly into
the file. With the .sb command and the soft spaces display (in the Screen
Settings dialog box) both turned on, the suppressed line displays on the screen
as shown here:

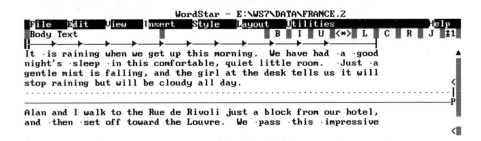

When the soft spaces are suppressed, the bar shown in the flag column is still
displayed.

To turn off the Suppress Blank Lines command enter **.sb off**, or deselect
the option in the Page Layout dialog box.

*Two other options on the Page Layout dialog box are discussed in later chapters. Paper
Bin is discussed in Chapter 8; and Orientation is discussed in Chapter 9.*

Note

Page Numbering

The commands discussed in this section control page numbering. From
the Layout menu, select Page Numbering. The screen displays this dialog box:

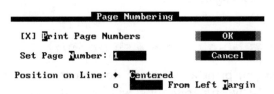

As usual, you can change your page numbering options from the dialog box or, if you find it more convenient, you can enter the dot commands individually. The dot commands associated with the page numbering dialog box are shown in Table 6-3.

Omit Page Numbers (.op)

You have probably noticed that for all the files you have printed so far, WordStar automatically printed the page number. To suppress page numbering, enter the dot command **.op** at the top of the page where you want page numbering turned off (or unmark the Print Page Numbers check box in the Page Numbering dialog box).

Note

Even if page numbers are not printed, WordStar continues sequential page numbering. You can also request to have a particular page printed in the usual manner when the document is printed.

Page Numbers On (.pg)

Page numbering is on by default. If you use .op to turn page number printing off, you can type **.pg** in the top line of the page where you want to turn page numbering back on.

6

Table 6-3. *Page Numbering Dot Commands*

Function	Command
Omit Page Number	.op
Set Page Number	pg/.pn n
Position on Line	.pc0 (centered) or
	.pc n (from left margin)

Set Page Numbers (.pn)

The .pn command allows you to set the first page number to be printed. WordStar automatically increments page numbering from the point of this command entry. If you wish to start printing page numbers on some page other than the first one, type **.op** on the first page; then, at the top of the page where you wish numbering to start, type **.pn** followed by the number you want that page to have.

You can also use this command with documents in two or more files. For example, suppose file A has 10 pages; file B, a continuation of A, has 7 pages. At the beginning of file B, type **.pn 11**. Numbering in file B will then begin at 11, and pages will be numbered sequentially through page 17.

Page Number Column (.pc *n*)

Page numbers are normally centered at the bottom of the page. The .pc command lets you change where the page number is printed. Type **.pc** followed by the column number in which you want the page number to appear. For example, **.pc 35** prints the page number in column 35. You may also indicate where the page number should be printed in terms of inches from the left margin. Follow the .pc command with the number of inches and then the inch symbol ("), just as you did with previous dot commands where inches were used.

A variation of the .pc command is .pc0. Inserting a zero after .pc causes the page number to print in the center of the current ruler line.

Remember

The # character can be used in either the header or footer commands to indicate page number placement, as described previously in "Special Header/Footer Format Commands."

New Page (.pa)

You have no doubt noticed that when your file has reached a certain length, you get a line across the screen with a *P* in column 80. The *P* is a flag character indicating where a page break will occur when you print your file.

Page breaks do not always occur where you want them, however. In long documents or documents with many charts or tables, for example, you almost always have to reposition page breaks to more appropriate places.

The .pa command allows you to force a page break at whatever line you select. Here's how to determine where you need to force a page break: Type your entire document, then return to the beginning and scroll through the document, entering the **.pa** command wherever you want a new page to begin. Never work from the end of the file to the beginning, or you may end up with a first page that is only a few lines long. Remember, too, that you can add up to six lines of text to a page by changing the bottom margin value.

Conditional Page (.cp *n*)

Another way to avoid unwanted page breaks is to use the Conditional Page command to specify the number of lines to remain on the page. This allows you to avoid breaking charts, tables, and so on. For example, if a table requires six lines, type **.cp 6** immediately above the table. Then, if there is not room for all six lines of the table on the page, printing of the table will start on the next page. On the screen, the page break, if displayed, appears as it does when the .pa command is specified.

6

Go to Page (^QI *n*, ^QI +/-*n*)

In previous chapters, you worked with commands that let you move long distances through a file. One of the most useful commands for long documents is ^QI *n*, which sends the cursor directly to the page specified by the number *n*. The cursor stops at the beginning of the requested page. A ^QI request to move to a page past the last numbered page will place the cursor at the beginning of the last page. If page numbering has been altered by a .pn command, a ^QI request to move to a page before numbering begins will move the cursor to the beginning of the file. By specifying +*n* or –*n* after ^QI, you move the cursor forward or backward *n* number of pages.

Next, Chapter 7 will complete your introduction to the basic features of WordStar. It deals with deleting, copying, and moving blocks, as well as a variety of Go To commands.

Exercises

1. Load EXAMPLE.2 from Chapter 2, and print it without a page number. Then print it again, with the page number in the header instead of the footer.

2. Using EXAMPLE.2, practice changing the page number column in both the header and footer.

3. Enter Example 6A. Experiment with the various Page Alignment features discussed in this chapter. Also, practice using the various ruler lines and paragraph margin settings discussed in Chapter 5.

4. Enter Example 6B, and use dot commands to print the filename and subdirectory name in the header. Print the page number in a footer in column 70.

5. Print Example 6B again, with page numbers at the top of the page.

6. Using a large file that you have saved, or using one that comes with WordStar, use an alternating odd/even offset to vary the left margins on odd and even pages.

Example 6A

```
                    STRAND HIGH SCHOOL
                     415 Green Street
                    Concord, CA 94520
                     (415) 798-5209

Dear Student Employer:

Please be advised that one of our students who has
been employed by you has applied for credit in the
Outside Work Experience Program.

We would like to acquaint you with the basic re-
quirements of this program so that there is no mis-
understanding at a later date.

Requirements

1.  The student must be regularly enrolled in the high
    school for no less than a minimum day, which
    consists of three classes.

2.  Absence from school automatically is considered
    absence from the Outside Work Experience job
    station. It is generally considered that if a
    student cannot attend school, he or she cannot go
    to work.

3.  A student cannot be employed in excess of eight
    hours per day, including school time.
```

6

Example 6A (*continued*)

For example:

If a student has four classes in the morning,
and works four hours after school, he or she is
within the requirements. However, if a student
has a full class schedule, he or she will be
entitled to work four hours after school.

4. All students under the age of eighteen must have
    a duly issued work permit.

I hope this letter is informative and that you and
your employee will be able to comply. We would
like to express our appreciation for your cooperation. If you have any questions, please call me at
666-1111.

                              Yours very truly,

                              JOHN SMITH

Example 6B

```
To:        Mr. John Sears      Mr. Peter Sherwood
           Mr. Jack Evans      Ms. Pat Gena

From:      Mr. Bob Harris

We have had discussions with several administrators
of the Martinez Unified School District during the
past year concerning projects to be implemented on
the microcomputer; for example:

     Mike Lena        Audio-Visual Inventory
     Laura Foster     Elementary School Testing
     Mary Aspen       High School Proficiency Tests
     Rich Laughlin    Elementary School Attendance
     Bill Smith       Word Processing
     Jack Evans       Title I Management

Some of these projects are well under way; others are
still in the discussion stage.

The implementation of these requests has relied
heavily on the use of the ROP equipment, some of which
is available for administrative use approximately two
hours each day.

Planning for these and future projects should be given
careful consideration by the administration. The main
points to consider are:

Hardware

We have at the high school now, or on order, the
hardware to implement these tasks at least at a minimal
level.

The correction of the elementary school tests with
the inclusion of data on each student and the Title
I Management program will probably exceed the capacity
of our 5 1/4-inch disks; therefore, consideration
```

6

Example 6B (*continued*)

should be given to the purchase of a hard disk (approximately $5,000).

Some of the projects (e.g., elementary school attendance, Title I Management) would be printed more efficiently on a high-speed printer (approximately $2,000).

When all of the above projects are on-line, along with others we have been using for some time, we will need full-time use of at least two terminals to obtain the output in a reasonable amount of time. (The cost of an additional terminal will be between $1,500 and $3,500, depending on some software information that should be available before the end of the school year.)

Software

There is also a variety of software required for the most efficient implementation of these projects.

The software should be compatible, not only for these projects, but also for those planned in the foreseeable future (two or three years). It would also be cost-effective to use the same software in the high school programming and business classes and for administrative word processing.

Facilities

Careful consideration should be given to housing the equipment required to perform these tasks. Because of the expense required for wiring and security, their location is not easily changed.

Since this cost can be considerable, the requirements to house this equipment, and to provide adequate,

Example 6B (*continued*)

secure storage, and ample space for personnel in the foreseeable future should be taken into account.

Planning is also important for the optimum utilization of the equipment. It is important that some equipment not be placed where it can be used only a small portion of the day while other equipment may be overtaxed.

Easy access by the departments that will make the most use of these facilities should be taken into account when locating the equipment.

Cost

The cost is, of course, an important factor. The district now spends in excess of $20,000 annually for computer-related services. (It may be considerably more than this; Mr. Lena would have to determine the exact amount.)

The district has potential savings from at least three sources:

1. Direct savings by performing some services on district computers that are currently done outside.

2. Indirect savings by using programs such as the inventory program, which allows better control over the audio-visual equipment, and would save some of the $6,000 in annual losses.

3. Indirect savings by increasing efficiency with computer programs and word processing. When some personnel leave, they would not have to be replaced.

6

Example 6B (*continued*)

```
Of course, only through a careful study of district
requirements and current expenses for computer ser-
vices can costs and benefits be determined.

RH/ljp

March 23, 1992
```

7

Block and Go To Commands

The Block and Go To commands allow you to quickly and accurately perform several functions that required a great deal of time and trouble prior to word processors. Using *blocks* in WordStar, you can manipulate large sections of text, instead of having to work with single characters, words, or lines of text.

Block Commands (Edit Menu)

Most of the Block and Go To commands you'll be working with in this chapter can be accessed from the Edit menu shown in Figure 7-1. (Other commands on the Edit menu and its submenus will be discussed in future chapters.)

Marking a Block (SHIFT-F9, SHIFT-F10)

Let's start with the commands to mark the beginning and end of a block. To have some sample text to work with, load the EXAMPLE.2 file. With insert mode on, place the cursor at the beginning of the file, over the *M* in *Most*, and press SHIFT-F9 (Begin Block). The symbol <B>, the beginning of the *block*

Figure 7-1.   *The Edit menu window*

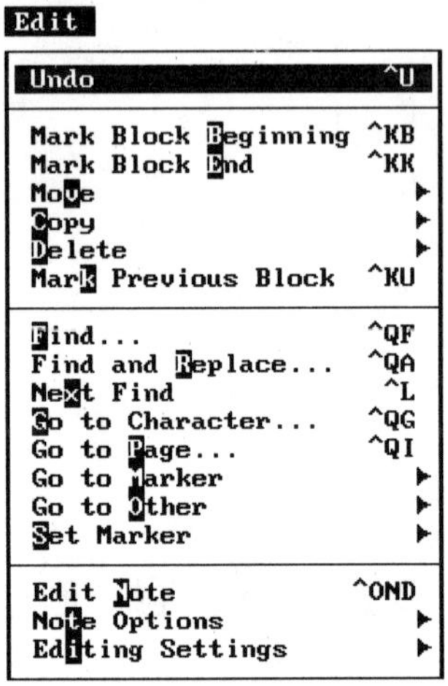

```
 Edit

 Undo                            ^U

 Mark Block Beginning  ^KB
 Mark Block End        ^KK
 Move                    ▶
 Copy                    ▶
 Delete                  ▶
 Mark Previous Block   ^KU

 Find...               ^QF
 Find and Replace...   ^QA
 Next Find             ^L
 Go to Character...    ^QG
 Go to Page...         ^QI
 Go to Marker            ▶
 Go to Other             ▶
 Set Marker              ▶

 Edit Note            ^OND
 Note Options            ▶
 Editing Settings        ▶
```

mark, appears on the screen in reverse video, and *Most* will have moved three spaces to the right.

Move the cursor to the end of the first paragraph, after the period, and press SHIFT-F10 (End Block). The beginning of the block mark, <B>, is gone, the blocked material appears in reverse video, and the symbols <B> <K> appear in the status line at the bottom of the screen. These two markers let you know a block is marked, even though you may be editing several pages away from the block. With the first paragraph blocked, you can now move it to the end of the file.

Moving a Block (SHIFT-F7)

Press the END key to move the cursor to the end of the file. Press ENTER to insert a blank line. Press SHIFT-F7, and the blocked paragraph is moved so that it begins at the cursor position.

Press the HOME key to move the cursor back to column 1 at the beginning of the file. Then press SHIFT-F7 again. The paragraph is returned to its original position.

With the SHIFT-F7 command you can move any blocked portion of your file—a phrase, sentence, paragraph, or more—to any position in the document.

Just place the cursor where you want the blocked material to be moved, and press SHIFT-F7. Note that a block remains defined until another block is specified. For practice, block the second paragraph and move it to the beginning of the file.

Note

The size of the block you wish to move is limited by the amount of memory available in the computer. If you try to move a block too large for your computer to handle, you will see the message "Block too long." You can then divide your material into two or three smaller blocks and move them one at a time.

Copying a Block (SHIFT-F8)

Instead of moving a block of material from one place to another, you may want to copy it, that is, to move it elsewhere and have it remain in its original position. To do this, mark the block as you did before, pressing SHIFT-F9 at the beginning of the block and SHIFT-F10 at the end. Then move the cursor to the position where you want the material copied, and press SHIFT-F8. The blocked material will be duplicated at the position of the cursor and will also remain as is in its original position.

To mark a new section of blocked text, move the cursor to the beginning of the new section and press SHIFT-F9. Then move the cursor to the end of the section and press SHIFT-F10. You can now move or copy this block. You can change the blocked section as often as you like.

Turning Block Highlighting On/Off (SHIFT-F6)

To eliminate the block highlighting from the screen display, press SHIFT-F6 (Block Hide). Normal video returns. Although the reverse video no longer identifies the block, WordStar remembers the blocked text for the remainder of the editing session or until you mark another block. The marks in the status line indicate that a block is defined. Press SHIFT-F6 again, and the reverse video will reappear—try it.

Unmarking a Block (^K<)

To unmark a block, press ^K<. (To access the < symbol, press SHIFT and the comma (,) key.) After you press ^K<, notice that the <B><K> block marks are no longer in the status line.

7

Note

There is a distinction between marking and unmarking a block and turning block highlighting on and off. The SHIFT-F6 *command (block highlighting) is a toggle. In contrast, to mark a block after you unmark it, you have to reset the beginning and end block marks by using* SHIFT-F9 *and* SHIFT-F10 *again.*

Blocking Columns On/Off (^KN)

To prepare to block columns, close EXAMPLE.2 and abandon your changes. Then open a new file.

To block columns of data, you must first turn on Column mode by pressing ^KN. Notice that "Column" now appears at the left end of the status line at the bottom of the screen.

Follow these instructions to enter section (1) of Example 7A: Enter the first row of characters. Then use the Block commands to copy in the next four rows. Next, with Column mode on, move the columns necessary to duplicate the pattern in section (2) of Example 7A. Place the cursor at the beginning of the file, in column 1, and press SHIFT-F9. Now move the cursor to the space after the last *C* in line 5; press SHIFT-F10. The three columns are blocked and in reverse video. Move the cursor to the end of line 1 and insert a space. Finally, press SHIFT-F7. Your screen should look like section (2) in Example 7A. Now follow the same procedure to produce section (3).

You can move or copy not only columns of characters but also columns of spaces, as was done in section (4) of Example 7A. This can be a very useful application when you have a long file with columns of names or numbers and you wish to change the spacing. To do this, you mark off a column of spaces and copy it to a new position, just as you would text.

Replacing Columns (^KI)

When you copy or move columns, existing material moves to the right as necessary to make room for the copied or moved columns. That is, all the columns are still there. If you wish to replace an existing column with new data, use the Column Replace command, ^KI. Column Replace can be invoked only if Column mode is already turned on.

With Column mode on, press **^KI**. Notice that following "Column" in the status line you now have "Replace." To experiment and familiarize yourself with the **^KI** command, use it to create pattern (5) in Example 7A. When you are finished, turn Column Replace mode off by pressing **^KN**.

Note

Pressing **^U** *(Undo) restores the block of data most recently deleted by Column Replace.*

Deleting a Block (SHIFT-F5)

Using Example 7A, block the first three rows. Press SHIFT-F5; the entire block is deleted. This is an easy way to delete large sections of material.

Just as you can undo other delete commands using ^U, you can undo block delete operations, provided the block is not too large. WordStar will advise you if the marked block is too large for the buffer and for the Undo command to restore, and will ask if the block should be deleted anyway.

Note

The size of the "unerase" buffer can be increased using WSCHANGE.

Marking a Previous Block (^KU)

You have seen how to block a section of your file, copy it or move it, and then mark a second block. After working with the second block, you can also quickly re-mark the first block by pressing **^KU**. To use ^KU, both blocks must have been set in the same manner—for example, with Column mode turned on or off for both blocks.

Writing a Block (^KW)

The Write Block command is used to take material from the file being edited and write it to another file on the disk. You can use this command when, for example, you have a section of a report that you want to use in several different documents.

The first time you type the material, block it and press **^KW**. The Copy to Another File dialog box shown in Figure 7-2 is displayed.

7

Figure 7-2.   *The Write Block window*

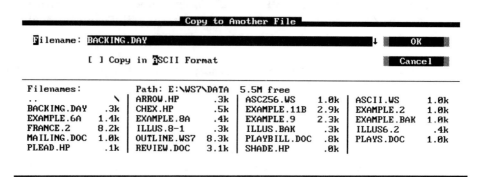

Enter the filename you wish to use for the blocked material. Press ENTER, and the blocked material is saved in that file.

If you use a filename that is already on your current directory, the following dialog box is displayed:

Select one of the following options:

Overwrite   To replace the contents of the disk file with the blocked material

Append   To add the blocked material to the end of the disk file

Cancel   To return to the file being edited

If you mark the Copy in ASCII Format check box in the Copy to Another File dialog box, all the formatting codes inserted by WordStar are stripped from the block. Mark this box only if the block being copied is intended for use by a program other than WordStar.

Note

Save EXAMPLE.7A. The next section will use EXAMPLE.7B.

Reading a File (^KR)

The Read File command is used to take material from the disk and add it to the file you are editing. The material could be something you have just written to the disk using ^KW, or a file that is already there. To try this, place the cursor where you want to add the material from the disk and press ^KR (Insert a File); WordStar will display the Insert File dialog box. After you supply the filename, press ENTER. The material from the disk will be inserted in the file you are editing at the position of the cursor. Your original disk file is left intact.

Try this now with one of the questions from the Physics test in Example 7B. Enter Example.7B and block one of the questions. Press ^KW, enter a new filename, **QUES.5**, and press ENTER. Press SHIFT-F5 to delete the question from the file you are editing. To reinsert the question, place the cursor where you want the question to appear, press ^KR, and type **QUES.5** (the filename used to save the question). Press ENTER, and the question is back in place. Now close EXAMPLE.7B.

In addition to reading in WordStar files, you can use ^KR to read in files created using MailList and most versions of Lotus 1-2-3, Quattro, Symphony, and dBASE. Once files or portions of files are read into WordStar, you may use all of the WordStar editing features to modify the file.

Note

When reading a file, whether created using WordStar or another program, be sure to enter the appropriate path if the file is not on the current directory.

Keep the following in mind when reading in a spreadsheet file:

- To prevent realignment of column material, Word Wrap (Off) should precede the data being read into your WordStar file.
- Be sure the section of your file where the spreadsheet is to be inserted is formatted in a nonproportional font.
- A dialog box will be displayed allowing you to select the desired spreadsheet range.
- Pressing ENTER without selecting the range selects the entire spreadsheet.
- If range names are used in a spreadsheet, they will be displayed and can be used to select the range.

Changing Case (^K", ^K!, ^K.)

Another application while working with blocks is to change the case of a letter, that is, to make it uppercase or lowercase within a block. Select Convert Case on the Style menu and the following screen appears:

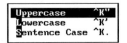

You have the three possibilities shown here:

^K"   Uppercase. Press **^K"** to change all the letters in the block to uppercase.

^K'   Lowercase. Press **^K'** to change all the letters in the block to lowercase.

^K.   Sentence Case. Press **^K.** to change the first letter of a sentence to uppercase and the remaining letters to lowercase. Some editing may be needed to check for missed uppercase letters.

Go To Commands (Edit Menu)

In Chapter 2 you used several keys associated with the keypad to move the cursor about the document you were editing. Now consider commands that make it easy to move to a block, or to a mark that you place in your file.

Moving to Beginning/End of Block (^QB, ^QK)

When a block is marked, you can quickly move to the beginning or end of the block with the commands ^QB (to the beginning) and ^QK (to the end), located under the Go to Other option on the Edit menu. These two commands are most useful with large blocks or large files when the cursor is some distance (several pages) away from the block you need. Now load EXAMPLE.7A and try these commands with a marked block.

Setting Marks (^K0 through 9)

In multiple-page documents, it is useful to set marks at appropriate intervals so that you can quickly go to any part of the document. Ten such marks can be set (0 through 9). These marks are most useful when working with a long file.

To experiment, open Example 7B or, if you like, use a long file of your own selection. There is no point in putting a mark at the beginning or end of a file since WordStar provides commands to move to these positions, so let's place the first mark at question 1. Put the cursor at the beginning of a paragraph on page 1 and press **^K0**. (Make sure you enter a zero, not a capital *O*.) A zero in reverse video will appear, and the number is displayed on the status line. Move the cursor to a likely spot on page 2 and press **^K1**. Continue in this manner until you have entered marks 2 through 4.

Note

If you enter a mark number that has already been set, the previously set mark will be repositioned at the present cursor placement and removed from the previous position.

Going to Marks (^Q0 through 9)

Now when you press **^Q** followed by one of the mark numbers you just entered, the cursor will move to that mark—try it. Again, this procedure is most useful for long documents.

7

Continuous Scrolling Up/Down (^QW and ^QZ)

You have previously used the PGUP and PGDN keys to scroll the screen up or down a full screen. With the commands ^QW and ^QZ, you can scroll the screen up or down continuously, or at least until the screen reaches the top or bottom of the file. Load a file that has three or four pages of material. Press **^QZ**, and the screen will begin scrolling towards the bottom of the file one line at a time. You can use this procedure to scroll through an entire file, looking for a particular entry. Once the ^QZ command has been given, you can control the rate of scrolling by pressing the numbers 0 through 9; 0 is the fastest and 9 the slowest. When you arrive at the end of the file, use **^QW** to scroll to the beginning of the file. Of course, the scroll rate is again controlled by the numbers 0 through 9. If any examples are open, close them now.

Exercises

1. Load EXAMPLE.2. Block the first half and write it to the disk. Do the same with the second half (using a different name from the first).

2. Using the Read File command, rejoin the two files you separated in Exercise 1.

3. Type five names and addresses with different zip codes (one name per line). Using the Block commands, rearrange the names and addresses so they are in alphabetical order.

4. Rearrange the names and addresses in Exercise 3 so they are in order by zip code, from lowest number to highest.

5. Open EXAMPLE.7B. Using Block commands, arrange the questions in reverse order.

6. Forms of one type or another are easy to create with WordStar by using the Block commands. To enter Example 7C, set the ruler line and tabs to conform to this form, and enter the form as far as the *B* on the right side in the example. (Do not enter the *A* or the *B*.) With the cursor at the position of the *B*, press SHIFT-F10. Move the cursor to the position of the *A* on the left side of the example and press SHIFT-F9. Move the cursor to the bottom of the file and press RETURN to place the cursor at the C position and press ^KC. Move the cursor back to position A and again press SHIFT-F9. Return to the end of the file and type ^KC. By repeating this process, you will move progressively larger blocks of material. Keep an eye on the line number in the status line so that you don't go past the end of the page.

Example 7A

```
(1)
AAAAA BBBBB CCCCC 11111 22222 33333
AAAAA BBBBB CCCCC 11111 22222 33333
AAAAA BBBBB CCCCC 11111 22222 33333
AAAAA BBBBB CCCCC 11111 22222 33333
AAAAA BBBBB CCCCC 11111 22222 33333

(2)
11111 22222 33333 AAAAA BBBBB CCCCC
11111 22222 33333 AAAAA BBBBB CCCCC
11111 22222 33333 AAAAA BBBBB CCCCC
11111 22222 33333 AAAAA BBBBB CCCCC
11111 22222 33333 AAAAA BBBBB CCCCC

(3)
11111 AAAAA 22222 BBBBB 33333 CCCCC
11111 AAAAA 22222 BBBBB 33333 CCCCC
11111 AAAAA 22222 BBBBB 33333 CCCCC
11111 AAAAA 22222 BBBBB 33333 CCCCC
11111 AAAAA 22222 BBBBB 33333 CCCCC

(4)
11111     AAAAA     22222     BBBBB     33333     CCCCC
11111     AAAAA     22222     BBBBB     33333     CCCCC
11111     AAAAA     22222     BBBBB     33333     CCCCC
11111     AAAAA     22222     BBBBB     33333     CCCCC
11111     AAAAA     22222     BBBBB     33333     CCCCC

(5)
AAAAA BBBBB CCCCC 11111 22222 33333
AAAAA BAAAB CAAAC 1AAA1 2AAA2 3AAA3
AAAAA BAAAB CAAAC 1AAA1 2AAA2 3AAA3
AAAAA BAAAB CAAAC 1AAA1 2AAA2 3AAA3
AAAAA BBBBB CCCCC 11111 22222 33333

          BBB   CCC   111   222   333
          BBB   CCC   111   222   333
          BBB   CCC   111   222   333
```

7

Example 7B

```
                        PHYSICS TEST

                        Chapters 7-8

Name _____  Period _____

1.  If a small planet were discovered whose distance
    from the sun was 16 times that of the earth, how
    many times longer than the earth takes would the
    new planet take to circle the sun?

2.  The radius of the moon's orbit is 60 times greater
    than the radius of the earth. How many times
    greater is the acceleration of a falling body on
    the earth than the acceleration of the moon toward
    the earth?

3.  At what height above the earth's surface will a
    rocket have 1/4 the force of gravitation on it
    that it would have at sea level? Express your
    answer in earth radii.

4.  A 75-kg boy stands 1 meter away from a 65-kg girl.
    Calculate the force of attraction (gravitational)
    between them.

5.  If you push a body with force of 4 newtons for
    1/2 sec, what impulse do you give the body?

6.  What average force is necessary to stop a hammer
    with 25 newton-sec momentum in .05 sec?

7.  What happens to the momentum of a car when it
    comes to a stop?

8.  What is the kinetic energy of a 2-kg hammer moving
    at 20 m/sec?
```

Example 7C

```
                          COMPUTER CENTER LOG

A JOB DESCRIPTION  |  IN DATE  | FROM  | OUT DATE  | TO
  -----------------|----------|------|----------|--
  -----------------|----------|------|----------|--
                                                   B
C -----------------|----------|------|----------|--
  -----------------|----------|------|----------|--
  -----------------|----------|------|----------|--
  -----------------|----------|------|----------|--
  -----------------|----------|------|----------|--
  -----------------|----------|------|----------|--
  -----------------|----------|------|----------|--
  -----------------|----------|------|----------|--
  -----------------|----------|------|----------|--
  -----------------|----------|------|----------|--
  -----------------|----------|------|----------|--
  -----------------|----------|------|----------|--
  -----------------|----------|------|----------|--
  -----------------|----------|------|----------|--
  -----------------|----------|------|----------|--
  -----------------|----------|------|----------|--
  -----------------|----------|------|----------|--
  -----------------|----------|------|----------|--
  -----------------|----------|------|----------|--
  -----------------|----------|------|----------|--
  -----------------|----------|------|----------|--
```

7

8

Printer Options

Today's market offers a wide variety of printers, with varying capabilities. The two most common types of printers used with personal computers are *dot-matrix* and *laser* printers. WordStar can take advantage of the characteristics of most of these and other printers. Consult your printer manual to see if your printer will work with the commands discussed in this chapter; most of the newer printers will. Also recall that a variety of commands that affect the appearance of your printed document are discussed in Chapter 6.

Many of the print functions discussed in this chapter can be accessed directly through the Style menu or its secondary windows, Other and Settings. The Print Controls menu, accessed by pressing **^P**, also lets you select the print functions. You can also enter the dot commands directly. WordStar offers print functions to print characters with underlining, boldface, double-strike, italic, and strikeout attributes, as well as subscript and superscript.

About Control Characters

As you try each of the print options, you will notice that each one causes the characters or text on the screen to be bracketed with different symbols, and the bracketed text is highlighted. These print option symbols or codes are called *control characters*. Control character displays can be toggled on and off by pressing SHIFT-F1. When you press SHIFT-F1, the screen returns to normal, with only the print feature itself (such as underlining or boldface) displayed. Pressing SHIFT-F1 again toggles the control character display back on. In addition to controlling the display of control characters, SHIFT-F1 can eliminate the display of any tabs or soft hyphens in your file. (Recall that in Chapter 3 you used SHIFT-F1, Command Tags, to toggle certain screen displays, such as dot commands, the flag column, and soft space dots, on and off.)

When you print a file, the control characters do not print, even if they appear on the screen. Generally, you will work with the control character display turned off. When you are working with several print-display formats and are unsure what the highlighting represents, you can turn the display on to view the symbols. Practice using these functions by entering the command characters before and after the text you want to affect. Use a single file, and then print it so you can see the appearance of the text.

Before you begin working with the print functions, enter Example 8A. As you encounter each of the print functions in this chapter, try it on an appropriate portion of the example. We will start with the two most commonly used print functions, underlining (F3) and boldfacing (F4).

Underline (F3)

You can underline a single letter or an entire document. All that is necessary is to bracket the text you want underlined with the appropriate print code. In Example 8A, let's underline the words *print functions*. First, position the cursor on the *p* in *print* and, with insert mode on, press F3. You will see that *everything* from that point on is underlined.

Note

The way your screen displays print options depends on the monitor you use. Not all monochrome monitors are capable of showing underline, for example. Also, color monitors will display the various print options in various colors.

Next, position the cursor immediately after the *s* in *functions* and press F3 again. Now only *print functions* is underlined. In addition to being underlined, notice that *print functions* is bracketed by two ^S control character symbols.

Note

When the control character symbols are displayed on the screen, the lines in which they appear may extend past the right end of the ruler line. Since the symbols will not be printed, however, your printed document will still be correctly justified.

When you print, the underlining will appear just as it does on the screen—only the words, not the spaces between words, are underlined; this is the default setting. You can also tell WordStar to use continuous underlining, as explained next.

Continuous Underline (.ul on/off)

Continuous underlining, that is, underlining both the words and the spaces between them, is achieved by inserting the dot commands .ul on and .ul off into the file, or by selecting Continuous Underline from the Settings window. To access the Settings window, open the Style menu and choose Settings; you will see this dialog box:

Using either the Settings window or the .ul dot command, enter **.ul on** at a convenient point before the text to be underlined. Remember that the dot goes in column 1, and no information but the command can be on that line. After you enter the dot command, bracket the desired text with ^S codes as you did before by pressing F3. Underlining will be continuous. To turn off continuous underlining, type **.ul off** on a line by itself at the end of the paragraph or section containing the underlined text. If you know you are

8

going to use continuous underlining throughout a file, just enter the dot command at the beginning of the file and leave it on. There will not be any distinction on the screen display between text with continuous underlining and text with individual words underlined.

Boldface (F4)

Next, make the last two words of the document in Example 8A boldface. Place the cursor over the first letter of the word *professional* and, with the insert mode on, press F4. Position the cursor under the period following *appearance* and again press F4. If the screen is set to display control characters, the words *professional appearance* are now bracketed by the ^B symbols and displayed in boldface. Remember, the symbols can be removed from the screen, as noted before, by pressing SHIFT-F1.

With the symbol display on, move the cursor several spaces to the left of the words *professional appearance*. Then, using the arrow keys, move the cursor one space at a time to the right. Watch the column number in the status line and notice that it does not change when the cursor crosses the ^B symbols (just as row numbers do not change when the cursor crosses lines containing dot commands).

Double-Strike (^PD)

Now try the double-strike attribute. *Double-striking* makes a word or phrase stand out, but it does not print as dark as boldface. To print text as double-strike, place the cursor in front of the selected text and press **^PD**. Move the cursor after the selected material and press **^PD** again. The text is now bracketed by ^D symbols.

Italic (^PY)

To print a section of your file in italic, place the cursor at the beginning of the section you want in italic and press **^PY**. Move the cursor to the end of the section, and press **^PY** again. On the screen, the bracketed section will appear in boldface or in a color.

Strikeout (^PX)

To use WordStar's strikeout capability, use ^PX to bracket a word or section of text with ^X codes. On screen, the enclosed text appears as "^XStrikeout^X." and when printed it appears as

~~Strikeout.~~

Change Strikeout Character (.xx)

You can change the strikeout character from the default (–) to some other character. To change the strikeout character, enter it in the Settings window (used previously to control underlining); or type the dot command **.xx**, followed by your new strikeout character. For example, **.xx#** causes the previous example to print as

#Strikeout#

Subscript/Superscript (^PV and ^PT)

8

Subscript characters are most commonly used in equations. Superscripts are used both in equations and to indicate footnotes. Here are two examples using equations. Type them in as they appear below.

Subscript Example: $m = a_1X + a_2Y + a_3Z$

Superscript Example: $X^2 + Y^2 = 36$

Now, to create the subscript and superscript characters, enter print codes just as you did in the previous examples. Place the cursor before the subscript number and press **^PV**. Move the cursor after the subscript and again press **^PV**. You use the same concept with superscript, except you use **^PT** to bracket the material. The examples should look like this on the screen:

```
                    Subscript Example
            m=a^V1^VX + a^V2^VY + a^V3^VZ


                    Superscript Example
            X^T2^T + Y^T2^T = 36
```

Not all printers can handle all of WordStar's special print options. Check your printer manual if you have difficulty using any of these functions.

Note

Ribbon Color (^P−)

If you work with a printer that offers a variety of print colors, you can easily select the color you want. Place the cursor at the beginning of the section where the color is to change and press **^P−**. The Color/Shading window for your printer is displayed. An example is shown here:

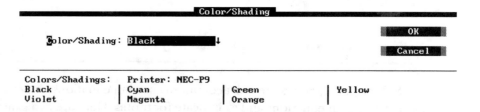

Select the desired color for the section of text. At the end of the section, press **^P−** again to return to the normal color. The color selected is displayed as a tag in your file, for example "<Light Blue>."

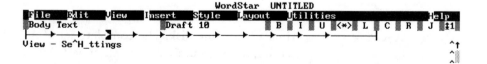

If you use a red-black ribbon, be sure the switch under the ribbon cartridge is set for red-black. WordStar can take advantage of this feature on your printer only if the color switch is properly set. When you switch back to multistrike ribbon, be sure to reset this switch, or you will get only half the use you should from your ribbon.

Tip

Print Pause (^PC)

At times you may find it convenient to pause while printing—maybe to insert an envelope or to change print wheels. Pressing **^PC** places a ^C code in a file so that printing will stop precisely where you want it to. You can then change print wheels to insert special characters or italic for a word or phrase, for example. Another ^C code must be inserted at the end of the special section so the printer will stop again, to allow you to reinsert the original print wheel.

To use the Print Pause feature, start the printing from the Opening screen. When the printer stops, "Print Wait" will appear in the status line. Display the Printing dialog box (select **P** from the File menu or from the traditional menu), and then press **C** to continue printing.

Overprint (^PH)

Overprint lets you print two or more characters in the same space. An example is a menu selection, such as View, Settings, where the accelerator letter **e** is underlined. To print "Settings," enter **Se^PH_tting**. On your screen it appears as

8

```
                        WordStar  UNTITLED
 File   Edit   View   Insert   Style   Layout   Utilities              Help
 Body Text              Draft 10        B   I   U  <*>  L    C   R   J  ±1
 |      →       →    ╡       →       →       →       →       →           ↑
 View - Se^H_ttings                                                      ^↑
                                                                         ^|
                                                                         ^||
```

Change Print Driver (^P?)

The documents you enter in the computer with WordStar can be printed on paper or saved (printed) on the hard disk. The software that operates your printer or prints to the disk is called a *driver*. Most people work with only one printer and, therefore, never have to change drivers. However, some of you may find it useful to change drivers for one of the following reasons:

- To use an alternate printer
- To save a file and print it at another computer
- To transfer a file to WordStar 4 format
- To view file format on screen before printing
- To prepare a fax file

To view the list of printer drivers available, press **^P?**. The display on your screen will depend on the printers you have installed. Here is an example:

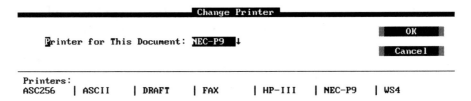

Use the arrow keys to make your selection and press ENTER.

There are two categories of drivers listed in the foregoing illustration: those you select when you install the printer and those supplied with WordStar. The following print drivers are supplied with WordStar to write a file to the disk for a specific purpose:

Driver	Purpose
ASC256	Prints a file to the disk. The complete set of ASCII codes, letters, numbers, and extended characters is printed. The extended characters are discussed in Chapter 16.

Driver	Purpose
ASCII	Prints the first 128 ASCII characters that all printers can handle.
Fax	Prepares files to send by facsimile.
WS4	Prints a file to the disk in WS4 format. The file may then be read and edited using WordStar 4.0. The file printed to the disk has the same name as the original, with the extension WS4.
Draft	A generic printer driver that will handle most printers. This driver has few, if any, special print-handling abilities.

Font Options

A font has several characteristics. Most prominent are its style, or how it looks; its size or pitch; and the symbols that make up the set. The fonts available to you are determined by your printer. Some examples of fonts available on WordStar 7.0 are:

```
Courier 10 850
Univers PC 12.2
Times PC12.2
```

Fonts are available as internal (built-in) fonts that come with the printer, cartridges that plug into the printer, and soft fonts. Laser printers and the newer dot-matrix printers have a wide variety of built-in fonts. Soft fonts are on a disk and can be loaded into the printer's memory.

Laser printers can handle *scalable* fonts. If you have this option available, you select the font and then indicate the desired size. The maximum size supported by WordStar is 999.75 points. The size can be changed in increments of .25 points.

8

Normal/Alternate Font Selection (^PN and ^PA)

The commands ^PN and ^PA give you a quick and easy way to change the font your printer uses. Again, the capability depends on your printer and its installation. All the printing you have done so far has been with your default or normal font, as shown in the style bar. To see the available alternate fonts, press **^PA**. With the cursor just past the Alternate tab, check the style bar to see which font is used. The standard installation is to have normal pitch set to 10 and alternate pitch set to 12.

The print tag for normal font doesn't show unless you press **^PN**. Usually this would only be done after a section was printed in alternate pitch. You can also use these commands to bracket a word or phrase for emphasis within a paragraph. The print tags are toggled on and off using SHIFT-F1. Figure 8-1 shows how the <ALTERNATE> and <NORMAL> print tags appear on screen.

In the figure, the first paragraph is 12 pitch and extends beyond the right edge of the ruler line. When the paragraphs are printed, the two fonts will print at the same line length. You can check the appearance of the printed file by using Preview, discussed in Chapter 9.

Figure 8-1.   *Edit screen with font tags*

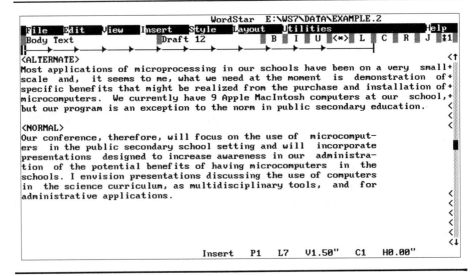

Font Selection (^P=)

If your printer offers a variety of fonts, you can change fonts within your document by pressing **^P=**. A sample Font window is displayed in **Figure 8-2**. (Of course, what you have displayed will depend on the printer you have installed.)

If you use a mouse, you can click the font in the style bar to display the Font window. You can then make the font selection by using the mouse.

To print a section of your file in another font, place the cursor at the beginning of the section, open the Font window, select the desired font, and press ENTER. If the font is scalable, fill in the desired point size when you are asked to do so, and press ENTER. Then move the cursor to the end of the section, display the Font window again, and select the original font or any other font style you wish. Press ENTER. You may bracket anything from a single character to a large portion of your file. When a different font is selected, a font description or tag is displayed at the beginning of the section, as shown in Figure 8-3.

After you have made your font selections, be sure to reformat the section with the new font. The reformat options are on the Utilities, Reformat menu. Paragraph reformatting was discussed in Chapter 3.

Note

The distance indicator in the status line will keep track of the distance between the cursor and the left margin. Also, even if the font size changes and a variety of fonts are used in the same line, the printout will remain justified if you are using that alignment.

Figure 8-2. *Font window*

8

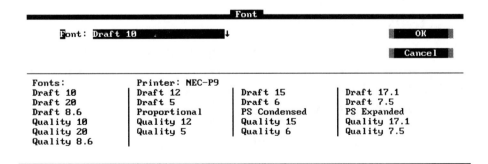

Figure 8-3.   Screen display with font tag

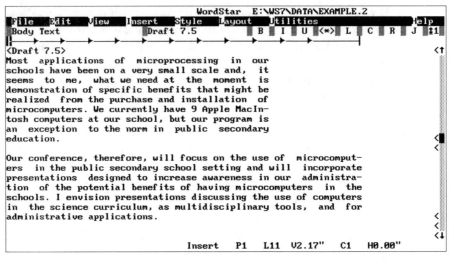

In Figure 8-3, the first paragraph has been reformatted. When printed, these two fonts will print at the same line length. As with the alternate pitch example, you can check the appearance of the printed file using Preview (Chapter 9). The font remains in effect until another font selection is made. If scalable fonts are available for your printer, they will be indicated on the Font window by three trailing dots (for example, Helvetica...). If a scalable font is chosen, a dialog box is displayed asking you to enter a point size.

Go To Font (^Q=)

You can advance the cursor quickly to the next font flag in your file by pressing ^Q=. The search is from the position of the cursor toward the end of the file. To search the entire document, place the cursor at the beginning of the file.

Additional Print Options

The following options are less commonly used, but you may find one or more of them useful for the type of work you do or because your printer has special requirements.

Microjustification (.uj on/off/dis)

If your printer supports *microjustification*, you can use the .uj command to set microjustification to *on*, *off*, or *dis*. The default value is dis (discretionary), which means the printer driver decides when to use microjustification. With microjustification on, spacing between words and (with some printers) between letters is adjusted in small increments. This slows printing to some extent. If speed is of primary importance, turn microjustification off (enter **.uj off**); if appearance is the main consideration, turn it on (enter **.uj on**). The default value, dis, is usually best for most printers that support this function. However, if you find that table columns are not aligned when printed, turn microjustification off before printing the tables and on again immediately after printing the tables.

Bidirectional Print (.bp)

The .bp command allows you to turn bidirectional printing on or off. Enter **.bp 0** (zero) to turn bidirectional printing off and cause printing to proceed from left to right only. Enter **.bp 1** to turn bidirectional printing back on. If your printer does not use bidirectional printing, it will not be affected by this command.

8

Proportional Spacing (.ps on/off)

The .ps command prints in *proportional spacing* the section of your document bracketed by .ps on and .ps off commands. Proportional spacing uses different amounts of space for different letters. For example, the letter *w* requires more space than the letter *a*. For printers that support this feature, WordStar maintains a table of spaces required for different letters. The appropriate wheel or thimble must be installed for this feature to work with daisy wheel and thimble printers.

Subscript/Superscript Roll (.sr *n*)

The .sr*n* command controls *subscript/superscript roll*—how far above or below the text line subscripts and superscripts are printed. The default value for this characteristic is 3 (3/48 of an inch). To change this value, enter **.sr** followed by the number of 48ths of an inch that you wish subscripts or superscripts to roll up or down.

Letter Quality (.lq on/off/dis)

The .lq command allows you to change print quality from draft- to letter-quality. You can set this command at the beginning of your document or within the document to print a section. Enter either **.lq off** or **.lq 0** to turn letter-quality printing off, and **.lq on** or **.lq 1** to turn it back on. The option dis stands for discretionary; WordStar will select letter-quality on or off depending on the font used.

Selecting Sheet Feeders (.bn *n*)

The .bn command allows you to select one of four sheet bins for your document. This allows you to feed into your printer letterhead, plain paper, envelopes, and other types of paper held in different paper bins, if your printer accommodates such a feature. The command to use is **.bn** followed by a number from 1 to 4 that is assigned by you or your printer to particular paper bins.

Ignore (.ig and ..)

Two commands, .ig (for ignore) and dot dot (..), allow you to insert remarks in your file that you can read on the screen but that are not printed. Enter the command and then your comments. Note that your comments must be confined to the line with the dot command on it. If your comment is longer than one line, use the command again at the beginning of the next line.

Exercises

1. Using Example 8A, try any of the special print commands introduced in this lesson that apply to your printer.
2. Enter Example 8B using the appropriate print functions, so that when you print it, your printout looks the same as the example.
3. Edit the Example 5A you typed in Chapter 5, changing the high school name and address to boldface and the words *Requirements* and *Example* to double-strike.
4. Use WordStar's subscript and superscript print enhancements to print the following equation:

   $y = a_1x^2 + a_2x + a_3$
5. Print a portion of one of your documents in alternate pitch. If you have a daisy wheel or thimble printer, use the Print Pause command (^PC) and change the print wheel to use both normal and alternate pitch.
6. If your printer supports different fonts, change the font for various sections of one of your files. Also, select a word or phrase and change the font.
7. Use the Go To Font command to quickly go through the file you used in Exercise 6 and change or remove the fonts you added there.

8

Example 8A

```
The print functions are listed on the command card
supplied with this book. In some documents they
are not only necessary but, when used appropri-
ately, give your work a very professional appear-
ance.
```

Example 8B

```
Mr. Bob Harris

As you requested, listed below are the AV school
identification codes.

AV INVENTORY — SCHOOL CODE

   AV1.........Martinez Elementary

   AV2.........John Swett

   AV3.........Las Juntas

   AV4.........Martinez Junior High

   AV5.........District Office

   AV6.........Adult School

   AV7.........Trailer

   AV8.........Alhambra High School
```

8

9

Preview and Fax

This chapter discusses WordStar's Preview feature first, and then the new fax capabilities offered by Preview.

The Preview Feature

Preview was introduced in WordStar 5. It lets you look at, or preview, the pages of a WordStar file before you print them. You can see how margins will appear and what the formatting will look like. If you use varying fonts or italic text in your file, you can see how they will appear. If you use scalable fonts, you will be particularly impressed with Preview. It allows you to see fonts up to 99.9 points, or about 1 1/3 inches, displayed in your file.

Although Preview has a size limit for displaying letter height of 99.9 points, WordStar correctly formats for horizontal spacing of point sizes up to 999.9.

Note

Another useful aspect of Preview is the ability to see files formatted using newspaper-style columns. Probably the most useful characteristic of Preview is to let you see how graphic material you create using Inset (see Chapter 19) will appear in your file. Finally, with version 7.0 you can use Preview to help you prepare fax files.

To use Preview, you will need a graphics adapter installed in your computer. Any one of the more common types—HGA, CGA, EGA, or VGA—works well. All of the screen displays shown in this chapter were produced on a computer with a VGA card and a color monitor. If you are using a different graphics card, your screen may show more or fewer pages on multiple-page displays.

For a useful trial of Preview, you need a file with several pages. The sample file used for the illustrations in this chapter has nine pages. As you read this chapter, try the ideas as they are presented using any multiple-page file.

About Portrait and Landscape Orientation (.pr or = p/l)

Normally you enter the text in your file so that it will print on paper that is 8 1/2 inches wide and 11 inches high. This orientation of text on the paper is called *portrait.* For special documents such as tables, spreadsheets, newsletters, and such, it is sometimes convenient to print on paper that is 11 inches wide and 8 1/2 inches high; this orientation is called *landscape.* Not all printers print in landscape, however. Consult your printer manual to see if yours has this capability.

Regardless of whether or not your printer handles landscape, Preview will display pages in either portrait or landscape. This can be useful when developing a file at one station that is to be printed at another. Note, however, that in Preview you can see only the text that will print on the standard-size paper, 8 1/2 by 11 inches—either in portrait or in landscape.

The default orientation is portrait. To change to landscape, enter the dot command **.pr or=l** (**or** stands for orientation; the letter **l** for landscape). To change back to portrait, enter **.pr or=p** at the top of the page. You'll see a screen sample of this shortly.

Figure 9-1 shows a display with the first page in portrait and the second, a spreadsheet page, in landscape.

Figure 9-1.   *Preview display showing portrait and landscape*

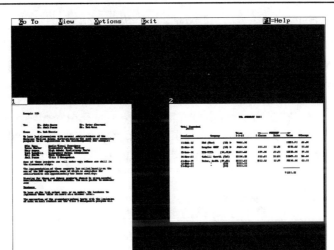

Using Preview (ALT-1)

To select Preview from Edit mode, you can use any one of the following methods:

- Press ALT-1
- Select the View menu, then Preview
- Press ^OP

When you start Preview, the screen will display the page the cursor was on.

In books, even-numbered pages are always on the left and odd-numbered pages are on the right. Preview is designed to show you how a document will appear if it is printed as a book. If the cursor is on an odd-numbered page when you invoke Preview, that page will appear on the left side of your screen. If you select Facing page from the View menu, the odd page will move to the right side of the screen and the left side will show the preceding even page.

9

Note

There is an exception to this rule. If the initial page displayed in Preview is page 1 and Facing Pages is selected, page 2 will display on the right half of the screen.

As always with WordStar, the best way to learn a new feature is to try it. Load a multiple-page file into WordStar. Move the cursor to page 2 of the file and press ALT-1. If the file you're loading uses any fonts in addition to the default font, the message "Building preview font" will appear briefly on the screen. Page 2 of your file will then appear on the left half of the screen in reverse video. Your display will be similar to the one shown in Figure 9-2. Note that the number of the page you are viewing is in the upper-right corner of the screen.

Note

If you have a mouse installed, the menu bar in Preview will contain a variety of mouse buttons. For an example, see "Using the Mouse with Preview," later in this chapter.

Figure 9-2.   *Preview display of single page*

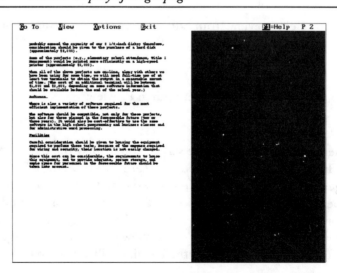

Keep in mind that the purpose of Preview is to examine the format and appearance of the page layout, not to edit or read the file. The text quality in the reduced page display does not compare to that available in WordStar's Edit mode.

View Menu

When you access Preview in any of the ways mentioned, you will see Preview's own set of pull-down menus—Go To, View, Options, and Exit. To make a selection, press the first letter of the menu title. To see the View pull-down menu, press **V**, and the following is displayed:

To select an item from the View menu, press the first character of the selection, or use the arrow keys to highlight the selection and press ENTER.

Viewing Entire, Facing, and Multiple Pages

The View menu gives you options to see one page, two facing pages, or multiple pages.

You can also step through these selections by pressing the gray plus (+) or minus (–) key on the keypad at the extreme right of the keyboard. (To use this method, you cannot have the View menu displayed.) Pressing the gray – key gives you progressively smaller views, down to Thumbnail display (discussed shortly). Pressing the gray + key gives you progressively larger views, up to a full page.

Try this now to see more pages of your file. Close the View menu if it is displayed. Then press the gray – key once; the screen appears as shown in Figure 9-3.

You now have page 2 and its facing page, page 3, on the screen. In this case, note that the page numbers are in the upper-left corner of each page.

9

Figure 9-3.   *Preview display of facing pages*

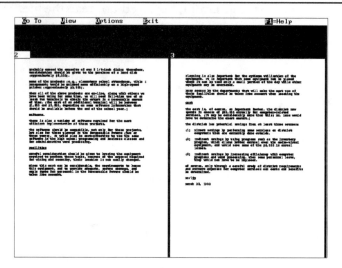

This occurs when there are two or more pages on the screen. The selected page is the one with the page number in reverse video. Use the LEFT ARROW and RIGHT ARROW keys to change the selected page. If two or more rows of pages are displayed, UP ARROW and DOWN ARROW may also be used. The selected page is the one that will be displayed when a single-page view is selected.

To view more pages, press the gray – key again. The screen now displays four pages or more, depending on your graphics card. The display starts from the selected page. At any time, you can move to progressively larger or smaller displays by pressing the gray + or – key, respectively.

Thumbnail Displays

The smallest set of pages your screen can display is referred to as the *Thumbnail* display. Select Thumbnail Display from the View menu or press the – key as many times as possible. A display with 21 pages appears on the screen—depending, of course, on the size of the file you are working with and the type of graphics adapter installed in your computer.

Figure 9-4. *Preview display enlarged*

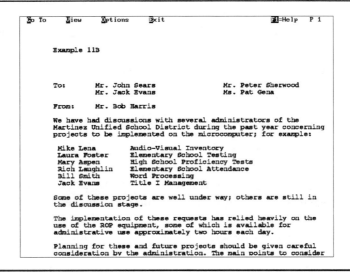

Enlarging the Image Size (2x Zoom, 4x Zoom)

To see larger-sized pages, press the gray + key or select one of the Zoom options directly from the View menu. If you use the gray + key, the pages appear in the reverse order from when you press the – key.

Try enlarging a page to twice its normal size (2x). Keep pressing the + key or choose 2x Zoom from the View menu. The display will look like Figure 9-4.

Pressing the + key again or choosing 4x Zoom gives you a four-times (4x) enlargement.

Adjust Window

The final selection on the View menu, Adjust Window, lets you move or adjust the screen to view a particular section of a page. It is available with an entire page display, and with 2x or 4x enlargements.

With a single page displayed on the screen, select Adjust Window. A window will open in the center of your screen, showing the page you are viewing. A rectangle outlines the upper half of the page. You can use the

9

following keys to help you position the rectangle over the desired portion of the page:

- Use the four arrow keys to move the rectangle in the direction of the arrows.
- Use the four corner keys on the numeric keypad, HOME, PGUP, END, and PGDN, to move the rectangle diagonally over the page.

If you use a mouse, you can use it to rapidly reposition the rectangle.

Note

When the rectangle is positioned correctly, press ENTER. The positioning window closes, and the portion of the page in the rectangle fills your entire screen. This gives you a very detailed view of that portion of the page. Return to the regular view by selecting Entire Page from the View menu.

Scrolling

Any time you have an enlarged page display, you can use the arrow keys to scroll the screen over the text.

Go To Menu

Regardless of what page is displayed when you start Preview, you can quickly move to any page in your file by making selections from the Go To menu (press **G** to display this menu). Its choices are shown here:

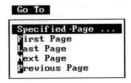

You can use the Go To menu for any View option, from 4x to Thumbnail. When you make your Go To selection, the View option does not change. Try going to different pages when you have different views on the screen.

Options Menu

Additional Preview selections are available from the Options menu, as shown here:

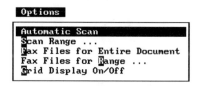

Automatic Scan moves you quickly through a file, from the first to the last page, giving you a brief look at each page. Scan Range allows you to select the range of pages to scan. Type the first page number, press ENTER, type the second page number, and press ENTER. Again you are provided with a brief look at each page. The choices on the Options menu, like those on the Go To menu, can be selected with any View option in effect; that view will be retained during the scanning process.

The next two choices (Fax Files...) on the Options menu deal with producing fax files. They are covered in the next section, "Working with Fax Files."

Note

The last choice on the Options menu, Grid Display On/Off, places a grid on the display that lets you accurately check the placement of any graphics or special formatting you have in the file. The grid display is available for full, 2x, and 4x page representation.

Exit

You can return to WordStar's Edit mode on either the page you were viewing while in Preview or the page you were on when you invoked Preview. From the Exit menu, select either Original Page or Current Page. You can also return to WordStar's Edit mode by selecting ALT-1 for Current Page or ALT-2 for Original Page; to enter these commands you must use the 1 and 2 keys on the top of the keyboard—not on the numeric keypad. Pressing ESC will also return you to WordStar's Edit mode on the original page.

Using the Mouse with Preview

If you access Preview with the mouse installed, the menu bar displayed will look like this:

With the mouse active you can click a menu option to display the pull-down menus, and then click an option to make your choice—just as you can at the WordStar Opening or Edit screen. You can also click the mouse options to the right of the Help title. The effect of clicking on each of these is described in Table 9-1.

Table 9-1. *Mouse Options*

Click	Action
+ and −	Corresponds to pressing the gray + or − key; that is, it increases or decreases the size of the display.
→ ←	Changes the active page (the one with the page number highlighted) to the one displayed right or left of the currently active page.
↑↓	Changes the active page to the one displayed above or below the current active page.
▲▼	Displays the previous or next screenful of pages. To display the previous screenful of pages, the active page must be the one in the upper-left of the screen. Otherwise, clicking ▲ is the same as clicking ↑. The same idea applies to displaying the next screenful of pages.

Working with Fax Files

Note

To prepare a fax file, you need a fax board and the accompanying software installed in your computer.

Another important use of Preview is to help you prepare *fax files*. Just as with a file you send to the printer, a fax file contains all the fonts and formatting provided by WordStar, and any graphics you prepared using Inset (Chapter 19).

WordStar creates a file in PCX format, the file format supported by most fax boards. If your fax board uses a different format, you will need a utility to convert from the PCX format to the one used by your board. This type of utility is normally supplied with the fax board. WordStar produces one PCX file for each page of your document and saves it on the WS/FAX directory (WS is the default directory with the WordStar files). The FAX directory is created the first time you produce a fax file.

Preparing a Fax File

To prepare a fax file from the Opening screen, select the File menu and then Fax. If you are working on the file in WordStar's Edit screen, you can select Fax from the Edit screen File menu or press the command ^K\. Either method produces the Fax dialog box shown in Figure 9-5.

Instructions for each field and button in the dialog box are described below.

Caution

Be sure to press TAB *to advance from option to option in the Fax dialog box. Pressing* ENTER *accepts the displayed options and produces the fax file.*

File to Fax   Specify the file to be faxed from the directory. If a file is located on another directory, be sure to include the path. The file used in this chapter is EXAMPLE.9. Enter and use Example 9 or a file of your own choosing.

Fax File Location   The Fax File Location field shows where the files you prepare to fax will be saved. The default directory you created when you saved

9

Figure 9-5.   *Fax dialog box*

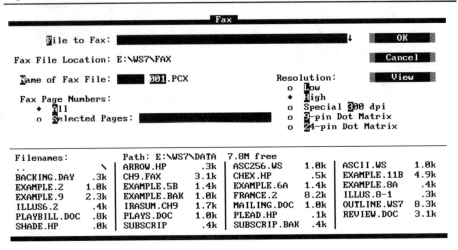

your first fax file is the subdirectory, FAX, which is attached to the directory
that contains WordStar. (This directory can be changed using WSCHANGE.)

Name of Fax File   The filename supplied by WordStar for fax files uses the
first five letters of the given filename, a page number starting with 001, and
the extension PCX. (If your fax filename has fewer than five letters, dashes
are used as fillers.) You may substitute any legal DOS filename in this field.
If the name you supply is already on the disk, you will be told:

```
"That file already exists.
Delete filename"
```

You then have the option to OK or Cancel the deletion.

Fax Page Numbers   The default is All. If you change to Selected Pages,
enter the pages just as you do when printing; for example, entering **1, 3, 5-8**
prints pages 1, 3, 5, 6, 7, and 8.

Note

Be sure page numbers you enter here are the physical page numbers, not numbers assigned using the dot command .pn.

Resolution The default resolution is High, but you must change it to correspond to the resolution of your fax board if it is different.

    ○   Low: (200x100 dots per inch, or dpi)
    ♦   High: (200x200 dpi)
    ○   Special 300 dpi
    ○   9-pin Dot Matrix
    ○   24-pin Dot Matrix

The last two options, 9-pin and 24-pin Dot Matrix, are drivers to create files used by dot-matrix printers to print PCX files.

View Button Selecting the View button transfers you to Preview, where you can check fonts, graphics, and formatting. After inspecting the file, you can press ESC to return to the Fax dialog box and select OK (described next) to produce the fax file.

Note

At the Preview screen, you can also use the Options menu items (described later) to complete the file.

OK Button Pressing ENTER with OK highlighted produces a fax file for each page selected. As the file for a page is produced, it is briefly displayed on the Preview screen. When the fax files are made, you return to the Opening screen.

Cancel Button Cancel interrupts the fax file operation and returns you to the screen where you started.

Fax Options

The following fax options are available on the Preview, Options menu.

9

Fax File for Entire Document   If you wish to produce files for each page of the document, select Fax File for Entire Document. You will see each page as the file for that page is produced. When you are finished, press ESC to return to your starting point.

Fax Files for Range   If you wish to send only selected pages of a document, you can make the choice here in the Options menu or in the Fax dialog box. From here, select Fax File for Range. A window is displayed where you can enter the page or page range of the file to send. If you haven't previously given the file a name, you can do so here using the same rules that apply in the Fax dialog box.

Returning to Preview

After you create the fax files for Preview, return to the screen where you started the process.

While the creation process takes place, you can press ESC once to interrupt the process at the end of the current page or press ESC twice to interrupt the process immediately.

Showing a PCX File

After fax files have been made, you can review them using the utility SHOWPCX. To try this, exit WordStar and enter this command at the DOS prompt: **SHOWPCX** *path\filename*. Here is a specific example if you are in the C:\WS directory: **SHOWPCX E\WS\FAX\CH9—001.PCX**. The file appears on the screen in enlarged format as shown in Figure 9-6.

With the file displayed, you can:

- Press the gray plus key (+) on the keypad to enlarge the print further.
- Use the arrow keys to position the file on the screen.

When you have finished reviewing the file, press ENTER to return to DOS.

While you are working with fax files, keep these points in mind:

- The largest point size available is 72 points.

- Merge print variables are substituted in the fax file.
- Use the FAX.PDF to prepare the fax file. The FAX.PDF is provided when you install WordStar. (You can add fonts to this PDF using PRCHANGE.)
- Use 4x resolution in Preview to determine how your fax will look. (It gives the best correspondence to the fax resolution.)
- 27K of memory is needed to create a fax file. (You may need to exit WordStar to send the file.)

Note

Fax files are graphics files and require large amounts of disk space. The fax file used as an example in this chapter required 3.1K of disk space as a WordStar file and 142K of disk space as a fax file–over 45 times as much space. Remember, after sending a fax file, to delete the fax format from the disk. (If necessary, you can re-create it quickly.)

Figure 9-6. *Example of SHOWPCX screen format*

MEMO

TO: ALL DIRECTORS

FROM: CHAIRMAN OF THE BOARD

DATE: March 23, 1992

A special meeting of all members of the Board of Dire
be held in the corporate headquarters on Monday, Apri
at 10:00 a.m. It is necessary that all Directors be
that meeting.

9

Exercises

1. Practice using all of the options on the Preview, View menu. Use the gray + and – keys to change the page size you are displaying.

2. Select at least two different sections of the multiple-page file you've been using with Preview and change the font to something other than the default font. Look at those sections of the file in Preview using 4x enlargement.

3. Practice using the View, Adjust Window option to get a close-up view of a particular portion of a page.

4. Use the Fax command from the Opening screen and select one of your large files to produce a fax file for pages 1 and 3.

5. Enter Example 9. Then, starting from the Edit screen, select Fax from the File menu, and then produce fax files for the complete document. In Exercises 4 and 5, compare the size of the WordStar files to the size of the fax files derived from them.

Example 9

MEMO

TO: ALL DIRECTORS
FROM: CHAIRMAN OF THE BOARD
DATE: March 23, 1992

A special meeting of all members of the Board of Directors will be held in the corporate headquarters on Monday, April 27, 1992, at 10:00 a.m. It is necessary that all Directors be present at that meeting.

The meeting will be held for the following purposes:

1. Discussing and voting upon the adoption by the corporation of a death benefit provision in the amount of $5,000.00 for its employees as provided under Internal Revenue Code Section 101(b). Attached to this memorandum is a copy of that code section. Please study it before the meeting to be thoroughly familiar with its contents and able to discuss it in detail.

2. Discussing and voting upon the appointment of John Blackwell to undertake the duties previously performed by James Johnson, effective immediately following the adoption of a resolution made at the meeting.

3. Discussion of the various duties that will be undertaken by John Blackwell, which will include:

    (a) Coordinating and facilitating all material deliveries to all job sites. In other words, John Blackwell shall be responsible for materials, equipment rentals, corporate equipment use, and equipment use by others on corporate jobs on all job sites.

9

Example 9 (*continued*)

(b)   Checking and cross-checking all incoming
       invoices for goods, services, supplies and
       materials received from vendors and suppli-
       ers and determining the accuracy of the use
       of said materials and supplies on corporation
       jobs.

(c)   Such other jobs on a day-to-day basis for
       the corporate operations on all job sites.

(d)   The Board of Directors shall determine the
       salary increase necessary to compensate John
       Blackwell for these extra duties which he
       has now been assigned over and above his
       present workload. The salary will be reviewed
       from time to time as operations continue in
       the future.

10

Find/Find and Replace

One of the most powerful features of any word processing system is the ability to find a given word or phrase in a file and automatically replace it with another word or phrase. WordStar provides two commands for these operations: the Find command and the Find and Replace command. You can access these two commands from the Edit pull-down menu and the Quick (^Q) traditional menu. You can also use accelerator keys. The commands shown after the headings in this chapter are the ones involving the fewest keystrokes—normally the accelerator keys.

Find (^F1)

To see how the Find command works, load Example 6B from Chapter 6 and place the cursor at the beginning of the file. To initiate the Find command, press CTRL followed by the F1 function key (^F1). The Find dialog box is shown in Figure 10-1.

Figure 10-1.   *Find dialog box*

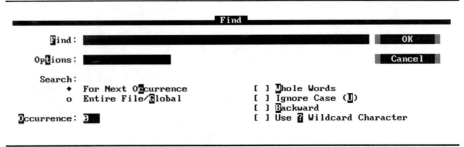

Your entry in the Find field can be any group of characters, or *string*—part of a word, a whole word, or a phrase up to 65 characters in length. Type the word **Facilities**, which occurs midway in the letter. For now, bypass the Options field and press F10; you'll read about the Find options shortly.

When you press F10, WordStar starts from the cursor position, and searches the file for the first occurrence of the word *Facilities*. If it finds the word, it stops there. If *Facilities* does not occur before WordStar reaches the end of the file, you'll see a window with the message "Can't find:"; press ENTER to continue. After you press ENTER, the cursor will be at the end of the file. You can return to where you started and search for another word or words, or resume editing.

Tip

After the search, you can return the cursor to where it was before the last command was given, by entering the command ^QP. If the Find command (^QF) was the last command entered, you will be returned to the position where that command was given.

The Find Options (G, *n*, W, U, B, ?)

From the Options field of the Find dialog box, you can specify exactly how you want to do a search. If you just press F10, selecting no options, WordStar will begin its search from the cursor position, searching for an exact match to the Find string you entered. To make your search more specific, you can enter letters that represent the search options.

Just below the Options field are two search choices: For Next Occurrence and Entire File/Global. For Next Occurrence is the default choice. This option searches forward from the position of the cursor to find the first occurrence of the entry in the Find field. If you wish to do a global search, enter **G** in the Option field. The global option starts the search from the beginning of the file, regardless of the position of the cursor when you pressed ^F1. For both of these options, you may enter the number of the occurrence you are looking for in the Occurrence field. (The entry you make in the Occurrence field will also appear above in the Options field, and if you enter the occurrence in the Options field, it will appear in the Occurrence field as well.) To keep the default search option, For Next Occurrence, Press TAB to move to the Occurrence field.

There are four additional search options: Whole Words (W), Ignore Case (U), Backward (B), and Use Wildcard Character (?). To use one or more of these options in the search, enter the highlighted letters, one after the other, with no spaces or punctuation marks between them, in the Options field. You can use either upper- or lowercase. Then press ENTER. These options will do the following:

Search Option	Find Operation
W	Finds whole words only. For example, *ace* will not match *race*.
U	Ignores the difference between upper- and lowercase letters. For example, *CASE* matches *case* or *Case*.
B	Searches backward from cursor position.
?	Treats the question mark as a wildcard. Enter the ? in the Options field as well as in the Find field. For example, if you enter **All?n** in the Find field and a ? in the Options field, WordStar will find the name *Allen* or *Allan*.

Finding Multiple Occurrences of a Word (^L)

The following exercise shows how to search for all occurrences of a word throughout an entire file. Press ^F1. In the Find box, type **cost** and press TAB. In the Options field, type **guw** with no spaces or punctuation. This selects the Entire File/Global (G), Ignore Case (U), and Whole Words (W) options. Then press the DOWN ARROW to move into the Search area. The screen is as shown in Figure 10-2.

10

Figure 10-2.   *Find dialog box with options entered*

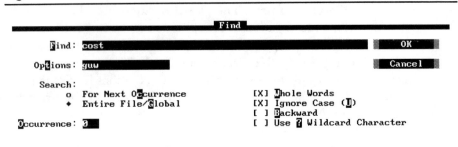

Press F10 to initiate the search. WordStar returns to the beginning of the file and starts looking for the word *cost*. It stops when it finds the string of characters you requested. To have WordStar find the next occurrence of *cost*, press ^L; again the cursor stops after the word. Each time the cursor stops, you may delete the word, add some text, or do whatever editing you wish. Then press ^L to continue the search for the next occurrence. Note that because you specified W for whole words only, the word *costs* in the last paragraph is bypassed in the search.

Finding a Specific Occurrence of a Word

WordStar's Find features also let you search for a specific occurrence of a word or words. For example, you can use the Find command's *n* option to find the third occurrence after the cursor of the word *cost*. Again using Example 6B, enter the information in the Find dialog box so your screen matches Figure 10-3.

Press F10. The cursor will go to where *cost* occurs for the third time.

Find and Replace (^F2)

In addition to finding words, WordStar can find a word (or string) and replace it with another word (or string). To use the Find command with a

Figure 10-3.   *Find dialog box illustrating global search*

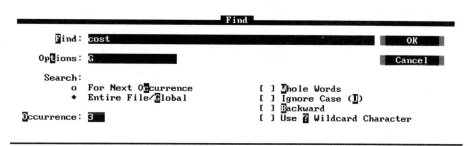

replace operation, return to the beginning of the Example 6B file. Press ^F2. You will see the Find and Replace dialog box. In the Find field, type **cost** and press TAB or the DOWN ARROW. In the Replace field, type **expense** and press the DOWN ARROW. Press the DOWN ARROW again. Your screen looks like Figure 10-4.

Press F10 to begin the search. The cursor advances to the first occurrence of *cost*. In the title bar is the question "Replace Y/N?" Type **Y**, and *cost* is replaced with *expense*. To continue the search, press ^L. The cursor advances to the next occurrence of *cost*, and the question is repeated. You can move through a file of any length in this manner, replacing the word (or not) by responding Y or N to the question.

Figure 10-4.   *Find and Replace dialog box*

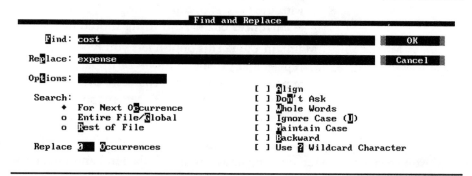

10

Find and Replace Options
(W, U, B, ?, G, *n*, A, M, N, R)

The Whole Words, Ignore Case, Backward, and Wildcard options that apply to the Find command also apply to the Find and Replace command. The *n* option, however, has a different function; and there are some additional options, as shown here:

Search Option	Find and Replace Operation
R	Starts the search from the position of the cursor and searches to the end of the file.
n	When you type *n*, where *n* is an integer in the Replace *n* Occurrences field, WordStar performs a Find and Replace operation *n* times. For example, if *n* is 4, WordStar finds and replaces the next 4 occurrences of the word. The "Not Found" message is displayed if the command cannot be performed *n* times.
A	Aligns paragraphs after the replacement is made. In most cases, the Replace string is not the same length as the Find string. WordStar does not hyphenate words during Find and Replace operations, even if Hyphen Help is on.
N	Don't Ask. Replaces a word or words without prompting you for confirmation. This feature is convenient to use with the G or R option, as long as you are sure all occurrences of the Find string should be replaced.
M	Maintain Case. This option lets you type the replacement string in lower- or uppercase but have it appear like the word it replaces. For example, even if you type **cash** for the replacement string, the word *Cash* would replace the word *Money*.

The Find and Replace command will find multiple-word strings, even if soft spaces have been inserted between the words. Find and Replace will also find a word or phrase that is split over two lines, and a word that is the first or last word in the file.

Using Find and Replace

For a timesaving application of the Find and Replace command (^F2), consider the following example. Suppose you are writing a letter or report that repeats the same phrase or long word several times. Each time that word or phrase occurs in the document, enter instead a single, uncommon character such as the ampersand (&). When you have finished the document, issue the Find and Replace command, ^F2. In the Find field, type &. For Replace, enter the repeated word or phrase. In Options, enter **GNA**. WordStar will then search through the entire file, automatically replacing all &'s with your Replace field text. Because you specified the Align option, paragraphs will automatically be reformatted after each replacement.

Now look at an example that uses some of the other Find and Replace options. In Figure 10-5, the option G causes the search to be global (through the whole file), U causes the search to ignore the distinction between upper- and lowercase letters, and W causes the search to find whole words only. Given this command, WordStar will find *Cost*, but not *costs*.

In addition to searching for words or phrases, you can search for special formats and characters, such as boldface, underline, and carriage returns. You can replace the format with other formats or special characters, or eliminate them by replacing them with nothing. In Figure 10-6, note that you must enter **^P^S** (^ must be pressed with both P and S) in the Find field, but

Figure 10-5.   *Find and Replace dialog box with sample options*

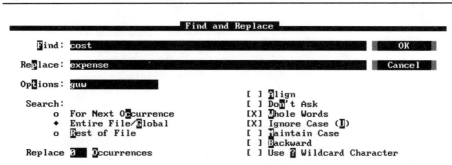

10

Figure 10-6.   *Find and Replace dialog box for a search for control characters*

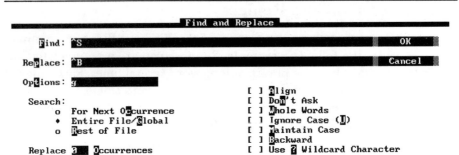

only ^S is displayed. Similarly, in the Replace field you must enter **^P^B**, but only ^B is displayed.

Exercises

1. Enter Example 10. Using the Find and Replace command, replace each occurrence of *John Philip Smith* with *Sara Lee Brown.*

2. Find every occurrence of *his,* and change it to *her* where appropriate.

Example 10

```
                LAST WILL AND TESTAMENT
                          OF
                  JOHN PHILIP SMITH


    I, JOHN PHILIP SMITH, presently residing in the
City of Walnut Creek, Contra Costa County, State of
California, being of sound and disposing mind and
memory, and not acting under duress, menace, or undue
influence of any kind or person whatsoever, do hereby
make, publish, and declare this to be my Last Will
and Testament in the following manner:

                     ARTICLE I

    I hereby revoke any and all former and other Wills
and Codicils made at any time heretofore by me.

                     ARTICLE II

    It is my intent hereby to dispose of all my
property, whether real or personal, tangible or
intangible, community or separate, wheresoever sit-
uated, that I have the right to dispose of by Will,
including all property in which I shall hereafter
acquire any interest, and further including any and
all property as to which I may hereafter acquire a
power of appointment by Will.

                     ARTICLE III

    I hereby declare that I am not married. I have no
children. I have no former marriages or issue of such.
```

10

Example 10 (*continued*)

ARTICLE IV

I hereby give, devise, and bequeath one-half (1/2) of the residue of my estate, real, personal, or mixed, of whatever kind and wheresoever situated, equally to my parents, JOHN SMITH and ANGELA SMITH, of Lovely Lane, Martinez, CA 94553. If one parent shall predecease me, then the surviving parent shall take all, and then to their issue by right of representation.

ARTICLE V

I give, devise, and bequeath one-half (1/2) of the residue of my estate, real, personal, or mixed, of whatever kind and wheresoever situated to my very good friend, MARCY SIMMONS. If MARCY SIMMONS shall predecease me, this gift shall lapse.

ARTICLE VI

I direct that all my debts, including funeral expenses, expenses of last illness, administration expenses, and all inheritance, estate, and other death taxes, and payment of a family allowance, if needed, be paid by the Executrix out of the residue of my estate from the first moneys coming into her hands and available therefor, and shall not be charged or collected from any beneficiary of my probate estate.

Example 10 (*continued*)

ARTICLE VII

I hereby nominate and request the court to appoint my friend, MARCY SIMMONS, as Executrix of this will, to serve without bond.

Should MARCY SIMMONS serve as Executrix, I authorize her to sell, lease, convey, transfer, encumber, hypothecate, or otherwise deal with the whole or any portion of my estate, either by public or private sale, with or without notice, and without securing any prior order of the court therefor.

I further authorize my Executrix either to continue the operation of any business belonging to my estate for such time and in such manner as she may deem advisable, and for the best interests of my estate, or to sell or liquidate the business at such time and on such terms as she may deem advisable, and for the best interests of my estate. Any operation, sale, or liquidation made in good faith shall be at the risk of my estate, without liability for any resulting losses against the Executrix.

ARTICLE VIII

If any beneficiary under this Will, in any manner, directly or indirectly, contests, objects, or attacks this Will or any of its provisions, any share or interest in my estate given to that contesting or objecting beneficiary under this Will is revoked and shall be disposed of in the same manner as if that beneficiary had predeceased me without issue.

10

Example 10 (*continued*)

ARTICLE IX

I have intentionally and purposely omitted and made no provision in this Will for any person not mentioned herein, whether an heir of mine or one claiming to be an heir of mine or not; and if any person, whether or not mentioned in this Will should object, contest, or attack this Will or any provision hereof, I give to such person, or to each of such persons, if more than one be so contesting or objecting, the sum of Ten Dollars ($10.00), and no more, in lieu of the provisions which I might have made for such person or persons so contesting, objecting, or attacking this Will.

IN WITNESS WHEREOF, I subscribe my name to this, my Last Will and Testament, this __ day of _____, 19___, at _____, Contra Costa County, California.

_____
JOHN PHILIP SMITH

Example 10 (*continued*)

    The foregoing instrument, consisting of four (4) pages and this fifth (5th) witness page, was, at this date, by the said JOHN PHILIP SMITH signed and published as and declared to be his Last Will and Testament in the presence of us, who, at his request, and in his presence, and in the presence of each other, have signed our names as witnesses hereto.

_____residing at_____

_____

_____residing at_____

_____

10

11

Windows

So far you have worked with one file at a time. WordStar, however, has the capability of opening and displaying two files at the same time. To do this, it divides or splits the screen into two sections, called *windows*.

Using WordStar Windows

The View menu shown below contains the command to open a window or switch to another window (^OK), and the command to change the size of a window (^OM).

```
 View 
┌──────────────────────────────┐
│ Preview              ^OP     │
├──────────────────────────────┤
│ Command Tags         ^OD     │
│ Block Highlighting   ^KH     │
├──────────────────────────────┤
│ Open/Switch Window   ^OK     │
│ Change Window Size...^OM     │
├──────────────────────────────┤
│ Screen Settings...   ^OB     │
└──────────────────────────────┘
```

Other commands you use with windows are accessed from the Edit menu.

To start to work with windows, read the sections below. You will find various examples for using the commands. Be sure to try opening two windows with a file in each one, and practice using the ^OK and ^OM commands.

Opening and Switching Between Windows (^OK)

The command ^OK has a dual function. If only one window is open, you use ^OK to open another window. If two windows are open, you use ^OK to move the cursor between the windows.

Let's try working with files in two windows. From the WordStar Opening screen, open a file. You will now be at the Edit screen. Next, press **^OK** to display the Open Document window shown in Figure 11-1.

Select a filename for the second file to open and press ENTER. The screen will be divided into two windows. One window will have your newly opened file, and the cursor will be in that window. The window where the cursor is located is the *active* window, the window where editing can be done. Figure 11-2 shows the screen with two files open.

Note

If you wish to compare sections of the same file, open the file again in the second window. When the same file is open in both windows, the copy in the second window will be in protected status. You can scroll the files independently to make comparisons. All editing, however, must be done in the first window.

Keep these points in mind when you're working with WordStar windows:

- All the information displayed in the title bar, style bar, and status line applies to the active window.

- The active window is shown in brackets on the far right of the title bar.

- Placing the mouse cursor in the second window and clicking the mouse will make that window the active one.

- In the second window you can edit one of the existing files on your disk, or you can open a new file altogether.

Figure 11-1.   *Open Document dialog box*

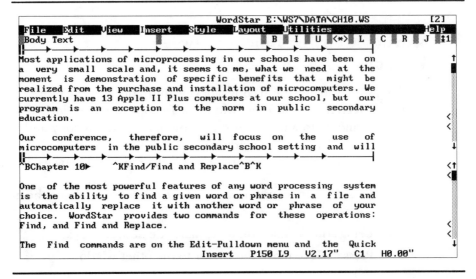

```
                              Open Document

     Filename: E:\WS7\DATA\EXAMPLE.2                                  OK
                                                                     Cancel


 Filenames:          Path: E:\WS7\DATA  7.5M free                 ▲ ▼ ↑ ↓
     ..           \  ARROW.HP     .3k   ASC256.WS    .1k   ASCII.WS     .1k
  BACKING.DAY  .3k   CH-10.WS7    18k   CH18-ABC     64k   CH9.FAX     3.1k
  CHEX.HP      .5k   EXAM.BAK    3.8k   EXAMPLE.11B  4.9k  EXAMPLE.2   1.5k
  EXAMPLE.5A  1.8k   EXAMPLE.5B  1.3k   EXAMPLE.5C   .8k   EXAMPLE.6A  1.4k
  EXAMPLE.8A   .4k   EXAMPLE.9   2.3k   EXAMPLE.BAK 1.3k   FRANCE.2    8.2k
  ILLUS.8-1    .3k   ILLUS6.2     .4k   IRASUM.CH9  1.7k   LETHEAD.14   .5k
  MAILING.DOC 1.0k   OUTLINE.WS7 8.3k   PLAYBILL.DOC .8k   PLAYS.DOC   1.0k
  PLEAD.HP     .1k   REVIEW.DOC  3.1k   SHADE.HP     .0k   SUBSCRIP     .4k
  SUBSCRIP.BAK .4k   TEST.256     .3k   TEST.BAK     .3k   TEST.C14     .3k
```

Figure 11-2.   *Screen with two files open*

```
                       WordStar E:\WS7\DATA\CH10.WS           [2]
  File   Edit   View   Insert   Style   Layout   Utilities          Help
  Body Text                              B  I  U <*> L   C  R  J  ↕1

 Most applications of microprocessing in our schools have been  on      ↑
 a  very  small  scale and, it seems to me, what we  need  at  the
 moment  is  demonstration  of  specific  benefits  that  might  be
 realized from the purchase and installation of microcomputers. We
 currently have 13 Apple II Plus computers at our school, but  our
 program  is  an  exception  to  the  norm  in  public   secondary
 education.                                                             <
                                                                       <
 Our   conference,   therefore,   will  focus  on   the   use  of
 microcomputers  in the public secondary school setting  and will      ↓

 ^BChapter 10▶     ^KFind/Find and Replace^B^K                         <↑
                                                                       <
 One  of  the most powerful features of any word processing  system
 is  the  ability  to find a given word or phrase in  a  file  and
 automatically  replace  it with another word or  phrase  of  your
 choice.  WordStar  provides two commands  for  these  operations:
 Find, and Find and Replace.                                           <
                                                                       <
 The   Find   commands are on the Edit-Pulldown menu and  the  Quick   ↓
                          Insert   P150 L9   V2.17"   C1   H0.00"
```

Changing Window Size (^OM)

When two windows are opened, WordStar automatically allocates ten lines for the first file (top window) and nine lines for the second file (bottom window). To change the size of a window, use **^OK** to move the cursor to that window, and then select the command **^OM**. Or, if you use the mouse, click the arrows next to the active window indicator. By either method, the Change Window Size dialog box will be displayed.

Half Screen is the default selection. You can select Full Screen, or you can specify the window size by entering a line number in the Lines field. The number of lines available in the Edit window will be one less than the number you enter, unless screen settings, the style bar, the status line, and so on, are toggled off. Even if you have one window (file) set to take up the full screen, the other file is still open, and you can switch between the two open files with **^OM**.

Moving/Copying Blocks Between Windows (^KA and ^KG)

Just as you can move and copy blocks within a file, you can move and copy blocks between files in different windows. To copy or move blocked material from one window to another, use the command **^KA** to copy and **^KG** to move the block. These commands can also be selected from the Edit menu.

Here are the steps to move or copy a block of material between windows:

1. Press **^OK** to move the cursor to the window containing the material you want to move or copy.

2. Using SHIFT-F9 and SHIFT-F10, mark the desired block.

3. Press **^OK** to move the cursor to the other window.

4. Position the cursor where you want the moved or copied block to begin.

5. Select **^KG** to move or **^KA** to copy the block.

For an example in copying and moving blocks between windows, look at Figure 11-3 and the following discussion:

Window 1 contains EXAMPLE.5A from Chapter 5. Window 2 was opened as a new file with the name EXAMPLE.XX. Notice the path and filename are displayed on the right in the title bar. Also notice the [2] that tells you window 2 is the active window. If you enter the command **^OK**, and the number 1 for window 1, the name of the file in that window would appear in place of EXAMPLE.XX. Then you could follow the procedure outlined above to copy or move material from one window to another.

Figure 11-3.   *Screen with two files open in two windows*

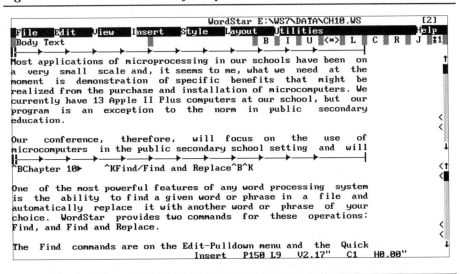

Saving with Two Files Open

The commands to save when two Edit windows are open are the same as those used when one file is open. As you might expect, however, there are some minor differences in how they work. The table below describes how each of the save commands works with two windows open.

Save Command	Function
^KD	Saves the active file, closes its window, and makes the remaining file active.
^KT	Allows you to change the name of the file being saved. After naming the file, the command works the same as ^KD.
^KQ	Abandons the active file, closes its window, and makes the remaining file active.
^KS	Saves the file and returns the cursor to the same position in the file, where you can resume editing (same as with a single window).
^KX	Saves the active file, closes its window, and makes the file in the other window active (same as ^KD).

Try each of these save operations with two files open. Use a couple of examples from earlier chapters, and check that each save operation works as expected.

Using the Windows Clipboard (^K] and ^K[)

If you use WordStar for DOS in the Microsoft Windows environment, you can copy blocks of text to and from the Windows Clipboard. Text copied from WordStar to the Clipboard replaces any material currently in the Clipboard. The commands to copy to and from the Clipboard are on the submenu for the Edit, Copy command, as shown here:

```
Block   .             ^KC
Block from Other Window ^KA
From Windows Clipboard  ^KI
To Windows Clipboard    ^KJ
To Another File...      ^KW
```

Note

To try this, you must be running Windows in the 386 enhanced mode.

The WordStar for DOS Clipboard copy commands have these limitations:

- Only text in ASCII format may be copied (no graphics).
- The Clipboard is limited to files 64K in size.
- Data copied to the Clipboard has all WordStar formatting removed.
- WordStar requires 64K of memory to copy to the Clipboard. If less than 64K is available, only part of the data will be copied.

Work with the various window commands, on the View menu and the Edit menu, until you feel comfortable with them. You will probably find many and frequent uses for them as you work with your files.

The next chapter describes how to set up the format of a file into almost any conceivable configuration.

Exercises

1. Copy some blocked material from one window to another: Open EXAMPLE.7B. Open a second window using the new filename TEST.PHY. Copy the heading, plus questions 2, 4-6, and 8, into window 2. Save both files, and open each again to verify that EXAMPLE.7B is unchanged and TEST.PHY contains the data you copied.

2. Try moving some material from one window to another: Open EXAMPLE.7A in one window and a new file in the other window.

Move sections 1 and 2 to the new window. Save both files and open each again to verify that the result is as you expect. Then move the sections back again to return EXAMPLE.7A to its original state.

3. Open the same file in both windows. Check that scrolling is independent in each window, and the file in the second window is in Protect mode.

4. If you use the mouse, practice using it to switch between windows and to access the Change Window Size dialog box.

5. If you work with Microsoft Windows, enter a brief message into the Clipboard and copy it to a WordStar file.

6. Again using Windows's Clipboard, try the copy process in reverse, copying one of your existing files from WordStar to the Clipboard. Keep in mind that the WordStar formatting is lost when you copy a file to the Clipboard.

12

Paragraph Styles

In previous chapters you have entered formatting commands individually or, with some dialog boxes, in small groups. In this chapter you will use dialog boxes to enter larger groups of formatting commands at one time to format a section of a file or an entire file. These special collections of formats are called *paragraph styles*.

WordStar supplies a library of predefined format styles, from which you can select the ones you want. You can also modify these supplied styles to suit the special requirements of a particular file. For example, you can make individual changes to fonts, margins, tabs, and other features. Changes you make to a paragraph style can be used in the file you are currently editing, called the *local* file, and can also be stored in the Paragraph Style library for use with any other file.

To see how paragraph styles can be used, look at Example 12 at the end of this lesson. Example 12 shows three styles commonly used in letters: <Title>, <Body text>, and <Hanging indent 1>. WordStar places the style names in angle brackets to indicate the style in effect for a particular section of a file.

Note

As with other tags displayed in WordStar–fonts, ribbon color, and so on–paragraph style tags can be toggled on and off using SHIFT-F1 *and, of course, they don't show when you print the file.*

The heading of the letter in Example 12 is centered and printed in boldface. This is a function of the <Title> style. Following the heading, the style changes to <Body text>. In the "Requirements" section of the letter there are four questions, formatted using the <Hanging indent 1> style. Finally the letter changes back to the WordStar default style, <Body text>. All three of these styles, along with several others, are in the Paragraph Style library that comes with WordStar for DOS.

The Paragraph Style Menu (^OF)

The Paragraph Style commands are on the Style pull-down menu and the Manage Paragraph Styles submenu. You can also select Paragraph Styles from the traditional menu (^OF). Since all of the Style options are on the traditional Paragraph Style menu, that will be the one used for reference in this chapter. Press ^OF now to see this menu:

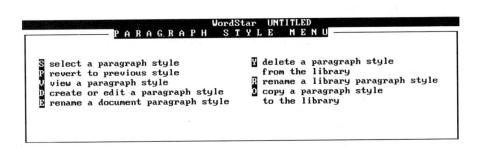

You select options from this menu by pressing the letter shown to the left of each option. As you get used to these commands and can press the option selections more quickly after the ^OF command, the menu will be bypassed. For example, pressing **^OFS** in quick succession immediately displays the Select Paragraph Style dialog box.

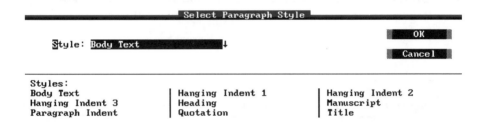

Note

The option to View a paragraph style (V) on the Paragraph Style menu is a carryover from earlier versions of WordStar. Therefore, you will not find the command ^OFV on the pull-down menus. If you are used to working with this command, you can select the V option from the Paragraph Style menu.

From the Paragraph Style menu, press **S** now to see all of the paragraph styles included in WordStar's Paragraph Style library displayed in the Select Paragraph Style dialog box.

```
                    ┌─ Select Paragraph Style ─┐
═══════════════════════════════════════════════════════════════
                                                    ┌────────────┐
  Style: Body Text                  ↓               │     OK     │
                                                    ├────────────┤
                                                    │   Cancel   │
                                                    └────────────┘
───────────────────────────────────────────────────────────────
  Styles:
  Body Text              │ Hanging Indent 1    │ Hanging Indent 2
  Hanging Indent 3       │ Heading             │ Manuscript
  Paragraph Indent       │ Quotation           │ Title
```

Notice that the styles associated with Example 12 are shown, along with several others.

There are two categories of paragraph styles: library styles and document styles. *Library styles* are available for all files. They are either WordStar supplied, or can be created by you and saved in the library. *Document styles* are styles you create—usually based on an existing library style—and use with a specific document. When you save a file, the document style is saved with the file but not in the library, and is not available for other files.

Before you try using a paragraph style, examine the format commands in the Define Paragraph Style dialog box. To do this, press ESC to return to the Edit screen, and press **^OF**.

Viewing, Editing, and Defining Paragraph Styles (^OFD)

On the Paragraph Style menu, select **D** to create or edit a paragraph style. This option lets you do three things:

- View, or examine, the formatting commands used by a particular style
- Edit an existing style
- Define, or create, a new style

On the Style pull-down menu this option is called Define Paragraph Style. Regardless of how you select this option, you see the screen display shown in Figure 12-1.

Figure 12-1.   *Define Paragraph Style dialog box*

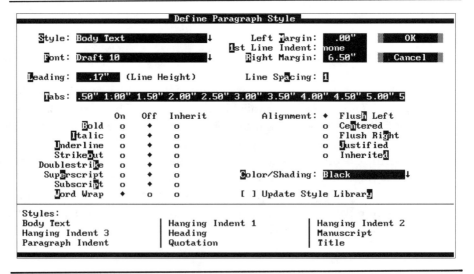

12

The Define Paragraph Style dialog box currently displays the format commands used by the Body Text style. The commands in the dialog box are for the style in effect when you selected Define Paragraph Style (^OFD). As you look through the commands used to create the Body Text style, you will recognize that they have all been discussed in earlier chapters, except for one, Inherited, which will be explained shortly.

Listed at the bottom of the Define Paragraph Style window is the directory of available styles. Use the arrow keys to highlight another style, and notice that the format settings and options change to reflect the selected style. For example, when Title is highlighted, the print style Bold is on, and the Alignment option changes to Centered. After you have reviewed the styles you are interested in, press ENTER to return to the local file. (You'll return to this dialog box shortly to work with Create and Edit.)

Selecting a Style (^OFS)

The S option on the Paragraph Style menu lets you choose the styles for your local file. It places all the style options that you saw in Figure 12-1 into your document at one time. To choose a style, return to the Paragraph Style menu by pressing ^OF at the Edit screen. Then select S. You can also press ALT-0 (zero) at the Edit screen, or choose Select Paragraph Style from the Style pull-down menu. In any case, you'll again see the Select Paragraph Style dialog box shown earlier.

Body Text is currently in the Style field because it was in effect when the command was given. Using the arrow keys, highlight the Title style. Press ENTER to return to the local file (the file being edited). A tag appears at the position of the cursor indicating the style (provided you haven't turned off Print Display, SHIFT-F1). Type your name and address, pressing ENTER at the end of each line. (If you start typing on the line with the style tag, your name will not appear to be centered properly. Press SHIFT-F1 and the centering will appear correctly.)

You can change paragraph styles in a file as often as you wish. To remove a paragraph style from your file, delete the tag.

Note

Editing a Paragraph Style

As pointed out earlier, the D option on the Paragraph Style menu (or Define Paragraph Style on the Style menu) lets you edit an existing style or create a new style. To begin, return to the Define Paragraph Style window (^OFD). First, you'll edit an existing style. Then you'll see how to create a new style.

Editing an Existing Style

To edit an existing style, display the style in the Define Paragraph Style dialog box. Using the TAB key, arrow keys, and accelerator keys, move the cursor to the settings and options you wish to change and make the necessary alterations. Press F10 to return to the local file.

Note

If you are making more than one change, it's probably best to create a new style from scratch, following the procedures in the section just below.

Now that you are in the local file, you need to select the style just edited, so press ^OFS, select the style, and press ENTER. Notice that the changes you made have been carried out. The following rules are in effect for an edited style:

- The changes made to a paragraph style affect only the local file.

- The *paragraph style* itself, with the changes, is saved with the local file and remains in effect for all future edits or until changed.

- In the Style library, an asterisk next to a style indicates the style has been modified for the local file, as shown below for Manuscript and Hanging Indent 2. (If this window were displayed for a different document, the asterisks would not appear.)

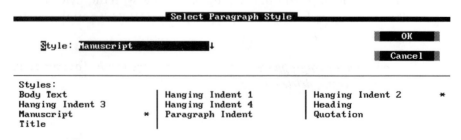

- You cannot save changes made to the default style, Body Text, in the library. Any changes made to Body Text only affect the local file.

Note

The alignment options, Centered and Flush Right, take effect automatically if Paragraph Align is on (^OA). If it is your habit to work with Paragraph Align off, then use Paragraph Reformat (^B) after entering text; the Centered or Flush Right option will then take effect.

Creating a New Style

To create a brand-new style to place in the library, you have two choices: (1) Start with an existing file and change it; or (2) start from scratch. In both cases you create the new style at the Define Paragraph Style window.

To try the first method, edit any existing style by first typing a new name in the Style field, and then changing one or more format settings in the style. When you finish the changes, mark the Update Style Library box by pressing the accelerator key (**y**), then F10. The style will be available to you for future documents.

For an exercise, you can change the Title style so that it prints text centered but not in boldface, and name the new style Centered. Select the create or edit option in the Paragraph Style menu (**^OFD**). In the Define Paragraph Style window, display the Title style settings. Change the Style name to Centered, turn Bold off, and mark the Update Style Library check box by pressing **y**. Press F10. If you then display the list of styles, you will see the new style, Centered.

Creating a New Style from Scratch

Again, the purpose here is to place a new style in the library. Suppose you have created a document style using individual dot commands that you feel will be useful in the future, and you want to add this set of commands to the style library. Follow this procedure:

1. Open the file as you normally would for editing, and place the cursor where all of the desired commands are in effect.
2. Press **^OFD** to display the Define Paragraph Style dialog box.

3. Delete the style name; with the cursor in the Style field, press **^Y**. The format settings in effect in the local file are displayed in their appropriate fields. (You can see that "starting from scratch" is a bit of a misnomer for this technique, since you always start with a default style.)

4. Enter the name that you want for this style.

Note

This is where the option Inherit applies. All the default format settings that were not changed are copied to this new file, and are thus "inherited." Inherited styles and line heights do not apply to headers, footers, or endnotes.

5. Move to the Update Style Library box and press **y**.

6. Press ENTER to accept the displayed settings.

This new style is now available for any future file that you create. If at some later time you wish to modify the new style, follow the procedure outlined in the earlier sections "Editing an Existing Style" and "Creating a New Style."

Rather than start with an existing style, if you know in advance what you want in the new style, you can create it directly. Open a new document, enter all desired dot commands and format settings, and follow the above procedure to name and place the style in the library.

Return to Previous Style (^OFP)

Frequently you will find it convenient to change to a new paragraph style for just a section of your file, and then return to whatever the previous style was. For example, you may start a document using the default Body Text style and then change to one of the hanging indent styles. To quickly change back to Body Text, press **^OFP**.

Also, it's not uncommon to start a file with a style other than the default, such as Title, and then change to Body Text. In this case, pressing **^OFP** will select the default style, Body Text.

Additional Style Options

The remaining options on the Paragraph Style menu handle the routine chores associated with maintaining paragraph styles. They are

E   Renames a document style in the local file. The style saved with the new menu will have the current format settings. The style in the Current Style Name field is still available and will have the original command settings.

Y   Deletes a paragraph style. (You cannot delete a style used in the current file.)

R   Renames a library style. This allows you to change the name of a style in the library. When you select this command, you will note the style Body Text is not displayed because its name cannot be changed.

O   Copy a paragraph style to the library. (If you specify a name already in the library, you will be asked to confirm the overwrite.)

All the above commands open a dialog box similar to that for **Rename Document Style**. Press **^OFE** now to see this dialog box:

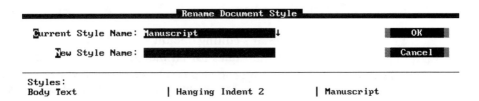

Type your selections and press ENTER to execute the command.

Keep in mind the following as you work with paragraph styles:

- If you insert text from a disk file into a local file (**^KR**), the style of the inserted text is retained.

- Since Body Text is the default style, changes to this format cannot be saved to the library.
- If you edit a style but do not use it or save it to the library, it will be deleted.
- If you delete a style from the library that is used in one of your files stored on disk, that style is still available and is displayed in the Styles, Library menu when the related file is edited.
- Because you can select a style from the library by pressing the first letter of its name, it is wise to use style names that start with different letters.

Tip

You might want to change a couple of the Hanging Indent style names—for example, Hanging Indent 1 could become 1st Hanging Indent.

Goto Next Style Tag (^Q<)

While working with styles, you may find it convenient to quickly move to the next style tag. The command to do this is ^Q<. The command only moves you *forward* in the file, so if you are looking for a particular style, be sure to start from the beginning of your file.

Changing Default Values

You can change WordStar's editing default values by using WSCHANGE (Appendix C). To change the values for an *individual file,* you can alter the Body Text paragraph style. You can also create a style with your own format settings and save it to the library. You will, of course, still find WSCHANGE essential for making a wide variety of default changes, as discussed in Appendix C.

Working with Newspaper-style Columns (.co *n,t,* .cb, .cc *n*)

Newspaper-style columns are appropriate for a variety of documents you might produce with WordStar. Club newsletters, company reports, and

12

annual statements are a few examples. Since version 5.0, WordStar has had the ability to produce newspaper-style columns. You can start the columns at any point in your file and edit them as frequently as you like throughout the document. You can add or delete information at any point and reformat it to fit the column format you have established.

Tip

Chapter 19 discusses the Inset feature of WordStar, which lets you develop graphical material to insert in a WordStar file. This combination of graphics and newspaper-style columns gives you the means to prepare professional newsletters and reports.

The three dot commands used to work with newspaper columns are described below:

Command	Purpose
.co n,t	Defines the number of columns on each page (*n*) and the spacing between columns (*t*). The space represented by *t* can be in character columns, inches,centimeters, or points.
.cb	Sets a column break; it corresponds to .pa in a standard WordStar file.
.cc n	Sets a conditional column break; places a page break if there are not *n* number of lines remaining on the page. It corresponds to .cp in a standard WordStar file.

The Column Layout Dialog Box (^OU)

An easy way to set up multiple columns is to use the Column Layout dialog box. To display this window, select Column from the Layout menu, or use the traditional command ^OU. You'll see this dialog box, with the settings shown for the local file:

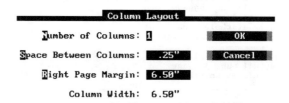

The values displayed here are determined by the values in the file when you display the dialog box. As soon as you enter a value in Number of Columns, the Column Width value at the bottom changes. As an example, if Number of Columns is 2, then Column Width changes to 3.13. The sum of the column widths, plus the space between columns, adds up to the right page margin:

$$3.13 + 3.13 + .25 = 6.5 \text{ (to the nearest tenth)}$$

which is the space between the left and right margins. The width of the text columns in this case is determined by the default left and right margins.

Columns do not appear side by side on the Edit screen, but do appear side by side when printed or when viewed using Preview. A sample Edit screen display is shown in Figure 12-2.

In this example, page breaks (.cb) were set after a few lines to display multicolumn breaks. Note the double line to show column 2 following the first .cb, and a single line to show column 1 following the second .cb. The

Figure 12-2.   Multiple-column display on Edit screen

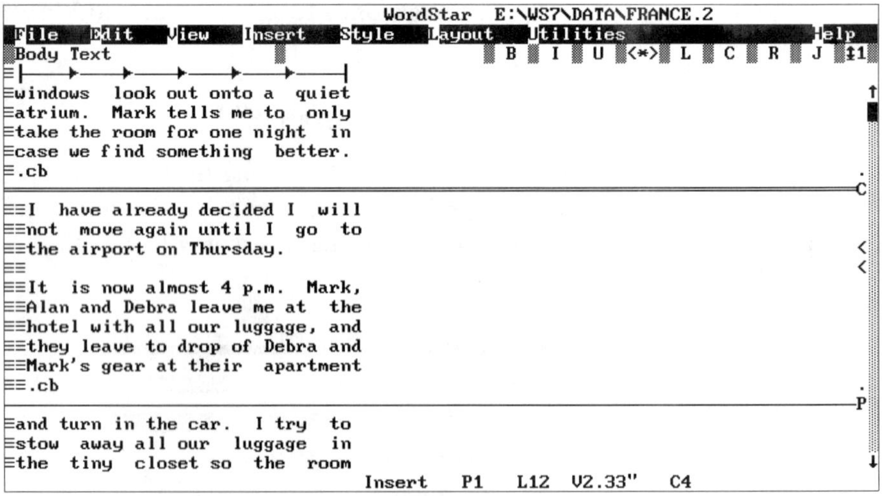

12

number of ☰ symbols on the left of the screen corresponds to the column you are working with. Notice that in the flag column a C is used to indicate the end of a column and, as usual, a P designates the end of a page. These flags, C and P, occur whether column- or page-ends happen by default or are forced by using .cb. A two-column display in Preview is shown in Figure 12-3.

Note

The space between columns is called the gutter. *When you are working with newspaper columns, whatever left margin you establish with the .lm command will be added to the gutter width. For example, if .lm .5" is used and you set the space between columns at .25", then the gutter will be .75". If you wish only the leftmost column indented, use the page offset command (.po) instead of the .lm command.*

To return to standard column structure, type **.co** or **.co 1**. You can also change any existing newspaper-style columns back to standard columns by deleting the dot commands associated with newspaper columns and then reformatting.

Figure 12-3.   *Multiple-column display using Preview*

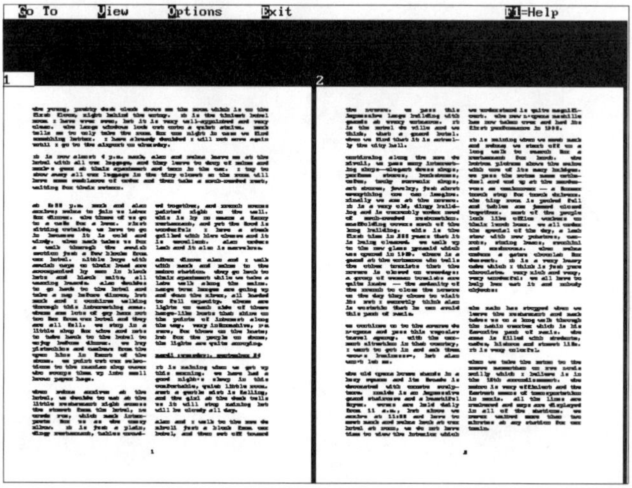

Exercises

1. Example 12 is a variation of Example 6A. Remove any dot commands you entered in Example 6A, and enter the styles shown in Example 12 to produce the same formatting.

2. Using one of your existing files, experiment with different numbers and widths of newspaper-style columns.

3. Use dot commands to create a hanging indent style different from the three styles supplied with WordStar. Use the procedures outlined in "Creating a New Style" in this chapter to design and save the style.

4. Create a three-column newsletter format and use Preview to display it in landscape mode.

Example 12

```
<Title>
                    STRAND HIGH SCHOOL
                      415 Green Street
                    Concord, CA 94520
                      (415) 798-5209

<Body text>
Dear Student Employer:

Please be advised that one of our students who has
been employed by you has applied for credit in the
Outside Work Experience Program.

We would like to acquaint you with the basic re-
quirements of this program so that there is no mis-
understanding at a later date.

Requirements
<Hanging indent 1>

1.  The student must be regularly enrolled in the high
    school for no less than a minimum day, which
    consists of three classes.

2.  Absence from school automatically is considered
    absence from the Outside Work Experience job
    station. It is generally considered that if a
    student cannot attend school, he or she cannot go
    to work.

3.  A student cannot be employed in excess of eight
    hours per day, including school time.
```

Example 12 (*continued*)

```
     For example:

     If a student has four classes in the morning, and
     works four hours after school, he or she is within
     the requirements. However, if a student has a full
     class schedule, he or she will be entitled to work
     four hours after school.

4.   All students under the age of eighteen must have
     a duly issued work permit.

<Body text>
I hope this letter is informative and that you and
your employee will be able to comply. We would
like to express our appreciation for your coopera-
tion. If you have any questions, please call me at
666-1111.

                         Yours very truly,

                         JOHN SMITH
```

13

Spelling Check, Definitions, and Thesaurus

Since version 5.0, WordStar has offered a Definitions dictionary in addition to the Spelling Check and Thesaurus features. All three are integral parts of WordStar and easy to use. Spelling Check and the Thesaurus are automatically installed with WordStar, but not Definitions. When you install WordStar using Setup, the Definitions are transferred to the hard disk; however, you will not have access to them (as part of the Spelling Check dialog box) unless you go into WSCHANGE and set "Definition during spelling check" to On. In WSCHANGE the path to Definitions is C/C/C. (You will find additional information for using WSCHANGE in Appendix C.)

Using Spelling Check

All of the commands related to word usage are on the Utilities menu and its submenu, Spelling Check Other, as shown in Figure 13-1.

Figure 13-1.   *Spelling and Thesaurus commands on the Utilities menu*

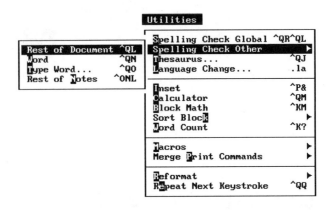

The Spelling Check commands, along with their functions, are listed here:

Spelling Command	Function
^QL	Checks the spelling in your document from the position of the cursor to the end of the file.
^Home, ^QL	To check an entire file, press ^HOME or ^QR to position the cursor at the beginning before selecting ^QL. Words on dot command lines are not checked. (Note that this is what SHIFT-F3 and Spelling Check Global, on the Utilities menu, do.)
^QN	Checks the word at the position of the cursor. Also displays the definition of the word if you have loaded Definitions and a definition is available.
^QO	Checks the spelling of a word entered from the keyboard. If you have loaded Definitions and a definition is available, it is also displayed.
^ONL	Checks the spelling in footnotes and endnotes from the position of the cursor to the end of the file.

The first two commands, ^QL and ^QN, can be selected from the Utilities menu or by using the macros SHIFT-F3 and SHIFT-F4. SHIFT-F3 performs a global spelling check by moving the cursor to the beginning of the file (^QR), then checking the complete file (^QL). SHIFT-F4 checks the spelling of the word the cursor is on.

When you press ^QL, the spell-check starts immediately. When WordStar encounters a word that is not in one of the Spelling Check dictionaries, the spell-check stops and the following Spelling Check dialog box is displayed:

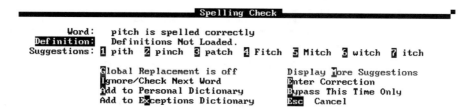

```
                        Spelling Check
        Word:     pitch is spelled correctly
  Definition:     Definitions Not Loaded.
 Suggestions: 1 pith  2 pinch  3 patch  4 Fitch  5 Mitch  6 witch  7 itch

             Global Replacement is off        Display More Suggestions
             Ignore/Check Next Word           Enter Correction
             Add to Personal Dictionary       Bypass This Time Only
             Add to Exceptions Dictionary     Esc  Cancel
```

Take a look at each of the Spelling Check options:

Option	Result
G	Toggles Global Replacement on or off. When Global Replacement is on, all words in the document with the same spelling as the word you corrected are replaced with the corrected word. When Global Replacement is off, only the current word is replaced. Default is off.
I	Causes WordStar to ignore the word and other occurrences of the same word in the document. When you are using ^QL, the word is ignored and the cursor proceeds to the next word not found in the dictionary. With ^QN, the cursor moves to the next word in the file. With ^QO, the window clears and you can enter a new word from the keyboard.
A	Adds the word to your Personal dictionary. Once the word is in that dictionary, WordStar no longer stops at the word.

13

X   Adds words to the Exceptions dictionary. This option only
           appears when you check the spelling of an individual
           word (^QN), or when you enter a word from the
           keyboard (^QO) and the word is spelled correctly.
           During regular spell-checks, the process always stops at
           any word in the Exceptions dictionary to check for
           correct usage. For example, it may stop at *nay*. You can
           check if that word is correct usage or a typing error of
           the word *any*.

M   The option to Display More Suggestions only appears
           when there are additional suggestions for an incorrectly
           spelled word. When the additional suggestions are
           displayed, the message changes to Redisplay First
           Suggestions.

E   Displays the Spelling Correction window, where you can
           edit the existing word or enter a new word. After you
           press ENTER, the word is rechecked against the dictionary.

B   Causes WordStar to bypass the word this time but to stop
           at the next occurrence of the word.

Check Individual Word (^QN)

To check the spelling of a single word, place the cursor on the word and
select ^QN. The Spelling Check dialog box shown previously is displayed. If
the word is spelled correctly, the definition is displayed immediately below
the word being checked (provided you have installed Definitions). Also, a list
of words with similar spellings may be displayed.

Check Keyboard Entry (^QO)

To check the spelling of a word entered from the keyboard, press ^QO.
This Spelling Check window appears:

```
                          Spelling Check
                                                        OK
Type Word to Check: _____         Cancel
```

Type a word and press ENTER; the Spelling Check dialog box is displayed. Again, when the word is spelled correctly, the definition, if available, is shown along with a list of correctly spelled similar words.

Multilingual Spelling and Hyphenation (.la *code*)

In addition to the American English spelling and hyphenation checker supplied with WordStar for DOS, medical, legal, and a variety of foreign language dictionaries (with appropriate hyphenation checking) are also available from WordStar International. Here is a sampling of the foreign language dictionaries:

British English	Portuguese
French	Brazilian Portuguese
French Canadian	Spanish
German	Mexican/Central American Spanish
Italian	

You can have several dictionaries available on your hard disk at the same time. By default, the dictionary used will be the American English one, but this can be reset with WSCHANGE. To select another dictionary for a particular file, you can insert the dot command .la, followed by the appropriate country code. The codes are supplied with the documentation that comes with the dictionaries, and can also be found in the IBM DOS manual.

Personal Dictionary and Exceptions Dictionary

WordStar comes with a dictionary that contains more than 100,000 words, plus two supplemental dictionaries to which you can add words—a Personal dictionary and an Exceptions dictionary. Initially, both supplemental dictionaries are empty. The purpose of the Personal dictionary is for you to add words that commonly occur in your work but that are not likely to be in the main dictionary. Examples of such words are your name, company names, names of people you deal with frequently, and product names. Of course, you need to be sure the words are spelled correctly when you enter them. The Exceptions dictionary lets you verify the use of particular words in the file you are checking. Examples are homonyms like *weather* and *whether* and typographical errors such as *chose* for *choose*.

13

To delete words from either supplemental dictionary, open that file (PERSONAL.DCT or EXCEPT.DCT) in Nondocument mode and make your deletions. Files with the extension .DCT do not appear in WordStar's directory, but you can access these files by entering their names in the Open Document window. (Nondocument files are discussed in Chapter 18.)

Here is a summary of the Personal dictionary properties:

- Words from your file are added to the Personal dictionary when the A option is selected from the Spelling Check dialog box.

- You may also add words directly to the Personal dictionary by opening the file PERSONAL.DCT in WordStar's nondocument mode and typing in the words. Be sure to enter the words in alphabetical order; or you can use the Sort command, ^KZ, to sort the words in ascending order. (Sort is discussed in Chapter 18.)

- Spell-checks go faster if the Personal dictionary is small. It is therefore better to have three or four small dictionaries than to have one large one. You can use WSCHANGE to have WordStar prompt you for the dictionary to use with a particular file. Appendix C shows the path through WSCHANGE to activate the prompt.

- To use a Personal dictionary from a version of WordStar prior to 5.0, be sure to sort the list in ascending order.

- Before you rely on a Personal dictionary from a previous version of WordStar, run a spell-check on the file to see if the words are included in WordStar's new expanded dictionary.

Using the Thesaurus (^QJ)

To select WordStar's Thesaurus, press ^QJ or choose it from the Utilities menu. You will see the Thesaurus dialog box as shown in Figure 13-2.

At the top-left of the window is the word for which you are seeking a synonym. Below this is a listing of available synonyms, and at the bottom of the window are the command options. If there are more synonyms than will fit in the window, a down arrow is displayed (as shown at the left of the screen in Figure 13-2). You can scroll the contents of the window a line at a time

Figure 13-2. *Thesaurus dialog box*

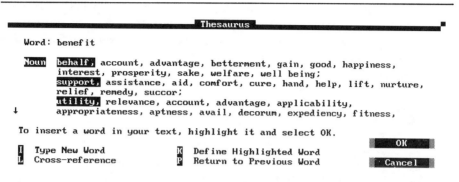

using the arrow keys, or scroll a full page, if enough additional options are available, using PGUP and PGDN. You can also scroll using the mouse.

The Thesaurus commands at the bottom of the screen, along with other keys useful with this window, are described next. In addition to using the keyboard, selection can also be made using the mouse.

Thesaurus Command	Function
LEFT ARROW/ RIGHT ARROW	Moves the cursor through the option list a word at a time in the direction of the arrow.
ENTER, F10	Replaces the word in your document with the Thesaurus word the cursor is on.
ESC	Exits the Thesaurus and returns you to your position in the file.
I	Displays the Type New Word window, where you can enter a word of your choice. If your entry is defined, synonyms are displayed.
L	Displays synonyms for the Thesaurus words shown in reverse video.
K	Defines the Thesaurus words shown in reverse video.
P	Redisplays synonyms for the previous word (usually used after the L option has been selected).

At times, the Thesaurus cannot find the word for which you are requesting a synonym. It will then display a list of similarly spelled words and allow you to select synonyms for any of these words. If you are not sure that the word you specified is spelled correctly, you can use Spelling Check before you use the Thesaurus.

Exercises

1. Check the spelling of one of your own files and, where appropriate, add words to the PERSONAL.DCT file. Run Spelling Check again to verify that WordStar no longer stops at any words you have added to your Personal dictionary.

2. Open a file and edit it, and use ^QO to check the spelling of a word entered from the keyboard. Note the difference in the E option here.

3. Add a couple of words that will be helpful to you to the Exceptions dictionary. (An example might be *fro* if you occasionally enter the typo *fro* for the word *for*.)

4. Use WSCHANGE to activate the Definitions dictionary during the spell-check if you haven't already done so. (When you are in WSCHANGE, the path is C/C/C. Check Appendix C if you are not familiar with WSCHANGE.)

14

Calculator and Macro Commands

This chapter introduces two capabilities that are common in word processors: using the WordStar Calculator while editing, and creating and using *macros* (a recorded combination of commands that can be executed by a single command).

In *Calculator mode*, you can interrupt the editing process, solve a math problem, return to your editing, and place the result of your calculation in your document. Calculator mode also allows you to block a section of your file and perform mathematical operations while editing.

The variety of available macros and the ease of developing them have been greatly improved with WordStar 7.0 for DOS. In WordStar 7.0 you can streamline the command entry process. You can create macros for frequently used command and text combinations and then later implement them by pressing a *hot key*. A hot key may be a single key or, more commonly, a two-key combination.

Using the Calculator in WordStar (^QM)

To try the Calculator features, open a new file. While working in the file at the Edit screen, you can transfer to the Calculator window and perform calculations using any of the 15 mathematical operators displayed. To do so now, press **^QM** or select Calculator from the Utilities menu. Your screen displays Figure 14-1.

WordStar follows standard mathematical convention in evaluating the formulas you enter. In general, operations are evaluated from left to right in order of precedence. Table 14-1 shows the order of precedence.

The order of precedence can be changed by placing parentheses around the operations you want to take place first. When there is one pair of parentheses within another, the operations in the innermost pair are evaluated first. For a more detailed review of this process, consult a book on algebra or BASIC programming.

Now let's use WordStar's Calculator to solve a problem—the amount of interest due on a loan during one month. The formula for interest is

Interest = principal x *rate* x *time*

Use this data:

principal = $14,364.71
rate = 7.5%
time = 1 month or 1/12 of a year

Figure 14-1.   *The Calculator window*

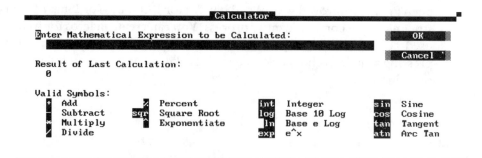

Table 14-1. *Order of Precedence in WordStar Calculator Evaluations*

Operator	Operation	Order
^	Exponentiation	Highest
* and /	Multiplication and division	Middle
+ and –	Addition and subtraction	Lowest

When you press **^QM** to display the Calculator window, the cursor is in the field Enter Mathematical Expression to be Calculated (the formula line). Type **14364.71*7.5%/12**. Press ENTER, and the result is displayed under Result of Last Calculation. The result is 89.7794375.

Note

As shown in the Valid Symbols list in the Calculator window, the multiplication symbol is an asterisk. The asterisk is universally used with computers to represent multiplication.

At this point, you can modify the formula either by making corrections or by entering new values. Use editing keys as you normally would in a document. You can press **^Y** and then **^R** at any time to replace the edited formula with the original. Pressing ENTER produces the results for the new formula.

Another function offered in the Calculator window is int (integer), which eliminates the decimal portion of a number. To see how this works, return the original interest formula to the formula line. With insert mode on, a square blinking cursor is in the formula line. Edit the formula so it reads

int(14364.71*7.5%/12)

and press ENTER. The result is 89. Note that the Calculator does not round the number to the nearest whole number, but eliminates the decimal portion of fractions; for example, the functions int(9.1) and int(9.9) both equal 9.

As with the int function, the other functions used in the calculator mode—cos (cosine) and tan (tangent), for example—require that the number you provide be enclosed in parentheses. Consult appropriate reference books if your work involves this type of material. Simple examples of how values are written for each function are shown in Example 14A at the end of this chapter.

14

Calculator mode produces results out to 14 decimal places. (For convenience, in Example 14A, the samples with ellipses have been shortened to three decimal places.) If WordStar's calculator can't handle a formula you provide, the program will ask you to check the formula.

Copying Calculator Results to a File (^M=, ^M$, ^M#)

To copy the results of your calculation to a file, press ENTER to close the Calculator window and return to the Edit screen. Press **^M=** to transfer the result of your calculation to the Edit screen at the position of the cursor. To insert the result in dollar format, press **^M$**. You may find it useful to insert the mathematical expression used to determine the result; you do this by pressing **^M#**. An example using this feature is described later in the "Macro Inserts" section.

Calculating in Blocks (^KM)

WordStar allows you to enter a mathematical expression (formula) directly into a file, block the expression, and press **^KM** to calculate the result. For example, at the Edit screen type

1250*8.75%*7=

and then block the expression. Your screen will look like this:

```
                          WordStar UNTITLED
 File    Edit    View    Insert    Style    Layout    Utilities          Help
 Body Text                 Draft 10            B   I  U <*> L    C   R  J ‡1
                      ▶       ▶     ▶        ▶         ▶
 1250*8.75%*7=                                                            ^↑
                                                                          ^:
```

Press **^KM**, and this window is displayed:

```
                          WordStar UNTITLED

 Block Math Result is:   765.625                         ▌ Continue ▌
```

Tip

*When you are working with an expression like the one in the foregoing **example**, be sure to block only the expression. If you want to find the sum of numbers **interspersed** throughout a file, block the entire section (the words and the numbers), press **^KM**, and the result is displayed. In either case, you can use ^M= or ^M$ to **print the result** at the cursor.*

Some examples of numbers that were added using the ^KM command and results printed using ^M= are shown in Table 14-2. The examples show the proper format for entering numbers to be added, and the method of indicating negative and exponential values.

About Macros

A *macro* is a series of keystrokes or commands, or a command-and-text entry, that you can give to a program by pressing a single key or a simple

Table 14-2. *Sample Block Operations in Calculator Mode*

Numbers	Result	Comments
5 6 7 8	= 26	A single space is sufficient to separate numbers.
5,6,7,8	= 5678	A comma between numbers is not a proper separator, so the numbers are not added.
5, 6, 7, 8	= 26	A comma plus a space properly separates numbers.
–5 6 7 8	= 16	A hyphen before a number is considered a minus sign.
–5 6 (7) 8	= 2	A number enclosed in parentheses is evaluated as a negative number.
3e3 6e3	= 9000	Numbers may be entered using exponential notation.

combination of keys. You started using macros in Chapter 1 when you pressed F1 to display the Help menu. Since then you have used most of the 40 macros already programmed by WordStar for your convenience.

Built-in Macros

Table 14-3 shows WordStar's 40 built-in macros. Two of these macros—F1 for help and F10 for accepting dialog box entries and returning to the Edit or Opening screen—are *reserved*. The two reserved macros cannot be changed; but the remaining 38 can be changed or edited at your discretion. As you can see from Table 14-3, the built-in macros are all implemented by using the function keys F1 through F10, either alone or in combination with SHIFT, CTRL, or ALT. In addition to these combinations, you can use the ALT key together with a letter or number key to create an additional 36 macros. If you use an extended keyboard, you can assign eight more macros, using F11 and F12 and their combinations with SHIFT, CTRL, and ALT.

Macro Hot Keys

Hot key is a term used by most software programs, including WordStar, to refer to a single key or two-key combination (such as those shown in Table

Table 14-3.   *WordStar's Built-in Macros*

F-Keys		SHIFT-F*n*	CTRL-F*n*	ALT-F*n*
F1	Help	Show/Hide Codes	Find		
F2	Undo	Center	Replace	—
F3	Undrline	Spellall	NextFind	⌐
F4	Bold	Spellword	Go-To-Pg	¬
F5	Del Line	Del Block	L-Margin	L
F6	Del Word	Hide Block	R-Margin	⌐
F7	Reform	Mov Block	P-Margin	⊤
F8	Ruler	Copy Block	New Page	⊥
F9	SaveFile	BegBlock	Line-Beg	⊢
F10	Continue	EndBlock	Line-End	⊣

14-3) that does the work of several, even several dozen, keystrokes. The purpose of a macro is to save you time. Consequently, for a macro to be worthwhile it must require fewer keystrokes to implement than the number of keystrokes it replaces. As an example, you press the single key F7 to reformat a paragraph. It replaces the traditional two-key WordStar command to reformat a paragraph, ^B. A more elaborate macro might let you press a two-key combination to execute all the commands necessary to insert a centered letterhead that includes your name, address, phone number, and the current date. You will design this macro shortly.

Note

In addition to executing macros using hot keys, you can display the Macro directory and select the macro from there.

14

The Macro Menu (^M)

You can select macro commands from the Macro menu, or with the Macro option on the Utilities pull-down menu. Display the Macro menu now by pressing **^M**. You have a display like Figure 14-2.

This menu has the macro commands listed under MACRO FUNCTIONS; under INSERT you'll find commands for inserting a variety of useful information into a document. Note that INSERT lists the math commands ^M= (the = on the menu) and ^M# (# on the menu) discussed earlier in this chapter.

Figure 14-2.   *Traditional Macro menu*

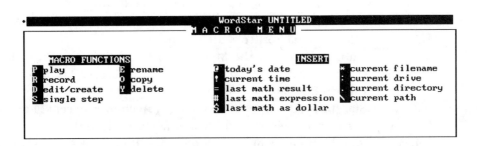

This Macro menu is convenient for reference because it has all the menu commands and inserts in one place. But like all traditional menus, you cannot make selections from it using the mouse.

As stated earlier, you can also select the macro commands from a pull-down menu. To do so, display the Utilities menu and select Macro. You'll see the macro commands shown here:

In the following section, you'll go through the steps necessary to *play* (or select) a macro, and to *record* (or define), a macro. After studying these commands, you will record three useful macros that will give you the experience you need to record your own macros. For the commands that follow, try different ways of selecting them—from the Macro menu, the Utilities pull-down menu, and the direct commands shown in parentheses in the following section headings.

Play (^MP)

When you are editing a document and wish to select a macro, the most common procedure is to press the appropriate hot key(s); but it is also possible to select a macro from the Macro menu. In fact, if you use macros extensively, and all possible hot key combinations have been assigned, you will have to select any additional macros from the menu.

To play a macro, display the Macro menu, and from the list of macro functions, select **P** for Play. The screen shown in Figure 14-3 is displayed.

Here you'll find an alphabetical list of all the macros that are supplied with WordStar (but you can redefine them if you choose, except F1 and F10).

The procedure to select a macro from the macro list is the same as if you select a file or other item from any WordStar list. Press DOWN ARROW to move

Figure 14-3. *Play Macro window and macro directory*

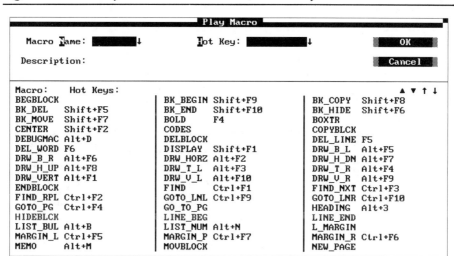

into the directory; as usual, the small down arrow next to the Macro Name
and Hot Key fields indicates that list selection is available. Notice that as you
move the cursor through the directory, the description of the macro, as well
as its name and hot key, are displayed in the fields above. This feature is useful
because the eight-letter restriction for the Macro Name field sometimes
results in a name's being too cryptic to describe the function of the macro.
When the desired macro is displayed, press F10. The macro performs its
function immediately, without any display of menus or dialog boxes—unless,
of course, it requires input from you.

Record (^MR)

WordStar provides two ways to define a macro: with the Record option,
or with the Edit/Create option. Using the Edit/Create option requires
knowledge of the macro programming language, which is similar to BASIC.
In this text we will create macros using Record.

Here is an outline of the procedure used to record a macro. **Read the procedure carefully; in the following section, you'll record three useful macros.** To record a new macro, follow these steps:

- Choose the Record command. The screen displays the Record Macro window, which is similar to the Play Macro window (Figure 14-3). The cursor is in the Macro Name field, which at this point is blank, waiting for you to enter the macro name.
- Enter the macro name and press TAB to move to the Hot Key field. The directory changes to a display similar to Figure 14-4. This screen shows the hot keys that have been assigned and those that are available in the range ALT-(0-9) and ALT-(A-Z).

Caution

It's not shown on the Record Macro window, but the hot keys ALT-F, -E, -U, -I, -S, -C, -U, and -H are assigned to display the pull-down menus. If you use any of these combinations for your macros, you will then have to display the associated pull-down menu using the mouse.

- Select the hot key you want to use and press TAB to move to the Description field.
- Enter the description for the macro (maximum of 48 characters).
- When the three entries, Macro Name, Hot Key, and Description, are correct, press F10 to move to the Edit screen.
- Now press the keys that execute all the WordStar commands and keystrokes that you want included in the macro, in the exact order that you wish them played back. If the macro will require keyboard input, such as a filename, press ALT- (hyphen) and any number of keystrokes as sample input. Enter ALT- (hyphen) again to terminate the input. Then continue entering the required macro commands.

Caution

Mouse clicks cannot be entered into a macro.

- When the macro is complete, hold down the ALT key and press = (equal sign) to end Macro Record.

Figure 14-4.   *Record Macro window with assigned and unassigned hot keys*

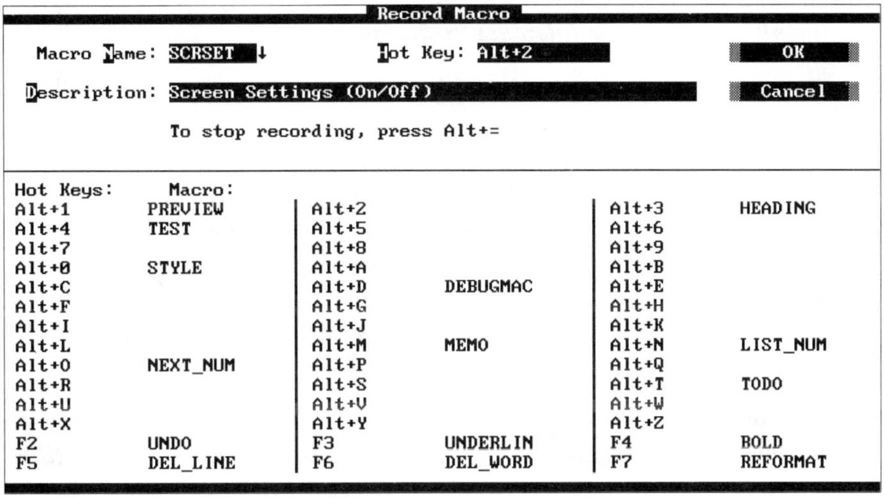

```
┌──────────────────────── Record Macro ─────────────────────────┐
│                                                                │
│     Macro Name: SCRSET ↓        Hot Key: Alt+2       ▐  OK  ▌  │
│                                                                │
│   Description: Screen Settings (On/Off)              ▐ Cancel ▌│
│                                                                │
│              To stop recording, press Alt+=                    │
│                                                                │
├────────────────────────────────────────────────────────────── │
│  Hot Keys:      Macro:                                         │
│  Alt+1        PREVIEW      Alt+2              Alt+3    HEADING  │
│  Alt+4        TEST         Alt+5              Alt+6             │
│  Alt+7                     Alt+8              Alt+9             │
│  Alt+0        STYLE        Alt+A              Alt+B             │
│  Alt+C                     Alt+D   DEBUGMAC   Alt+E             │
│  Alt+F                     Alt+G              Alt+H             │
│  Alt+I                     Alt+J              Alt+K             │
│  Alt+L                     Alt+M   MEMO       Alt+N    LIST_NUM │
│  Alt+O        NEXT_NUM     Alt+P              Alt+Q             │
│  Alt+R                     Alt+S              Alt+T    TODO     │
│  Alt+U                     Alt+V              Alt+W             │
│  Alt+X                     Alt+Y              Alt+Z             │
│  F2           UNDO         F3     UNDERLIN    F4       BOLD     │
│  F5           DEL_LINE     F6     DEL_WORD    F7       REFORMAT │
└────────────────────────────────────────────────────────────── ┘
```

The macro is now ready to try at the appropriate spot in your document.

Recording Your Own Macros

You have probably found use for most of the built-in macros. You may also be wondering why there's no macro to perform some other particular operation that you use frequently. Using the Record command, it may be possible for you to produce that macro. Three macros are presented now that you may find useful and that will also give you the experience to create other custom macros that will save you considerable time.

Turn Off Screen Settings

The first macro you'll write here is one that turns off all the screen settings—ruler line, style bar, and so on—with the press of a single hot key.

Note

When a macro "plays," it reproduces all the keystrokes you entered when you recorded it. That includes any errors and corrections. Therefore, it's a good idea to practice entering the keystrokes before you create the macro.

Although it's not necessary, it is easier to record a macro without having text on the Edit screen. Therefore, open a new file now to record your first macro. Then select **Record** on the Macro menu (**^MR**). In the Macro Name field, enter **SCRSET** (for Screen Settings) and press TAB to move to the Hot Key field. The screen directory changes to show the hot keys that have been assigned and those still available in the range ALT- (0-9) and ALT- (A-Z). For this macro, select Alt+2. Press TAB to advance to the Description field, and type **Screen Settings (On/Off)**. The Record Macro window will look like this:

```
▄▄▄▄▄▄▄▄▄▄▄▄▄▄▄▄▄▄▄▄▄▄▄▄ Record Macro ▄▄▄▄▄▄▄▄▄▄▄▄▄▄▄▄▄▄▄▄▄▄▄▄

  Macro Name: SCRSET ↵          Hot Key: Alt+2            ▓ OK ▓

  Description: Screen Settings (On/Off)                  ▓ Cancel ▓

            To stop recording, press Alt+=
```

Press F10. You are now in the Edit screen ready to record the SCRSET macro. Note the instruction "To end recording, press Alt+=" in the title bar.

Note

As you go through the process of recording the macro, you can use the View menu and the Screen Settings window just as you would normally.

Here is the exact sequence of the keys you press and what happens when you press them. These keystrokes will be saved as a macro for you to use any time you are working with WordStar.

Keys Pressed	Purpose
ALT-V	Opens the View menu
S	Selects Screen Settings
STLR	Turns off scroll bar, style bar, status line, and ruler line
F10	Returns to the Edit screen
ALT-=	Terminates recording the macro

When you press the last key, **=**, you are returned to the Edit screen, and the scroll bar, style bar, status line, and ruler line are turned off. Press the hot key ALT-2 now, and watch the four information lines reappear. With this macro, you are getting two for one, because the macro works as a toggle. Each time you select the macro, it turns the screen settings on or off, because all the commands that make up this macro are toggles. You can use this macro any time you are editing a file in WordStar.

Create Centered Letterhead

Now try a more elaborate macro that uses both text and commands. If you look ahead at what you enter in this macro, you'll see an unfamiliar command, ^M@, which will be discussed shortly. Begin by choosing Record, and enter **HEADING** as the macro name. Press TAB and select the hot key Alt+3. Press TAB and enter the description **Centered Letterhead**. Press F10 to return to the Edit screen. Type the following, using appropriate punctuation between the items you enter, and pressing ENTER after every line:

^OC, *(your name)* ENTER
^OC, *(your address)* ENTER
^OC, *(your city, state, zipcode)* ENTER
^OC, *(your phone number)* ENTER
ENTER
^OC ^M@ ENTER

Finally, press ALT-= to terminate the recording process.

You are back at the Edit screen, and now can use this macro to enter your letterhead any time you start a new file, a letter, and so on. Because of the ^M@ command, the date will always be correct, provided it is set correctly in the computer. Try the macro: Press ALT-3, and the letterhead prints similar to the display below:

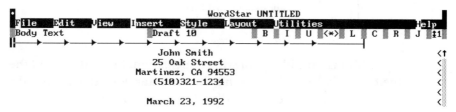

Rounding to the Nearest Penny

If you use the Calculator frequently, you may find this macro for rounding dollar numbers to the nearest penny to be helpful. To see how useful the macro will be, try this simple example. At the Edit screen, enter

7.464 + 8.795 =

Block the numbers and press **^KM**. The result, 16.259, is displayed and stored in the computer. Press ENTER. Place the cursor after the = sign, and press **^M=**. The result 16.259 is printed. Delete the 16.259 and press **^M$**, and the result 16.25 is printed. It is close to being exact, but is not correct to the nearest penny.

The macro below will round the result of any calculator result to the nearest penny. To record the macro, display the Record Macro window. Enter **Round** in the Macro Name field. Press TAB, and select Alt+R for the Hot Key field. Press TAB, and type **Round to the nearest penny** in the Description field. Press F10. Enter the following, leaving out the commas:

^KB, ^M=, press SPACEBAR once, **005, ^KK, ^KM**, ESC, **^KY, ^M$**

Press ALT-= to stop recording. The purpose of each entry is shown in the diagram below.

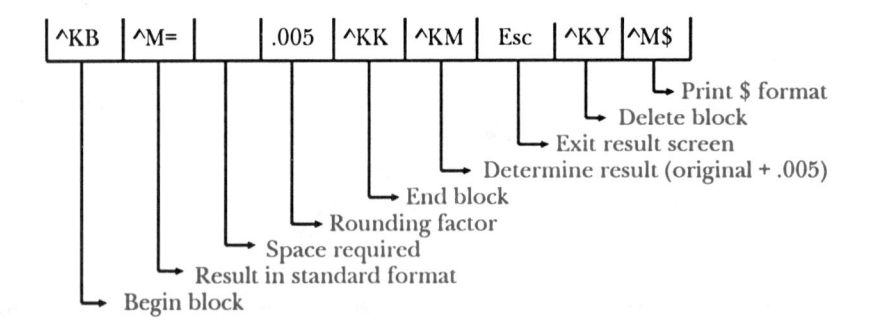

Try this macro with the previous calculation. Press ALT-R, and the display at the cursor is 16.26. To use the macro, enter your calculation, then press ALT-R. The result will be rounded to the nearest penny.

More Macro Functions

Now that you have had some experience recording macros, let's continue exploring the remaining macro functions on the Macro menu.

Edit/Create (^MD)

The Edit/Create command is used to edit an existing macro, or create a new macro using WordStar's macro language. As mentioned earlier, we will not use the macro language in this text. However, let's look at the steps for using the Edit portion of the Edit/Create command to edit an existing macro:

1. Choose the Edit/Create command. A window similar to Figure 14-3 is displayed.

2. Select the macro you want to edit, by name or hot key, and press F10. The macro is displayed in the Edit screen. For this example, SCRSET, the macro you recorded earlier, is shown in Figure 14-5.

3. If you wish, edit the macro and press F10 to save the file. WordStar saves the files and informs you if any errors were made during the edit. If there were, you must edit the macro again to correct the error.

Figure 14-5.   *Edit screen showing SCRSET macro*

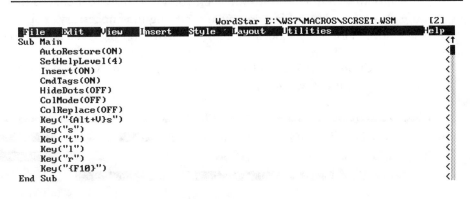

Note

If you wish to copy a block of data from one macro to another, start at the Opening screen. Select Macro from the Utilities menu and open two windows. Display the material to copy in one window. Display the macro you are copying to in the second window. Block the material to be copied, and copy it to the target macro just as you would any text.

Single Step (^MS)

The Single Step command is used to verify that a new macro operates as you expected. To single-step through a macro, follow this procedure:

1. Choose the Single Step command. From the directory displayed, select the desired macro by name or hot key and press F10.

2. You are now in the Edit screen with the macro name in the title bar. Press the SPACEBAR to advance through the macro a single character or command at a time. It may require eight to ten presses before you see anything on the screen, depending on the macro.

3. To end the single-step process at or before its normal termination, press ESC or ^BREAK. (If the macro is paused for input, you must use ^BREAK to terminate the process.)

Copy (^MO)

The Copy command is useful when you want to create a macro similar to an existing one, by making a copy and editing it as necessary. You can also use Copy to provide a macro for another WordStar user. To copy a macro:

1. Choose the Macro Copy command, and the Copy Macro window shown below will open.

```
                          Copy Macro
   Macro Jame: ▉▉▉▉▉↓        Iot Key: ▉▉▉▉▉▉↓              ▉ OK ▉

   Description: Screen Settings (On\Off)                 ▉ Cancel ▉

   Name of Copy: ▉▉▉▉▉▉▉▉▉▉▉▉▉▉▉▉▉▉▉▉▉
```

2. Using the arrow keys, select the macro to be copied. In the field Name of Copy, enter a new name for the copied macro, up to eight letters. There is room in the field if you need to enter the path. WordStar supplies the extension .WSM. If the name you enter is already in use, you will need to confirm that you wish to overwrite.

3. When all entries in the window are correct, press F10.

A copied macro has the same description as the original, but the same hot key is not assigned. Use Rename Macro, discussed shortly, to assign the hot key.

Delete Macro (^MY)

Delete Macro is used to remove an existing macro. To delete a macro:

1. Choose the Macro Delete command to see the Delete Macro window.

2. Select the macro by name or hot key and press F10. A window is displayed asking you to confirm your choice.

3. Press ENTER or F10 to confirm your request, and the macro is deleted.

Rename Macro (^ME)

Rename Macro lets you change a macro's name, hot key, and/or description.

1. Choose the Macro Rename command, and the window shown below is displayed.

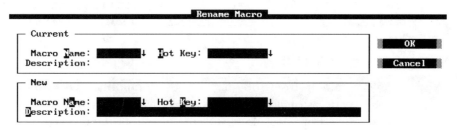

2. Select the macro to be renamed and press TAB to move to the New fields of the Rename window. Enter the desired new macro name, hot key, and description. Again, if the name or hot key is already in use, you will be asked to confirm the overwrite.

3. With all New fields correct, press F10 to complete the renaming process and return to the Edit screen.

Macro Inserts

On the Macro menu there are nine Macro inserts—macros that insert items into your document. You used three of these while working with the Calculator to print the last math expression, the last math result, and the last math result in dollar format. Before you go any further, notice these commands can also be accessed from the Insert pull-down menu:

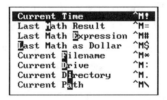

Today's Date Value has its own place on the Insert menu because it is so frequently used. The remaining eight insert commands are on the submenu that you see when you select Other Value.

Tip

You used the option Today's Date in the Heading macro for a centered letterhead, recorded earlier. If you have the date set properly, it displays at the position of the cursor in this format: March 23, 1992. The format can be changed using WSCHANGE—for example, to 23 March 1992.

The remaining Insert options are not commonly used by most people, but you may occasionally have a document where they will be helpful. Here are all the Insert options, along with the format of the display:

Access Command	Insert Item	Format
^M@	Current date	March 23, 1992
^M!	Current time	9:54 a.m.
^M=	Last math result	89.7794375
^M#	Last math expression	14364.71*7.5%/12
^M$	Last math as dollar	$89.77
^M*	Current filename	INSERT.14
^M:	Current drive	C:
^M.	Current directory	\BOOK
^M\	Current path	C:\BOOK\INSERT.14

Notice that the information for current filename, drive, directory, and path is the same information shown in the title bar to the right of "WordStar."

To try some of these macros, open a file with the name EXAMPLE.14B. Then press **^QM**, enter the interest equation presented earlier, **14364.71*7.5%/12**, and return to the Edit screen. Type in Example 14B, using the **^M** macros, as shown at the end of this chapter. If you use the same dot commands, your screen should look similar to Figure 14-6.

Figure 14-6.   *Example using Insert options*

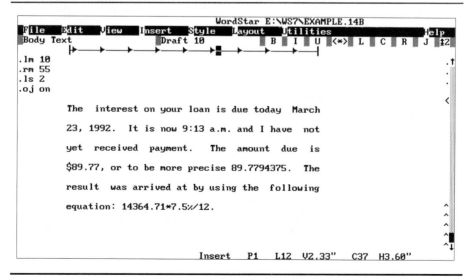

```
                           WordStar E:\WS7\EXAMPLE.14B
 File    Edit    View    Insert   Style    Layout    Utilities              Help
 Body Text              Draft 10           B   I   U  <*>  L   C   R   J  ±2
        |+————→————→————→————■————→————→————→————|
.lm 10                                                                      .↑
.rm 55                                                                      .
.ls 2                                                                       .
.oj on                                                                      <

        The   interest on your loan is due today   March

        23, 1992.  It is now 9:13 a.m. and I have   not

        yet  received  payment.   The   amount  due   is

        $89.77, or to be more precise 89.7794375.   The

        result   was arrived at by using the   following
                                                                            ^
        equation: 14364.71*7.5%/12.                                         ^
                                                                            ^
                                                                            ^■
                                                                            ^↓
                      Insert    P1    L12   V2.33"   C37   H3.60"
```

Exercises

1. Write a macro to print a complimentary closing for a letter, including three carriage returns for blank lines before your name, as in this example:

   Sincerely,

   John Smith

2. Write a macro to move the cursor to the space after the last letter of a word (instead of to the first letter of the next word, as ^F does).

3. Use the Single Step macro command with your Screen Settings macro, and observe how the command single-steps through the macro.

4. Create a macro that turns off the command tags as well as the screen settings.

Example 14A

```
ln(10) = 2.302...  exp(3) = 20.085... atn(1) = 45
log(100) = 2       sqr(64) = 8        sin(45) = .707...
cos(60) = .5       tan(45) = 1
```

14

Example 14B

The interest on your loan is due today, ^M@. It is
now ^M! and I have not yet received payment. The
amount due is ^{M}, or to be more precise ^M=. The
result was arrived at by using the following equation:
^M#.

15

Indexing, Tables of Contents, Footnotes/Endnotes, and Paragraph/Line Numbers

This Chapter includes a variety of specialized topics. Some users may only find occasional use for these topics; others may find one or more of the procedures useful on a daily basis. If the work you do includes producing manuals, documentation, or books, you will find WordStar's Indexing and Table of Contents features very useful. Also used with this type of writing are footnotes and endnotes. Those working with contracts or legal documents in general will have use at one time or another for paragraph and line numbering. Let's start with indexing.

An *index* is an alphabetical list of words or topics in a document, along with the page numbers where each can be found. A *table of contents* is a sequential list of the sections in a document, also including page numbers. Because page numbers are part of both an index and a table of contents, these items are the final pieces of a document that you create. That is, you must complete all formatting and editing, which could affect page numbering, before starting the index and table of contents.

Indexing

There are two methods of indexing a document with WordStar. One is similar to traditional index-card indexing. The other is called exclusion indexing.

Traditional Indexing (^PK, .ix, ^ONI)

Here is an outline of the steps in doing traditional—manual—indexing:

1. Read your document, marking the words or phrases you want in the index.
2. Read the document again, copying each word or phrase, along with the page number, onto an index card.
3. Sort the cards alphabetically.
4. For all cards with identical entries, collect the page numbers on one card.
5. Type the list of entries in the proper format for your index.

With WordStar, you use the same approach. You begin by marking the items you want in the index, but you mark them electronically, using the command ^PK, .ix, or ^ONI. The command ^PK is used to bracket with ^K codes the words or phrases you want in the index. As usual, the ^K symbols can be removed with the print display toggle, SHIFT-F1.

If a topic you want to include in the index does not appear in the text, you can enter it in one of two ways:

- Enter the dot command **.ix** in the proper position and follow it with the index entry on the same line.
- Select Index/TOC Entry from the Insert menu or enter the command **^ONI**. In either case, you are presented with the Index Entry window where you can then type your index entry.

```
┌──────────────────────────── Index Entry ────────────────────────────■
│                                                                      │
│                                                           ▓▓▓ OK ▓▓▓ │
│  Index Entry: ▓▓▓▓▓▓▓▓▓▓▓▓▓▓▓▓▓▓▓▓▓▓▓▓▓▓▓▓▓▓▓▓▓▓▓▓▓▓▓▓▓▓             │
│                                                         ▓▓ Cancel ▓▓ │
└──────────────────────────────────────────────────────────────────────┘
```

Tip

If you wish the page number for your index entry to appear in boldface, enter a + (plus sign) before the entry.

Be sure to enter the **.ix** or **^ONI** command *before* the paragraph or section containing what you want indexed. Avoid placing it in the middle of a paragraph; otherwise, the command may be included in the paragraph during a paragraph reformatting operation.

If you wish, try the following exercise using the traditional method of indexing. To produce a useful illustration of an index, you will need a long document that is edited and formatted. For this example, you might enter the text of Chapter 10 from this book and save it as document file CH10.WS. Then follow these steps:

1. Bracket the words and phrases you want in the index, using **^PK** to insert **^K** codes. Or enter the **.ix** or **^ONI** command, followed by the topic you want included.

2. After all the index entries are marked and/or added, save the document and return to the Opening menu.

Figure 15-1 shows two sections of Chapter 10, and is similar to what you would obtain if you marked Chapter 10 for indexing.

You are now ready to index. With the marked file saved and closed and the Opening screen showing, display the Utilities menu and select **I** (Index). You'll see this window:

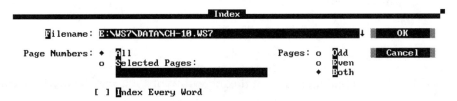

Figure 15-1.   *Edit screen view of file marked for indexing*

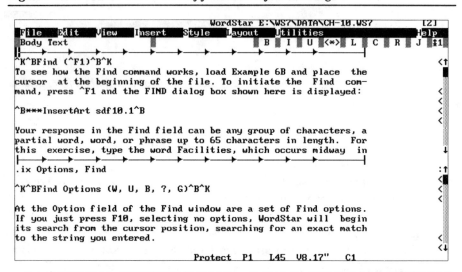

```
                            WordStar E:\WS7\DATA\CH-10.WS7            [Z]
  File   Edit   View   Insert   Style   Layout   Utilities            Help
 Body Text                                B   I   U  <*> L    C    R   J  ±1
 ┃
 ^K^BFind (^F1)^B^K                                                       <↑
 To see how the Find command works, load Example 6B and place  the
 cursor  at the beginning of the file. To initiate the  Find  com-
 mand, press ^F1 and the FIND dialog box shown here is displayed:        <
                                                                         <
 ^B***InsertArt sdf10.1^B                                                <
                                                                         <
 Your response in the Find field can be any group of characters, a
 partial word, word, or phrase up to 65 characters in length.  For
 this  exercise, type the word Facilities, which occurs midway   in      ↓
 ┣──▶──┬──▶──┬──▶──┬──▶──┬──▶──┬──▶──┬──▶──┬──▶──┬──▶──┬──▶──┤
 .ix Options, Find                                                       :↑
                                                                         <
 ^K^BFind Options (W, U, B, ?, G)^B^K                                    <
                                                                         <
 At the Option field of the Find window are a set of Find options.
 If you just press F10, selecting no options, WordStar will  begin
 its search from the cursor position, searching for an exact match
 to the string you entered.                                              <
                                                                         <↓
                          Protect  P1   L45  V8.17"   C1
```

If the name of your file to be indexed does not appear in the Filename field, enter it. Leave the Index Every Word check box unmarked, and use the default values, All and Both, in the Page Numbers and Pages fields, respectively. Press F10. Indexing starts immediately and takes only a second or two for a document of 2000 words. On the title bar, the page number advances as indexing proceeds. When indexing is finished, an index file is produced with the same name as your file but with the extension .IDX.

The index file produced for Chapter 10 is shown in Figure 15-2. Notice that the page references are off because, to create this example, an arbitrary page number, 150, was introduced with the .pn command.

An index file can be loaded into WordStar like any other document. You then have all the WordStar editing features available to you to modify it in any manner you please.

Exclusion Indexing

The second method of indexing with WordStar may seem a little cumbersome at first; but once you've tried it, you will find it an efficient and easy method of indexing. We will refer to it as *exclusion indexing*, because it requires

Figure 15-2.   *Index for Chapter 10*

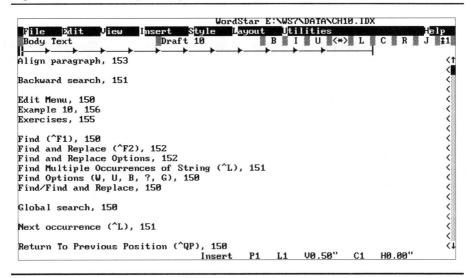

two "exclusion files"—files that contain the words you *don't* want in the index. One exclusion file is provided by WordStar, and the other is created by you (with the help of WordStar).

The exclusion file provided by WordStar is named WSINDEX.XCL and should be with your WordStar files. It is a list of words that are almost never included in an index. You can examine this file using the Open Nondocument command to see the type of words it contains.

You will create the second exclusion file using WordStar, as described next. (Again, the document to be indexed should be in final form with formatting and editing done.) From the Utilities menu on the Opening screen, select **I**. As before, enter the filename for the document. Then press TAB to move to the Index Every Word field, and press the SPACEBAR to enable this option. Then press F10. Indexing starts immediately; this time every word is indexed. This process takes only a few seconds for a file of 2000 words. Again, an index file is produced with the same name as your document, with the extension .IDX. A small section of this long file, again using Chapter 10, is shown in Figure 15-3. This file is the first step in producing your exclusion file.

Figure 15-3.   *Edit screen showing part of a file with Index Every Word option enabled*

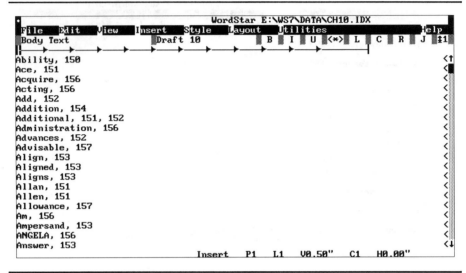

```
                                      WordStar E:\WS7\DATA\CH10.IDX
 File     Edit     View     Insert    Style    Layout    Utilities          Help
 Body Text                        Draft 10              B  I  U <*>  L   C   R  J  ‡1
 ├───►────────►─────────►───────►──────►──────►──────►──────►───────►
Ability, 150                                                                    <↑
Ace, 151                                                                        <█
Acquire, 156                                                                    <
Acting, 156                                                                     <
Add, 152                                                                        <
Addition, 154                                                                   <
Additional, 151, 152                                                            <
Administration, 156                                                             <
Advances, 152                                                                   <
Advisable, 157                                                                  <
Align, 153                                                                      <
Aligned, 153                                                                    <
Aligns, 153                                                                     <
Allan, 151                                                                      <
Allen, 151                                                                      <
Allowance, 157                                                                  <
Am, 156                                                                         <
Ampersand, 153                                                                  <
ANGELA, 156                                                                     <
Answer, 153                                                                     <↓
                         Insert    P1    L1    V0.50"    C1    H0.00"
```

The next step is to scroll through this index file, *deleting all the words you want to have in your index*. Then save the file and make it an exclusion file, by changing the extension from .IDX to .XCL. (Use Rename on the File menu of the Opening screen.)

Now, go back and index the same document, again enabling the Index Every Word option, accepting the default values for the Page Numbers and Pages entries, and pressing F10. This time you will have the appropriate index of your document, because all the words in WordStar's exclusion file and the exclusion file you created are omitted, leaving only those words you deleted from the previous index file.

Subreferences and Cross-references

Here is an example of an .ix command to create entries in the subreference format:

.ix Commands, Dot commands

When the file containing this example command is indexed, the printout will look like this:

Commands
   Dot commands, (*page number*)

To use an index topic as a cross-reference, precede it with a hyphen in the .ix command, as in

.ix-Indexing commands. *See* Dot commands

With an index entry of this type, no page number is included.

When using either ^PK or .ix, the maximum length of the word or phrase to be indexed is 150 characters, including any subreferences.

Note

15

Tables of Contents (.tc)

The procedure for producing a table of contents is similar to the traditional method for producing an index. When your document is in final form, go through it and enter the dot command **.tc** above each of the items you want in the table of contents. With the .tc command, you have to tell WordStar if you want page numbers included. You do this by placing a number sign (#) on the same line with the .tc command, in the column where the numbers will be.

As an example, using file CH10.WS, follow these steps:

1. Enter a **.rr** or **.tb** command to set up a ruler line, with a TAB at the column where you want the page numbers to appear. (If you use .rr, be sure at least one hyphen follows the TAB, and terminate the ruler line with an R.) The ruler line and tab commands are discussed in Chapter 5.

2. Enter **.tc** above the items you want in the table of contents.

3. Place the cursor on the line containing the item to be included, delete the item, and then reenter it with the Undo command, ^U.

4. Position the cursor after the .tc command, and press **^U** to also place the deleted item on the line with the .tc command.

5. Press **^P.** (period) to enter periods (dot leaders) all the way over to the tab mark you entered in step 1.

6. Enter the # symbol at the end of the .tc command line.

7. Repeat steps 3 through 6 for each table of contents entry.

An example of how a table of contents entry will appear, with dot leaders, is shown here:

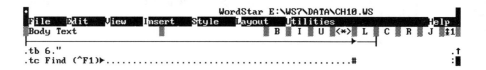

```
                              WordStar E:\WS7\DATA\CH10.WS
 File    Edit    View    Insert    Style    Layout    Utilities            Help
 Body Text                                B   I   U  <*>  L    C   R   J  ‡1

.tb 6."                                                                    .↑
.tc Find (^F1)►...............................................#           :█
```

Note

If you use Undo (^U) to place text after .tc or .ix, the flag (:) will be deleted if the line terminates with a soft carriage return. Move the cursor to the end of the line and press ENTER *(with insert on), and the flag will reappear in column 80.*

You can use the special print commands—underline (F3), boldface (F4), and so on—in the .tc line. These commands do not change the display on the Edit screen but will be in effect when the TOC files are printed. One space after the .tc command produces no indentation. Any additional spaces are retained when the TOC is printed. These spaces can be used to specify different indentations in the TOC entries.

You can have up to nine separate table of contents listing files for a single document. For example, you can use .tc commands for the table of contents, .tc1 commands for a list of all illustrations, .tc2 commands for a list of tables, and so on. Figure 15-4 shows a portion of a file (CH10.WS) with a .tc command and a .tc1 command.

Creating the .TOC File

Once you have finished with the .tc commands and text, save and close the document. Select **T** from the Utilities menu at the Opening screen, and you'll see this screen:

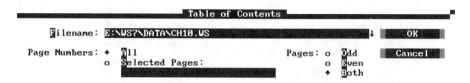

Enter the name of the document file (**CH10.WS**), and mark the appropriate options. Press F10 to prepare the table of contents file for the document. On completion, a file with the same name as the document but with the extension .TOC is written to the disk. If more than one table of contents is produced,

Figure 15-4. *Edit screen showing .tc commands to produce two different TOC files*

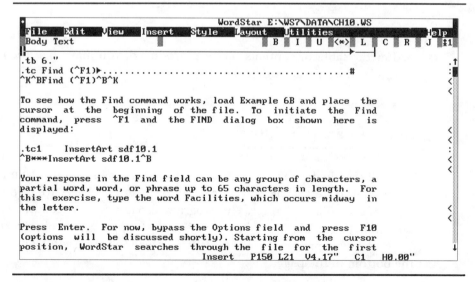

15

additional table of contents files are labeled in numerical order—.TO1, .TO2, and so on.

The table of contents produced from Chapter 10 is shown here:

```
                               WordStar E:\WS7\DATA\CH10.TOC
 File   Edit   View   Insert   Style   Layout   Utilities              Help
 Body Text                    Draft 10             B   I   U  <*>  L    C    R   J  ±1

     ▶      ▶      ▶      ▶           ▶      ▶           ▶

 Find (^F1)▶..............................................150            <↑
 Return To Previous Position (^QP)▶......................150            <
 Find Options (W, U, B, ?, G)▶...........................150            <
 Find Multiple Occurrences of String (^L)▶..............151            <
 InsertArt sdf10.3▶.....................................152            <
 Find and Replace (^F2)▶................................152            <
 Find and Replace Options▶.............................152            ∧
```

The following sample, also from Chapter 10, shows a list of illustrations:

```
      Printing                  WordStar E:\WS7\DATA\CH10.TO1
 File   Edit   View   Insert   Style   Layout   Utilities              Help
 Body Text                    Draft 10             B   I   U  <*>  L    C    R   J  ±1

     ▶      ▶      ▶      ▶           ▶      ▶

 Figure 10.1....................................150            <↑
 Figure 10.2....................................151            <
 Figure 10.4....................................152            <
 Figure 10.5....................................153            <
 Figure 10.6....................................154            <
```

After the table of contents files are produced, you may open them for editing as you would any other file.

Footnotes and Endnotes

WordStar allows you to enter footnotes and endnotes in your documents. *Footnotes* are printed at the bottom of each page, and *endnotes* are printed at the end of each file or chapter. The program also lets you use comments and annotations to explain items in a file. *Comments* appear only on screen, to enhance the explanation of items. *Annotations* print like footnotes, appearing at the bottom of the page.

The Notes Menu (^ON)

The commands to select the various note options are scattered throughout the pull-down menus. The traditional Notes menu (^ON) has all the commands organized on a single menu, so we'll use it for reference; see Figure 15-5.

Entering Notes

All four types of notes are entered and edited in the same manner. To enter a note, place the cursor next to the item in your file that the note will reference. Then you can press **^ON** and select the type of note from the Notes menu (**F** for footnote, **E** for endnote, **A** for annotation, or **C** for comment). Or, from the Insert menu select Note and choose the type of note from the Insert Note window shown here:

By either method, when you make your note type selection the Edit screen splits into two windows. The cursor is in the lower window waiting for you to enter the note. An example is shown in Figure 15-6.

Figure 15-5.   *Notes menu*

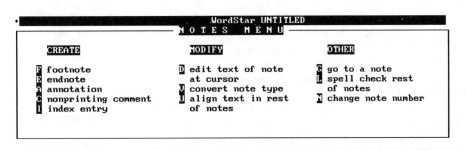

15

Figure 15-6.   *Edit screen split with Note window open at bottom*

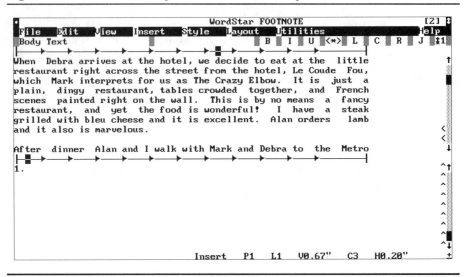

Keep in mind the following guidelines as you work with notes:

- The title bar shows the note type (in Figure 15.6, FOOTNOTE).

- For footnotes and endnotes, the upper-left corner of the bottom note window contains the note number. The default numbering sequence starts with 1. (How to modify the starting number and its format is discussed later under "Note Characteristics.")

- If you select Annotation, the following window opens, where you can enter a *, #, or whatever symbol you wish to use to mark your annotations in the document.

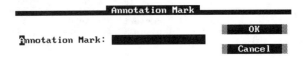

- Comments do not have a marker.

- To abandon the note while in the Note window, press **^KQ**, just as you would to abandon any file.
- Any combination of notes, including all four types together, may be used in a single document.

When you have finished entering a note, press F10. The note is saved, the Note window is closed, and the cursor is back at the Edit screen. A tag appears next to the item referenced by the note, showing the first few words of the note. As with other tags, this can be toggled on or off using SHIFT-F1. When screen tags are turned off, the footnote and endnote numbers and the annotation marks are displayed in place of the tags, but nothing is displayed for comment notes.

Now let's take a look at the remaining items on the Notes menu. As we said, these options are spread throughout the pull-down menus. At the end of each paragraph describing the option is a reference to the pull-down menu containing the command. For example, after the paragraph on Display and Edit Note, (Edit-N) tells you that you can access the Edit menu and press the accelerator key **N**.

Display and Edit Note (^OND)

You can display and edit any previously entered note by placing the cursor on the desired note and pressing **^OND**. Press F10 when you are finished editing. WordStar's full range of editing options is available to edit notes. (Edit-N)

Convert Note Type (^ONV)

Pressing **^ONV** lets you change a note from one type to another. Place the cursor on a note, then press **^ONV**. A dialog box is displayed where you select the new type of note. WordStar renumbers the notes automatically. (Edit-T-C)

Align Text in Notes(^ONU)

If you change the margins for your notes, pressing **^ONU** will reformat your notes within those margins, starting at the note the cursor is on and proceeding through the notes to the end of the file. (Utility-R-N)

15

Go To a Note (^ONG)

You can quickly locate a note by pressing **^ONG**. A dialog box appears where you can select the type of note to find. After you make your selection, you see the Find Note dialog box, which is similar in appearance and function to the Find dialog box used with a document search. In the Find field enter any word or phrase in the note, and in the Options field choose any of the options displayed—G, U, ?, and so on. (Edit-O-N)

Check Note Spelling (^ONL)

To check the spelling of notes, press **^ONL**. The spelling is checked in each type of note from the position of the cursor to the end of the file. (Utility-O-N)

Create Index Entry for a Note (^ONI)

In order to have an index entry for a footnote, endnote, or an annotation, press **^ONI**. A dialog box opens where you can enter the index item. The index entry for the note will print along with the other index entries. (I-I-I)

Automatic Numbering (^ONN)

In each file the notes are, by default, automatically numbered beginning with 1. To change the sequence of numbering for footnotes and endnotes, select **^ONN**. In this dialog box:

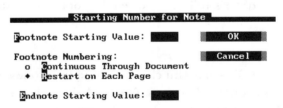

enter the starting value for either or both endnotes and footnotes, and select the desired numbering option (continuous or page-by-page). Press F10. (Edit-T-S)

Note Sequence Options   You have the option of using either numeric or alphabetical sequencing for your notes. For example:

Numbers: 1, 2, 3, etc.
Alpha: A–Z, AA–ZZ, AAA–ZZZ

You can also start footnote and endnote numbering at whatever initial value you choose, by entering the dot commands .f# and .e# directly. For example, the command .f# 5 will start the footnote numbering with 5 rather than 1. The .f# and .e# commands may also be used to select the initial letter in a lettering sequence. To change to a lettering sequence, use a command like .f# A.

Note Characteristics

The general characteristics for the four types of notes are described in the paragraphs that follow.

Footnote Separator   When a file is printed, a line of dashes is automatically inserted between text and footnotes on each page. (You can change the separator line character with WSCHANGE.)

Size Limitation   There is effectively no size limit on any of the four types of notes; each note can be up to 40K, or approximately 15 pages.

Full Editing Capabilities   When in any of the note windows, you may use all of WordStar's editing capabilities.

Automatic Renumbering   If you add or delete notes, or move a block of text in your file that contains a note, all notes are automatically resequenced, regardless of whether they are numbered or lettered.

Converting Notes at Print Time (.cv)   The dot command .cv may be used to convert notes from one type to another. Place one of these commands at the beginning of your file:

.cv f>e	Print footnotes as endnotes
.cv e>f	Print endnotes as footnotes
.cv c>f	Print comments as footnotes
.cv c>e	Print comments as endnotes

15

If you are working with newspaper-style columns, footnotes are automatically converted to endnotes.

Placement of Endnotes (.pe)   You can use the dot command .pe (print endnote) to control where endnotes are printed. As an example, suppose you have more than one chapter in a file, with endnotes for each chapter. To have the endnotes print at the end of each chapter, place a .pe command at the end of each chapter. Endnotes print on the last page of the file (or following a .pe). If you would like them printed on a separate page, place the dot command .pa at the end of the file followed by the .pe command.

Customizing the Note Format   You can customize the format for printing notes using WSCHANGE. The primary items you can customize are printer font, default margins, line spacing, line height, position on page, title line, and separator line. (In WSCHANGE, select **D/A/D**.)

Paragraph/Line Numbering

Some types of legal documents require paragraph and/or line numbers.

Paragraph Numbering (^OZ)

The paragraph numbering feature offers a wide variety of formats. To enter a paragraph number, place the cursor where you want the number to appear; then press **^OZ**, or from the Insert menu select **O** for Paragraph Outline Number. The following dialog box is displayed. In this case, it displays the default starting value, 1.

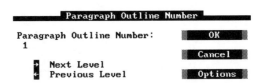

As you progress through a file numbering the paragraphs, the numbers automatically increase. To change to the next level of paragraph numbering, press the RIGHT ARROW. If 2 is the current level, it would change to 1.1. To return to the previous level, press the LEFT ARROW. If 1.1 is the current level, it returns to 2. Press F10 when the number you want is displayed. The paragraph number in the dialog box is printed next to the paragraph.

Setting the Paragraph Number (.p#)

To start paragraph numbering at a set value, you can enter the dot command **.p#** and the desired value. For example, **.p# 2.7** will number the next paragraph 2.7 when you select **^OZ** (Paragraph Outline Number) and press F10. The value 2.7 may be changed to the next or previous level by pressing RIGHT ARROW or LEFT ARROW.

You can also set both the format and starting number of paragraph numbers using the dot command .p# or the Paragraph Outline Options dialog box. To open this box, press **^OZ** to go to the Paragraph Outline Number window, then select Options to see this:

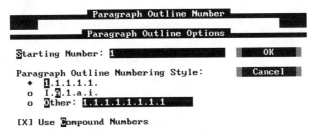

In the Starting Number field, enter the starting number, and select or enter a numbering style as you wish. Enable the Use Compound Numbers option if you use a style with more than one style code. The style codes are described in the next section.

Paragraph Number Formatting

When you use the Paragraph Outline Options, WordStar inserts a dot command in your file. The dot command has this format:

.p# *start number, style codes, number type*

where *start number* is the number used for the next paragraph number. The *style code*s are the codes used to set characters for paragraph numbers (see the table below). There are two *number types*: **c**, compound numbers, allows a mixture of upper- and lowercase letters, roman numerals, and arabic numbers; **o** is for outline numbers using a single code.

If you enter .p# commands directly, make sure the format options following the .p# are separated by commas.

Note

In addition to numbers, a letter or roman numeral format can be used; letters and numbers may be mixed in the same sequence. The following table lists style codes and their definitions when used with the .p# command:

Style Code	Definition
Z	Uppercase letters
z	Lowercase letters
I	Uppercase roman numerals
i	Lowercase roman numerals
9	Arabic numbers

Several examples of .p# commands are shown here:

- **.p#,Z.9.z, c**   The first paragraph will be A, since no start number is indicated; the second paragraph, if you press RIGHT ARROW once, will be A.0; the third paragraph will be A.0.a, if you press RIGHT ARROW again. The *c* indicates a compound number.

- **.p#,[9.9]**   Starts the paragraph numbering with 0 and encloses all subsequent paragraph numbers in brackets. Note that if other symbols are entered in the .p# command, WordStar assumes they should be printed as entered.

- **.p#1,§9,c**   Starts the paragraph numbers with §1. The paragraph symbol, ¶, or the section symbol, §, can be entered in the .p# command by selecting 20 or 21 from the Extended Character menu. (Extended characters are discussed in Chapter 16. Check your printer manual to be sure it can print these symbols.)

Line Numbering (.l#)

Line numbers can also be set, either directly with a dot command or with the aid of a dialog box. The dot command used to print line numbers is .l# (that's the letter *l*, not the arabic number 1).

To display the Line Numbering window, select Layout, Line Numbering. The screen displays

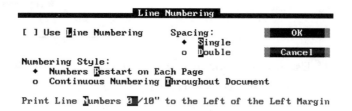

Press F10 to accept the entries, or make appropriate selections. The dot command determined by these entries is placed in the file.

Three options in the .l# command control the format of line numbers: *style*, *spacing*, and *distance*. The line number command takes this form:

.l# *style spacing distance*

The *style* option has two possible values:

d   Line numbers start at 1 and are continuous from page to page.

p   Line numbers start from 1 at the beginning of each page.

The *spacing* option can be any of the following values:

1   Single-spaced numbering
2   Double-spaced numbering
0 or blank   Turns line numbering off

The *distance* option denotes the number of columns to the left of the text where the line number will print. The default value for *distance* is 3. For example, if you are using the default left margin of 8, a *distance* value of 3 will print the numbers 3 columns to the left of the text, or 5 columns from the paper's left edge.

As an example, the command **.l# d2 3** causes line numbers to print consecutively from page to page (**d**), double-spaced (**2**), and three columns to the left of the text (**3**). (There can be no space between the **d** and the **2**. There must be a space and *no* comma between the **2** and the **3**.)

Exercises

1. Use one of your own documents or enter the text of one of the chapters in this book, and use the traditional method to produce an index. If you use a chapter from this or another text, use the .pn command to start at an appropriate page number. Remember, if you use the .pn command to set the page number, it must be inserted before any text or blank lines in your file.

2. Use the same document and produce another index, this time using the exclusion indexing method.

3. For a document that contains tables or figures, create a standard table of contents and at the same time a list of tables or figures.

4. Use an existing file to experiment with paragraph numbering. Start with the default values; also use format codes to start the numbering with roman numerals and a letter/number combination.

5. Using an existing file, create line numbers. Have the numbers begin with 1 on each page, and make the lines double-spaced.

6. In a long document, create some endnotes and footnotes.

7. Using the file from the previous exercise, convert all the footnotes to endnotes when the document is printed.

16

Drawing with Extended Characters

In this chapter, you will see how to incorporate a variety of special characters other than letters and numbers into a WordStar file. This chapter deals only with the standard IBM character set that displays on a nongraphics monitor; it can be printed by most newer printers.

Chapter 19, which introduces Inset, will describe the more elaborate graphics capabilities of WordStar. But even if you have a printer and monitor that allow you to take full advantage of Inset, you will find the line-drawing capabilities of the characters introduced in this chapter useful for generating forms. And if you don't have a graphics monitor, you may find the special characters a convenient method for incorporating simple charts and graphs into your work. How you utilize the character sets introduced in this chapter will depend upon the type of work you do and the type of equipment you use.

ASCII, Special, and Extended Character Sets

All computers and office software packages—word processors, spreadsheets, databases, and so on—give you access to 128 characters; 96 are printable, and 32 are called *special characters*. Printable characters include the upper- and lowercase letters, numbers, and punctuation marks that make up the ASCII (American Standard Code for Information Interchange) character set. These characters are used in standard screen displays for all microcomputers. Some software packages give you access to another 128 characters, referred to as the *extended character set*. WordStar gives you access to both sets of characters.

The complete set of special, ASCII, and extended characters is listed in Appendix B, after the tables of WordStar codes and characters. Take a look at Appendix B now. The extended character set is composed of the characters numbered from 128 to 255. As you can see, a variety of characters are included—math and graphics symbols, Greek letters, and most of the letters with diacriticals used in many European languages. In this chapter, we will be concerned primarily with characters useful with graphics, but the same procedures discussed here are used to access any of the 128 extended characters and the 32 special characters.

The Extended Character Menu (^P0)

To display the Extended Character menu (Figure 16-1), press **^P0** (zero, not capital *O*). This menu shows the entire extended character set, plus the special character set that has the ASCII values from 0 to 31 (0 prints a blank). Also included are a few of the standard ASCII characters that are accessible directly from the keyboard and that may be useful to you.

At the top of this menu is a field where you enter the code number for the character you wish displayed on the Edit screen. For example, to print the math symbol for pi, π, you would type **227** and press ENTER. π is printed at the position of the cursor. When working with this menu, either set of number keys on your keyboard can be used to enter the code.

Tip

If you use the mouse, you'll find it a convenient way to select extended characters. With the Extended Character menu displayed, click on the character you want. You are immediately back at the Edit screen with the selected character displayed.

Figure 16-1.   *Extended Character menu*

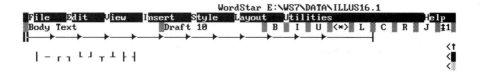

Using Graphics Characters

Ten graphics characters are available using the macros ALT-F1 **through** ALT-F10. When one of these key combinations is pressed, a graphics symbol is displayed. Try this now by pressing ALT and F1 simultaneously; a vertical line is displayed after you release the keys. Press the SPACEBAR, and repeat this process, trying each of the ALT-F*n* key-combinations. Separate the graphics characters with spaces so they don't run together. If you pressed the ALT-F*n* key combinations in sequence, your screen will be similar to the one shown here:

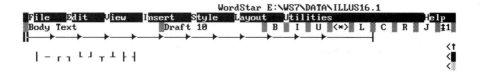

Examine the following chart, which shows the graphics symbols produced by each of the ALT-F*n* key combinations:

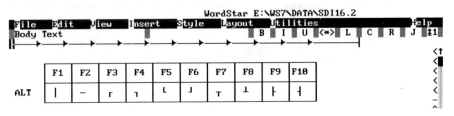

This chart was created with WordStar by using all of the graphics symbols from the first illustration, plus an additional one, the +. (This symbol resembles a plus sign but is actually extended character code 197.)

Tip

If you frequently use extended character code 197, or any other member of the extended character set, you can define a macro to produce the symbol.

The following illustration shows a portion of the chart from the preceding illustration, with some blank rows and columns inserted. It lets you see the individual graphics symbols used in the table's construction.

Producing Graphs Using Extended Characters

Symbols 176, 177, and 178, and 219 through 223 lend themselves very nicely to graphs, as shown in the following illustration:

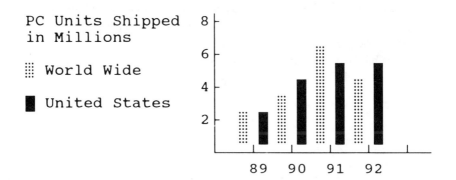

The x- and y-axes in this chart were produced using the built-in graphics character codes (the ones produced with the ALT-F*n* key combinations discussed previously). The vertical bars in the chart were made using character codes 176 and 219.

If you have use for these types of graphical elements and you don't have a specific graphics software package, you might consider creating the x- and y-axes and the column bars shown in the foregoing illustration, and then saving them in a file so you can pull them in whenever you need them. You can further simplify this process if, when you complete one set of bars, you use the Block Copy command (in Column mode) to place them in various positions. You can then add or delete individual symbol characters to obtain the right column height. You can also create a macro that inserts multiple symbols at one time.

As a final example of the usefulness of graphics symbols, look at the following illustration of a box placed around text:

```
╔══════════════════════════════════════════════╗
║                   It's not a bug,             ║
║           it's an undocumented feature        ║
╚══════════════════════════════════════════════╝
```

You can facilitate your use of boxes by creating a box large enough to contain the contents of a standard page and storing it in a disk file. When you want to box text (be sure to type the text first, before attempting to box it), you can read the box into the current document (by pressing **^KR**) and then cut it

16

down to the desired size with appropriate Block and Column Delete operations. Then, using the Column Replace command (^KN followed by ^KI), you can block the text and place it in the box.

What would happen if you blocked the box and tried to place it around the material? Try it if you want to—and remember the Undo command!

Exercises

1. Create a set of macros that will produce the graphics symbols used to "draw" the box in the last illustration of this chapter.

2. Table 16-1 shows most of the built-in macro commands provided with WordStar. Re-create this table on your screen and save it in a file. Then print it for reference. (If you customize these macros to perform functions best suited to your work, don't forget to modify this chart accordingly.)

3. If you use an extended keyboard, add rows in Table 16-1 for function keys F11 and F12.

Table 16-1.   *WordStar Macros*

F-Keys		SHIFT-F*n*	CTRL-F*n*	ALT-F*n*
F1	**Help**	Show/Hide Codes	Find	│
F2	Undo	Center	Replace	─
F3	Undrline	Spellall	NextFind	┌
F4	Bold	Spellword	Go-To-Pg	┐
F5	Del Line	Del Block	L-Margin	└
F6	Del Word	Hide Block	R-Margin	┘
F7	Reform	Mov Block	P-Margin	┬
F8	Ruler	Copy Block	New Page	┴
F9	SaveFile	BegBlock	Line-Beg	├
F10	**Continue**	EndBlock	Line-End	┤

4. Create a large rectangle, using either graphics symbols provided with WordStar or those you worked with in Exercise 1. Save the rectangle in a file for later use.

5. Reenter Example 7C, this time using appropriate extended characters in place of the keyboard characters used in Chapter 7.

6. Construct a graphics function-key chart, like the one shown in the "Using Graphics Characters" section of this chapter. Where you see the + symbol, select character code 197 from the Extended Character menu.

16

17

Miscellaneous Commands/ Traditional Menus

The purpose of this chapter is twofold: First, it briefly discusses the WordStar commands not yet introduced in this book. Though these remaining commands are not used frequently by many people, you may just find a nugget here that will be useful in your work. Second, the chapter presents a brief description and an illustration of each of WordStar's traditional menus. You'll find the illustrations are useful for quick reference as you work.

Miscellaneous WordStar Commands

Review all the miscellaneous commands in this section so you are aware of what they do. This way, should you ever need to perform a particular operation, you will know WordStar has a command to help you.

Repeat Command (^QQ)

The ^QQ command is used to repeat a command at a controlled rate. For instance, if you wish to scroll through a file from beginning to end in order to proofread it, place the cursor at the beginning of the file, and press ^QQ and then DOWN ARROW. The text will advance on the screen one line at a time. The speed at which the text scrolls can be increased or decreased by typing a number from 1 to 9 after the UP or DOWN ARROW; 1 is the fastest rate, 9 is the slowest rate, and 3 is the default value. For example, to slow down the scrolling, press ^QQ, DOWN ARROW, and then **9**. To scroll backwards, press ^QQ, UP ARROW, and then **9**. You can also display successive screens, either forward or backward, by pressing ^QQ and then PGDN or PGUP. Setting the rate at which the command repeats applies to any command used in conjunction with ^QQ, not just scrolling.

Load one of your examples and try this command. To interrupt the scrolling process, press ESC.

Tip

Another useful application of ^QQ is to reformat an entire document. You must exercise caution here to be sure each section has the appropriate dot commands. For example, tables, charts, and bulleted lists can have an unexpected appearance if your reformatting changes them to double-spacing when that was not what you intended.

Word and Byte Count (^K?)

At times you may want to determine the number of words and bytes in a file or a section of a file. To find out the word and byte count for an entire file, place the cursor anywhere in the file and press ^K?. A window like the following one will appear:

```
Words:  2508   Bytes:  18318                      Continue
```

When the count is finished, the cursor will be at the end of the file.

To determine the word and byte count for a section, first use ^KB and ^KK to block the section. Then, with the cursor anywhere in the file, press

^K?. The same window shown above is displayed, giving the word and byte count for the blocked section.

Memory Usage (^O?)

Whenever you are using one of WordStar's supplementary programs in conjunction with WordStar, it is useful to be able to check the memory available for editing. You can obtain this information by pulling down the File menu at the Opening screen and selecting Status. In addition, you can now get statistical information on WordStar's memory usage while you are editing, by pressing ^O?. To see a sample display when this command is used, look at Figure 1-5 in Chapter 1.

Assign/Change Form Feed (^PL and .xl)

You can place a form-feed character in a file by pressing ^PL. The symbol ^L will appear at the left of the screen along with a line across the page (just as with a page break). An *F* will appear in the flag column. When you print the file and the printing reaches this command in the document, the printer will scroll to the next page and begin printing. No page number or footer will print on a page containing a ^PL command.

Your printer may require a form-feed character different from the one provided by WordStar's printer driver. In that case you can enter the dot command .xl (that's the letter *l*, not an arabic number 1), followed by the correct form-feed character for your printer. You will have to consult your printer manual to determine whether your printer supports this feature and what the proper symbol is.

Running a DOS Command While Editing (^KF)

To issue a DOS command while you're editing in WordStar, press ^KF, and the screen displays this:

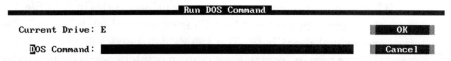

In the DOS Command field, type the DOS command you wish to execute. On its completion, you will be asked to press any key to return to WordStar.

Defining Custom Printer Controls (^PF, ^PG, ^PQ,^PW, ^PE, ^PR, ^P!, .xq, .xw, .xe, .xr)

Here are more printer commands that depend on the printer you use. These commands allow you to access, through WordStar, print features such as double-width printing. WordStar offers six custom printer codes, plus one special code entered only at the Edit screen. The feature assigned to each code depends on your printer. To access these seven codes, select Custom Printer Code from the Insert menu, and you'll see this submenu:

An example of when you might use custom printer controls is with daisy wheel and thimble printers, which sometimes have special characters on their wheels or thimbles. Such characters are designated by ASCII codes 32 and 127, and you can access them by using the WordStar commands ^PF and ^PG (if WordStar has supplied codes for your particular printer). The symbols ^F and ^G will be displayed on the screen. If you use either of these printer types, try these commands and see what prints.

There are two ways to control WordStar's custom printer commands: by using the appropriate dot commands, or with WSCHANGE. The commands ^PF and ^PG can be modified only by using WSCHANGE. The remaining four printer commands can be modified at the Edit screen, as well as with WSCHANGE. The dot commands .xq, .xw, .xe, and .xr modify the corresponding commands ^PQ, ^PW, ^PE, and ^PR. The codes entered using the dot commands override any custom codes entered through WSCHANGE.

When you use dot commands to enter printer codes in your file, you must enter these codes in the form WordStar expects, which is base 16. *Base 16* is the hexadecimal (hex) base. The values you need will be in your printer manual in the proper format. Each custom printer code is limited to 24 bytes.

For example, the hex values 1B 0E turn on double-width printing for an Epson or compatible printer, and the hex value 14 turns it off. Therefore, if the dot commands .xq 1B 0E and .xw 14 are in your file, entering the command **^PQ YOUR NAME ^PW** will print "YOUR NAME" in double-width on an Epson printer (or another printer that uses Epson printer codes). Your screen will look like this:

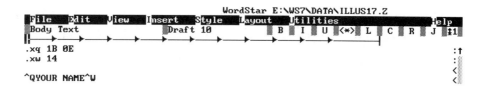

The output produced by the preceding file is as follows:

YOUR NAME

You can use ^P! to define the custom printer code at the time of entry. This procedure is normally used only with a one-time-only code entry. Press ^P! to display the following dialog box; its fields are explained just below.

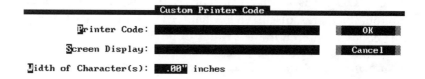

Printer Code   Enter the ASCII codes or the filename that contains the codes to be sent to your printer. Some codes must be preceded by special symbols.

- To enter a filename, type *%F"filename"*. You must include the quotation marks. For example, to use the file ARROW.HP mentioned at the end of this section, in the Printer Code field enter **%F"ARROW.HP"**.

- The caret (^) symbol must precede a control code.
- To enter a hex value, type **%x** before the number; for example, to enter 1B type **%x1B**.
- To enter %, type **%%**.

If appropriate, you can enter the name of a file that contains your printer codes. For an HP LaserJet or compatible printer, WordStar supplies four such files:

Printer Code Filename	Prints
ARROW.HP	A small arrow
CHEX.HP	A checkered pattern used in the WordStar logo
PLEAD.HP	The vertical bars on legal pleading paper
SHADE.HP	Shades an entire page a light gray. You can control the size of the shaded area by changing the page size.

Screen Display   Enter the character you wish to display on the screen to indicate a custom printer code. For example, an *x* is the symbol that displays when ^OD turns display off. This is the same concept that is used for annotation marks, discussed in Chapter 15. With display turned on, you'll see the codes as entered in the Printer Code field.

Width of Character(s)   If characters are printed by the codes, enter the width in inches here.

Sorting Text (^KZ)

You can sort lines of text in a WordStar file by blocking the text and pressing **^KZ**, the Sort command. This operation is particularly useful with a list. For example, you might have a list of family members and friends with their names, phone numbers, birthdays, ages, and addresses. To sort the list, first press **^KB** and **^KK** to block the list, and then press **^KZ** to sort it. As soon as you press ^KZ a message appears on the screen asking, "Sort into ascending or descending order (A/D)?" Enter your choice and the list is immediately sorted.

You can also select Column mode, enter ^KN, block any column, and then sort the column in ascending or descending order based on the items in that column. The associated items on the same lines but in other columns will remain on the same lines with the items being sorted. With this idea in mind, whenever you create a columnar list, it's wise to give careful consideration to the data in each column. For example, if you think that at some point you might want to sort the list based on street names, put the street numbers and street names in separate columns. Additional information about sorting is in Chapter 18 in the sections on MailList.

Note

If you have any special codes in your list to be sorted, even if their display is toggled off by ^OD, they will be read when alphabetization takes place. If you use such codes, you probably won't get the sort result you want.

Reprinting the Screen (^\)

Although uncommon, sometimes electrical interference or DOS (the disk operating system) can place extraneous characters on the screen. These extra characters are not in your WordStar file. To reprint your screen without these characters, press ^\. The screen is reprinted with only those characters contained in the file.

17

WordStar's Traditional Menus

As you are aware, there are two sets of menus with WordStar: the traditional menus and the pull-down menus. Throughout this book, we emphasize selecting commands from the pull-down menus. The advantages of the pull-down menus are that their names are on the menu bar, and you can select commands using the mouse. On the other hand, though you cannot use the mouse from the traditional menus, they do offer the advantage of displaying all of WordStar's Edit commands on five windows.

To set WordStar to display the traditional opening menus, set the help level at 3. Display the Help menu, select Change Help Level, and set the help level to 3 or less. (To display the Help Level window at the traditional menu, press ^JJ.)

In addition to the Edit menu, WordStar has five other traditional command menus and three special menus. The basic command menus are

^O	Onscreen Format menu
^K	Block and Save menu
^M	Macro menu
^P	Print Controls menu
^Q	Quick Functions menu

The three special menus listed below were demonstrated in their own respective chapters of this book, because of their usefulness in organizing the commands on each subject. The special menus are

^OF	Paragraph Style menu (Chapter 12)
^ON	Notes menu (Chapter 15)
^QM	Calculator menu (Chapter 14)

Edit Menu

After pressing **S** or **D** and loading a file, at the Opening screen the Edit menu appears. As with all the traditional menus, it is divided into branches—in this case Cursor, Scroll, Delete, Other, and Menus.

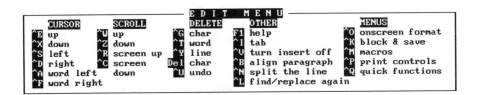

To access one of the other traditional menus, enter the menu prefix (for instance, **^K**, **^M**, and so forth), and that menu's options will be displayed. To

select an option, press the letter adjacent to the command. When you select an option, the command is entered in your file, and the screen again displays your text.

Block & Save Menu (^K)

This menu contains commands for saving files, block operations, and other file and disk operations.

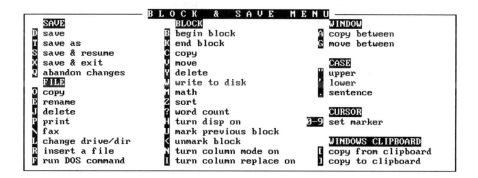

Macro Menu (^M)

This menu lets you access the macros supplied by WordStar, as well as create your own macros. It also displays WordStar's full list of inserts.

17

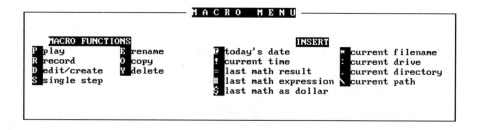

Onscreen Format Menu (^O)

This menu contains commands for setting margins, tabs, and typing and screen displays.

Print Controls Menu (^P)

This menu contains commands for special print effects.

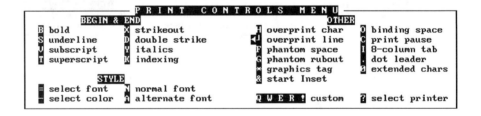

Quick Menu (^Q)

This menu contains commands for cursor movement; commands for the find, delete, scroll, spelling, and thesaurus operations; and a few other handy commands.

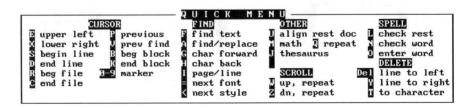

Paragraph Style Menu (^OF)

This menu lists several choices. Each option displays a dialog box where you make further entries. From each dialog box you return directly to your file.

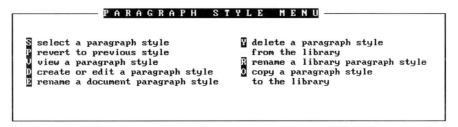

Notes Menu (^ON)

This menu lists all the commands to insert the four types of notes, plus the commands related to their use.

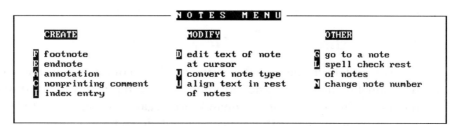

Calculator Menu (^QM)

This menu displays all the math functions available to you through Calculator mode.

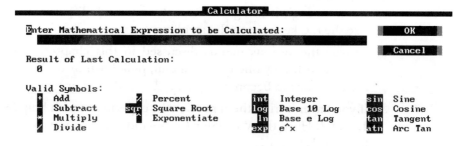

Figure 17-1.   *Edit screen with available pull-down menus*

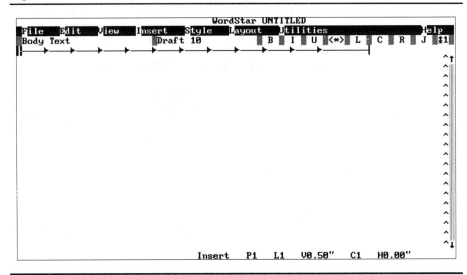

A Word About the Pull-Down Menus

The pull-down menus offer virtually all the commands available on the traditional menus. The basic differences between pull-down and traditional menus are in the way the commands are organized. Figure 17-1 shows the Edit screen menu bar with the available pull-down menus.

Exercises

1. Type and save Example 17. Return to the beginning of the file and scroll through it using the Repeat command. Try various speeds. Use the ESC key to stop the scrolling.

2. Display the various menus discussed in this chapter. If you are familiar with only one type of menu, pull-down or traditional, take the time now to become acquainted with the other type.

3. If you haven't tried them previously, experiment with help levels 0, 1, and 2. Have the WordStar Command Card handy to work with help levels 0 and 1.

Example 17

```
    SUGGESTIONS FOR COMPUTER CONFIGURATION AND USE IN M.U.S.D.

CLASSROOM I       Formal Programming Class
                  Six Stations, Printer (High Quality)
                  Dual Disk
                  Word Processing

CLASSROOM II      Formal Programming, CAI
                  Six Stations, Printer (High Speed)
                  Dual Disk
                  Open for Individual Teachers

ADMINISTRATION    Two Stations: Printer
                  Dual Disk—Hard Disk
                  Word Processing

MOBILE UNIT       Four stations to be used in various classrooms
                  and schools for short periods

USES:

1. TEACH     a. Basic Programming        - All Students
             b. Assembly Language        - MGM
             c. Word Processing          - Business Students
             d. Accounting (Bookkeeping) - Business Students
             e. Computer "Literacy"      - Bus. & Gen. Students
             f. Special Projects         - e.g., Plotter
             g. Journalism               - English Students

2. Computer Assisted Instruction (CAI)
        Useful in all areas - particularly for remedial work

3. ADMINISTRATION
   a. Attendance (H.S.)*        f. Physical Performance Test*
   b. Attendance & State Reports g. WASC*
      (elem.)*                  h. District Handbook
   c. Scholarships*             i. District Directory
   d. Voc. Ed. (records)*       j. Reports
   e. OWE (records)*            k. Recordkeeping (misc.)

While building towards the desired computer facilities in the
school district, careful planning should be maintained to ensure
maximum compatibility of software between systems.

*Projects completed or in progress.
```

17

18

Merge Printing and MailList

Merge printing is a powerful supplement to WordStar's primary function, word processing. Merge printing allows you to generate form letters with names, addresses, or other information automatically inserted, in the format you wish. In general, the information comes to the document from a data (nondocument) file or is entered from the keyboard at the appropriate time.

To merge information from a data file into a document, you will need two files:

- A *master document* that contains instructions for the information that will be inserted, and the text into which the data will be inserted
- A *data file*—a nondocument file containing all the information to be inserted in the master document

We will begin by working with WordStar's MailList companion program to produce the data file you will be using.

About Nondocument Files

You can create a data (nondocument) file in three ways: (1) type the data directly into WordStar using Nondocument mode; (2) use a commercial database program such as Q&A; or (3) use the MailList program that comes with WordStar. Each method has its advantages and disadvantages:

- Entering data directly into a nondocument file is useful if you only have a limited amount of information for about 10 or 20 people or items.

- MailList works well to maintain a list with just a few names or with large numbers of names, even up to several hundred—provided the data you wish to maintain is in the predefined MailList or Inventory form, as explained later in this chapter.

- A commercial database program is necessary if you have an extremely large amount of data or a greater variety of data than MailList can accommodate.

In this chapter you will use MailList to create your nondocument file. Nondocument files contain only the characters you enter from the keyboard. They do not contain the special characters, such as soft spaces and soft carriage returns, that WordStar places in document files. MailList adds the extension .DTA to its nondocument filenames. In fact, it's a good practice to use this extension for any data files you create. This helps you remember they are data files and should not be opened using WordStar's standard Document mode.

Note

If you open a nondocument file accidentally, abandon the file—don't save it.

In this chapter you'll work with MailList and learn how to do the following:

- Use MailList for data entry

- Apply the various MailList functions such as sorting and filtering data to be viewed or printed
- Use MailList programs to print envelopes, address labels, and a proof report
- Use the Merge Print commands to design your own reports

Using MailList

MailList gives you an easy way to maintain a list of names, addresses, phone numbers, or any other information you may want to have available for use with master documents. The data you place in the list may be sorted in any order. Any information kept in a MailList data file can be used with WordStar's Merge Print commands and master documents that you create.

If you have not installed MailList with WordStar, do so now. To run MailList, at the Opening screen display the Additional menu as shown here:

The MailList option is highlighted, so press ENTER to see the MailList menu.

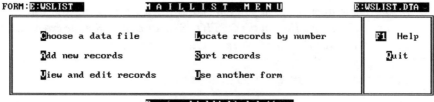

Let's examine the six options available to you, starting with choosing a data file.

Choose a Data File

Press **C** to select the Choose a data file option. MailList switches to the Options subdirectory and displays the names of the two blank files, INVENTORY.DTA and WSLIST.DTA, that are supplied with WordStar. The Choose a Data File dialog box and the screen appear as follows:

Notice that in the upper-left corner of the dialog box the form name WSLIST is displayed, and in the upper-right corner the data filename (WSLIST.DTA) is displayed. WordStar's default file for MailList is WSLIST.DTA; this is the file that you will use in this chapter. The E: before each filename indicates the hard drive that contains the file. All the procedures for working with the WSLIST file also apply to the Inventory file; more on this later.

Highlight WSLIST in the directory, press ENTER to select it, and you return to the MailList menu. The next step is to add names to the WSLIST file.

Note

If you choose another name for your data file, it's a good idea to use the filename extension .DTA. All files on the OPTIONS subdirectory with the extension .DTA are automatically listed on the Choose a Data File directory.

Adding Names to a Data File

To add names to your mailing list data file, select **A**, Add New Records, on the MailList menu; you'll see the Add New Records window and data form shown in Figure 18-1.

For each name on your data file, you need to fill in the Add New Records *data form*. This screen contains the fields for all the possible information that

Figure 18-1. *MailList record screen for adding new records*

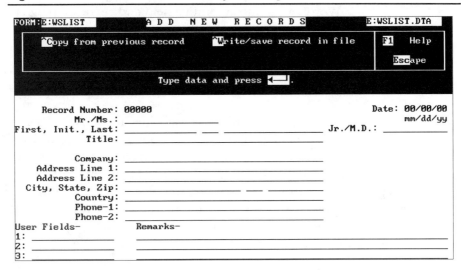

can be entered for each person in the mailing list. The characteristics of this data file are as follows:

- Each line on the screen represents an item of information, and each item is called a *field*. Notice where you enter the name there are three fields—one each for first name, middle initial, and last name.

- Each field has a fixed length represented by the number of underline characters in the field.

- All the information for each person entered into a data form, shown in Figure 18-1, makes up a *record*.

- You assign the first record number, usually 1; thereafter, WordStar assigns the record numbers sequentially.

- After entering information into each field, press ENTER. The cursor moves to the next field.

- All fields are optional, except the Record Number field.

- When you enter data in a field, always start in the first space of the field; otherwise, sorting cannot work properly.

18

- Use the LEFT ARROW and RIGHT ARROW keys, just as you normally do with WordStar, to move within a field and correct typing errors.

- ^RIGHT ARROW and ^LEFT ARROW move the cursor to the next or previous field.

- From any field in the form you can move directly to the first field by pressing the HOME key or directly to the last field by pressing END.

There are two helpful commands available in the Add New Records window at the top of the screen: Copy from previous record (^C) and Write/save record in file (^W). Copy from previous record helps you minimize data entry time. By pressing ^C, you can quickly fill in any field by copying in the entry from the corresponding field of the previous record. To save a record, press ^W in any field, and then press ENTER; or you can press ENTER in the last field on the record. After finishing the data entry, press ESC to return to the MailList menu.

Entering Sample Data Records

To gain some experience with the data record form, use the names, addresses, and other information in Example 18A at the end of this chapter to enter records in the WSLIST.DTA file. This example also gives you data that you'll use in trying the other options from the MailList menu. In order to match the examples, enter the data just as presented, even though there are several empty fields. It's obvious which fields most of the data belongs in, except for a couple: Enter the phone numbers in the field labeled Phone-1, and enter the profession (legal, medical, and so forth) in the field labeled User Field 1. Also, notice that after you enter the first and last names and press ENTER, the full name appears next to the record number.

Viewing and Editing Records

Once you have entered records into a MailList data file, it is a simple matter to view or edit the records in that file. Just select **V**, the View and edit records option, from the MailList menu. Here is the View and Edit Records window, which shows a menu of commands you can use to edit or update your data records:

Below the menu is the MailList form with the data you just entered for the first record. Following are descriptions of each View and Edit Records option. These options remain in view at the top of the screen as you are viewing and editing records.

Previous/Next Record (^P, ^N)

Press ^P or ^N to move to the previous or next record. Try this now. Press ^N to advance through the file and press ^P to move backwards through the file.

Write/Save Modified Record (^W)

To practice, edit a record now. Add a middle initial or change some other item of information in the record. Use the same keys as when you entered the data. When you have completed editing, press ^W to save the record. If you advance to a new record or go back to a previous record without pressing ^W, your edits are lost. When you press ^W, you will see a window display giving you these options:

- Press ENTER to save. The next record appears.
- Press the SPACEBAR to return to the record and continue editing.
- Press ESC to go to the MailList menu (this does not save the edit).

Create/Change Record Filter (^C)

Perhaps you want to work with only certain people in your mailing list—for example, only those with a particular zip code or from a particular city or state. To select a particular record or group of records, from the View and

Edit Records menu press ^C for Create/change record filter. You will see the Record Filter window and screen shown in Figure 18-2.

In this screen all the fields are filled with asterisks (*). Think of the asterisks as wildcard characters; any character you substitute for an asterisk is the character MailList will search for in the data file. Each record that has a match in the corresponding position will be displayed.

The rules for working with the Record Filter are as follows:

- Press ENTER to advance the cursor from field to field.

- Use the LEFT ARROW and RIGHT ARROW keys to move the cursor within a field.

- Use the ^LEFT ARROW and ^RIGHT ARROW to move the cursor to the previous or next field.

- From any field in the form you can move directly to the first field by pressing the HOME key or directly to the last field by pressing END.

- The letters you enter as the filter criteria are case-sensitive.

Now move the cursor to the State field and enter **OR** as the filter criteria. (Remember, the letters are case-sensitive.)

Figure 18-2.   *MailList screen for creating a record filter*

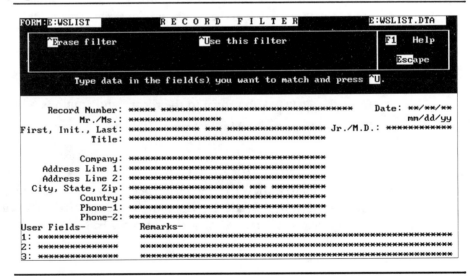

You can call for a match in more than one field of the record filter. Also, you can match a portion of a field–for example, all zip codes that start with 945.

Use This Filter (^U)

After you enter information in the record filter, press ^U. The first record in the data file that matches the filter will be displayed. Use ^N or ^P to display the next or previous record that matches the filter.

Erase Filter (^E)

When you create a filter, as you just did, it stays in effect until you change it, erase it, or until you leave MailList. You've already seen how to change the filter by selecting Create/change record filter on the View and Edit Records window, and then making your change. To erase the current filter, select ^E, Erase filter, from the Record Filter window.

Locate Records by Number

To find a record by record number, from the MailList menu select L, Locate records by number. The Locate Records by Number window is displayed as shown here:

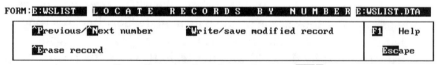

All the options in this window are the same as or similar to the previously discussed MailList windows.

- When the Locate Records by Number screen is displayed, the cursor is at the Record Number field waiting for your entry. Enter the desired number, press ENTER, and the record will be displayed.

- Press ^N and ^P to advance to the next or previous record, which you can view or edit.

18

- Press ^W to save the edited record. The save options here are the same as those for the ^W command on the View and Edit Records window.

- Press ^E to erase a record. This displays a window where you must confirm your erase command. Again, you have the option to press the SPACEBAR to return to the record for editing, or ESC to go to the MailList menu.

Sorting Your MailList Data File

When you view the data in the mailing list file, the records appear in the same order they were entered, by record number. Selecting **S**, Sort records, from the MailList menu allows you to sort the records in any order you wish. For one data file, you can create and use up to 32 different sort orders, for example, alphabetically by name or company, by zip code, or a variety of other possibilities. Initially the mailing list has one sort order—by record number.

Sorting Records (S)

If you add, edit, or erase records from the data file, the list must be re-sorted to put the records back into record number order. To sort the mailing list by record number, select Sort records from the MailList menu. Figure 18-3 shows the Sort Records window and screen that is displayed.

There are six Sort Records options. We will go over each of them shortly, but first take a look at the MailList form in the Sort Records window. Notice that the Record Number field has the entry 1111A. This code tells you the primary sort is by the field with the 1s, in this case the record number. The A indicates the sort will be in ascending order, from smallest to largest record number. As shown in the Sort Records window at the top, you press ^U to use the displayed sort order. When you press ^U, the file shown at the upper-right corner of the window, WSLIST.DTA, will be sorted according to the sort order, RECORDNO, shown in the upper-left corner of the window.

The sort takes place very quickly. A window informs you when the sort is completed and tells you the number of records sorted. When you see this window, press ESC to return to the MailList menu to make your next selection. Now let's take a look at creating a different sort order.

Figure 18-3.   *MailList Sort screen to sort by record numbers*

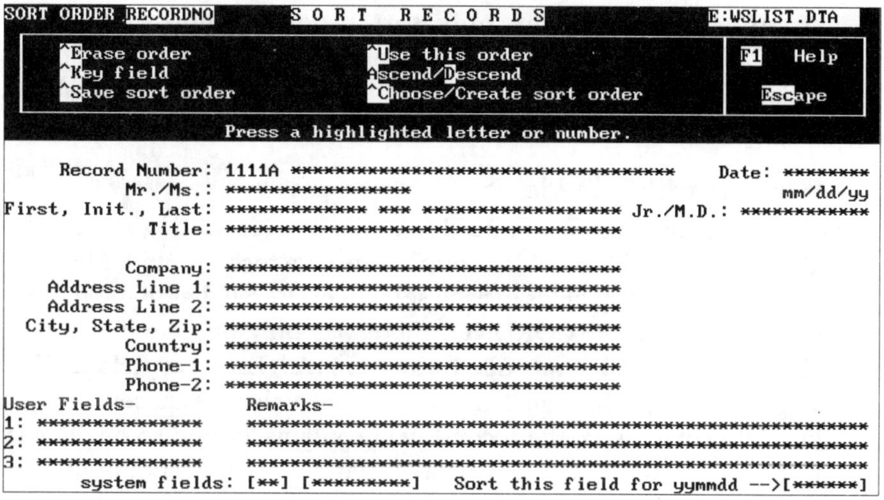

```
SORT ORDER RECORDNO      S O R T   R E C O R D S        E:WSLIST.DTA
  ^Erase order          ^Use this order            F1   Help
  ^Key field            ^Ascend/Descend
  ^Save sort order      ^Choose/Create sort order       Escape
              Press a highlighted letter or number.
   Record Number: 1111A ****************************** Date: ********
         Mr./Ms.: ******************                          mm/dd/yy
First, Init., Last: ************* *** ****************** Jr./M.D.: ************
           Title: ******************************
         Company: ******************************
  Address Line 1: ******************************
  Address Line 2: ******************************
 City, State, Zip: ****************** *** **********
         Country: ******************************
         Phone-1: ******************************
         Phone-2: ******************************
User Fields-        Remarks-
1: ****************   ***********************************************
2: ****************   ***********************************************
3: ****************   ***********************************************
     system fields: [**] [*********]   Sort this field for yymmdd -->[******]
```

Choose/Create a Sort Order (^C)

To create your own sort order, select Sort records from the MailList menu and, if necessary, select the data file WSLIST.DTA. Select Choose/Create sort order, ^C. A screen similar to Figure 18-4 is displayed, asking you what sort

Figure 18-4.   *MailList Sort screen for choosing a sort order*

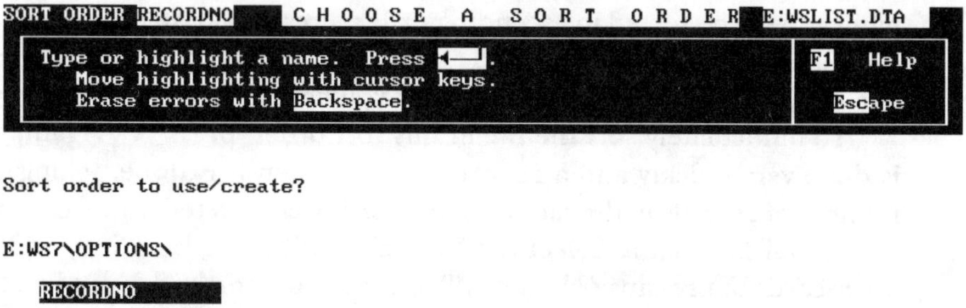

```
SORT ORDER RECORDNO    C H O O S E   A   S O R T   O R D E R  E:WSLIST.DTA
  Type or highlight a name.  Press  <---- .         F1   Help
  Move highlighting with cursor keys.
  Erase errors with Backspace.                           Escape
```

Sort order to use/create?

E:WS7\OPTIONS\

RECORDNO

18

order you want to use or create. Below that is the drive letter and path to the sort order files, and a list of possible sort orders.

As shown here, the only sort order to choose at this point is RECORDNO—record number. You are going to create a sort order in this example that will sort the file alphabetically by state name, with all the people in each state listed in alphabetical order.

Working with Key Fields

The main concept you need to understand in sorting is that of *key fields*. These are the fields by which you sort the data records. With MailList you can have up to nine key fields in each sort order. Recall that in the first sort order you used, called RECORDNO, there was only one key field, the Record Number field, and it was filled with "1111A." Each key field is filled with a single number, 1 through 9, in the order the fields are chosen; that is, the first key field contains 1s, the second field contains 2s, and so on. The last place in each field will have an A or a D, standing for ascending or descending order. Ascending order is the default.

To create the sort order described above, you must first give it a name. In the Choose a Sort Order screen, after "Sort order to use/create?" type **STATNAME,** representing a sort by state and name, and press ENTER. (You can use a maximum of eight letters to name the sort order.) The Sort Records menu and MailList form are redisplayed on the screen. Move the cursor to the first key field—in our example, the State field—and press ^K. The field will display "11A," indicating it is the first key field, and the state name abbreviations will be sorted in ascending order, A to Z. Press ^LEFT ARROW to get the cursor back to the Last Name field. Again, press ^K. The field fills up with 2s, indicating it is the second key field. The last character is an A, indicating the names are to be sorted in ascending order. Press ^LEFT ARROW twice to move the cursor to the First Name field and again press ^K. Your screen now looks like Figure 18-5. To save the sort order you have created, press ^S.

To immediately sort the file in this sort order, press ^U. Again, the sort is done very quickly and a report is issued when it is done, telling you the number of records in the file. With the sorting completed, press ESC to return to the MailList menu. Select the View and edit records option, and display the records by pressing ^N; they will appear in the sort order you just created.

Figure 18-5.   *MailList Sort screen to sort records by state and alphabetically by*
                 name

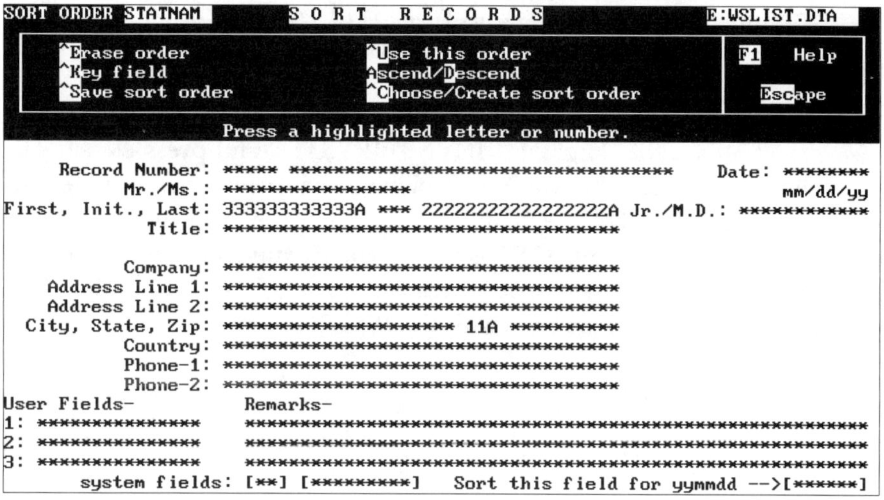

```
SORT ORDER STATNAM         S O R T   R E C O R D S          E:WSLIST.DTA

    ▓rase order            ▓se this order              F1    Help
    ^▓ey field             ▓scend/▓escend
    ^▓ave sort order       ^▓hoose/Create sort order    Es▓ape

              Press a highlighted letter or number.

    Record Number: *****  *************************************  Date: ********
          Mr./Ms.: *****************                                  mm/dd/yy
First, Init., Last: 333333333333A *** 222222222222222222A Jr./M.D.: ************
            Title: *****************************************

          Company: ************************************
   Address Line 1: ************************************
   Address Line 2: ************************************
   City, State, Zip: ********************** 11A ***********
          Country: ************************************
          Phone-1: ************************************
          Phone-2: ************************************
User Fields—        Remarks—
1: ****************  ******************************************************
2: ****************  ******************************************************
3: ****************  ******************************************************
     system fields: [**] [*********]    Sort this field for yymmdd -->[******]
```

Editing a Sort Order

After you have created a sort order, you can do some minor editing of it.
Choose Sort records from the MailList menu. On the Sort Records screen,
you can add key fields. Or, for each key field, you can change the ascend-
ing/descending order by placing the cursor at the beginning of the key field
and pressing **A** or **D**. You cannot, however, change the order of the key fields
by editing. (If this is necessary, create a new sort order.)

Erasing a Sort Order (^E)

The maximum number of sort orders maintained for a data file is 32.
When you reach that number, you must erase an existing sort order to create
a new one. To erase a sort order, at the Sort Records window press **^E**. A
window is opened asking you to confirm your request; answer **Yes** to complete
the erasing of the sort order. Press ESC to return to the previous screen. (The
Record Number sort order, RECORDNO, cannot be erased.)

18

Working with the Inventory File

As we said, the procedures used to work with the Inventory data file form are the same as those used with WSLIST. To choose the Inventory form, select **U**, Use another form, from the MailList menu. The screen shown in Figure 18-6 is displayed.

Highlight INVNTORY.DEF and press ENTER. The screen then asks you to select a data file. Highlight INVNTORY.DTA and press ENTER. The screen clears except for the window displaying the form name and filename in the upper corners. On the MailList menu, choose Add new records, and the screen shown in Figure 18-7 is displayed. The inventory form is different, but the menu options and procedures for moving from field to field in the form are the same as those used with the WSLIST form.

Exiting MailList

When you are through working with MailList, press ESC to return to the MailList menu, and then Q to quit. You return to WordStar's Opening screen.

About the MailList Index Files

Each data file you create with MailList produces an index file with the same name as the data file but with an .NDX extension, for example, WSLIST.DTA and WSLIST.NDX. If something should happen to the index file, when you attempt to work with the data file a message will indicate the index is missing. You can press **R** to rebuild the index file.

Figure 18-6.   *MailList window and screen to select the Inventory form*

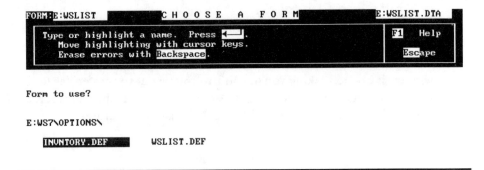

Figure 18-7.   *MailList Inventory form*

```
FORM:E:INVNTORY          A D D   N E W   R E C O R D S        E:INVNTORY.DTA
   ┌──────────────────────────────────────────────────────────────────────┐
   │  ⁀Copy from previous record      ⁀Write/save record in file   F1  Help │
   │                                                                        │
   │                                                               Escape   │
   └──────────────────────────────────────────────────────────────────────┘
                        Type data and press ◀──┘.

     Record Number: 00000                     Date: 00/00/00  mm/dd/yy
     Item: _____     Code: _____   Status: _____
   Description: _____
   _____

        Account:  _____      _____     _____

       Quantity:  _____      _____     _____

          Price:  _____      _____     _____

   User Fields─            Remarks─
   1: _____     _____
   2: _____     _____
   3: _____     _____
```

Caution

It is important to be in the habit of backing up your hard disk frequently. Database programs like MailList normally develop large files. The loss of such a file because of hard disk failure or other reasons would be a serious misfortune. When backing up your system, be sure to back up both the data and the index files, those with the extensions .DTA and .NDX.

Merge Printing with a Data File

18

Now that you have a data file to work with, you are almost ready to try merge printing. One more file is needed, however—a master document. The sequence of information in this section is as follows:

- Creating the master document
- Printing the file (to the disk)
- A review of the Merge Print file, including special merge commands, dot commands, and variables

Creating a Master Document

As mentioned at the beginning of this chapter, there are two sections to a master document: the commands or instructions (mostly dot commands) telling WordStar what data to use and where to find it; and the text or form letter where the data will be inserted. For the master document to merge print with the WSLIST.DTA data file used here, WordStar provides the necessary commands in the file MAILLIST.DOT; the form letter is in Example 18B at the end of this chapter.

Follow these steps to create the master document:

1. Open a new file and call it POLIT1.MRG.

2. Read (^KR) the file MAILLIST.DOT into the file POLIT1.MRG. MAILLIST.DOT is in the Options subdirectory under the WordStar directory.

3. Type Example 18B into the file POLIT1.MRG.

A printout of your master document should be the same as the listing below.

```
.oj on
.op
.df wslist.dta
.rv x, number, full-name, first, mi, last, Mr-Ms, title
.rv company, addr1, addr2, city, state, zip, country
.rv phone1, date, Jr-MD
.rv user1, phone2, user2, x, user3, remark1, remark2, remark3, ymd



                    DESERT SPRINGS COUNTY SUPERVISOR'S OFFICE
                         COUNTY BUILDING—SUITE 3001A
                            2105 WEST ACACIA BLVD.
                     DESERT SPRINGS, CALIFORNIA  94562


                                   &@&

&Mr-Ms& &first& &last&
&addr1/O&
&addr2/O&
&city& &state& &zip&
```

```
Dear &Mr-Ms& &last&:

In my three terms serving as your County Supervisor, I hope my
honest support of the &user1& profession has earned your trust
and your vote. More than that, &Mr-Ms& &last&, I hope you can see
your way clear to the modest campaign contribution of 25 tax
deductible dollars.


Sincerely,



Jerome P. Hunnycutt
County Supervisor


JH:sb
.pa
```

Notice one dot command, .oj on, is added at the top of the file. Also, look at the .df command; the data file WSLIST.DTA has no path indicated. This is fine as long as you are in the directory that contains the file. Unless you changed it or moved it, the default is normally C:\WS\OPTIONS\WS-LIST.DTA. Finally, notice the command &@&, which we will discuss shortly.

Tip

If you will be working with MailList and Merge Print frequently, it is wise to keep printouts of your master files for reference. In order to print a listing like the one shown above, at the Print dialog box mark the Print Unformatted Text check box, and unmark the Interpret Merge Variables check box.

18

Printing to Disk

When you are learning a new technique, in this case merge printing, there are apt to be a few mistakes along the way. And each trial run of the example in this chapter will use ten sheets of paper (if you entered all the names in Example 18A). A handy way to save paper as you work through this chapter is to use the ASCII driver when printing. It prints the output to your hard disk. You can then open the output file, ASCII.WS, as a WordStar file and see if there are any errors in your work. This also has the advantage of being much faster than your printer.

Tip

If you print to the hard disk a file that contains extended characters, use the ASC256 driver.

     Let's try printing to the hard disk. At the Opening screen, choose File. Then select Print. Choose the master document POLIT.MRG, and include the path. In the Printer field select ASCII, and press F10. The hard disk will be active for a few seconds. Your output is saved to the disk with the filename ASCII.WS. (This filename is always used unless you change it in the Redirect To field of the Print dialog box. On subsequent uses you will be asked if it's OK to overwrite the file.)

     Now open the file ASCII.WS in WordStar and check that the output of your merge print is what you expected. If necessary, make corrections to the master document POLIT1.MRG, and repeat the printing process. A printout of the first letter is shown in Example 18C.

Note

When you print to disk, the .pa command does not determine page breaks as it does when you print to a printer. Disregard the lines showing page breaks with this type of output. When the document is printed, the .pa command will take effect as usual.

Understanding Merge Print Dot Commands

     Merge Print uses a variety of dot commands. All of the commands you have used previously are available. In addition, there are a few that work exclusively with Merge Print; these are accessed from the Utility menu on the Edit screen by selecting Merge Print Commands, or you can enter them directly. Here is the Merge Print Commands menu:

```
┌──────────────────────────────────────────┐
│ Data File...                           .df│
│ Name Variables...                      .rv│
│ Set Variable...                        .sv│
│ Set Variable to Math Result...         .ma│
│ Ask for Variable...                    .av│
│                                           │
│ If...                                  .if│
│ Else                                   .el│
│ End If                                 .ei│
│ Go to Top of Document               .go t│
│ Go to Bottom of Document            .go b│
│                                           │
│ Clear Screen While Printing...         .cs│
│ Display Message...                     .dm│
│ Print File n Times...                  .rp│
└──────────────────────────────────────────┘
```

Let's consider the special Merge Print commands used in POLIT1.MRG—the two dot commands .df and .rv and the symbols & and /O are used only with **Merge Print.** You'll learn more about them as you work through this section.

Special Merge Print Commands/Symbols	Function
.df	Specifies name of data file
.rv	Assigns variable names
&	Brackets inserted variable data
/O	Omits line with no data

Page Numbering with Merge Print (.op, .pn)

When you generate a master document for merge printing, it's important to pay special attention to page numbering. Because it is assumed you are going to print the text of your file more than once, you can use either .op or .pn to control page numbering. If your letter or document is one page, enter **.op,** which omits page numbers altogether. If your letter or document is more than one page long and you want page numbers printed starting with page 1 each time the file is printed, enter **.pn 1.** As usual, you'll want to enter the command at the beginning of the file, before you enter any text.

18

Page Breaks with Merge Print (.pa)

It's also important to consider page breaks in a merge print. Be sure the
.pa command is included at the end of your file, so each letter will begin on
a new page.

Name of Data File (.df)

Use .df to tell WordStar the name of the data file to get data from for the
merge print. In POLIT1.MRG, we used the data file you entered previously,
WSLIST.DTA. In the merge file, the command would be

```
.df wslist.dta
```

If you use MailList to create your own data list, substitute the name of that
file after the .df command. Entries may be upper- or lowercase. Be sure to
include the path if the data file is not on the current directory.

Read Variable (.rv)

The .rv command, always used in conjunction with .df, assigns variable
names to each item in the data file record. These variable names must be
listed in the same order as the fields within the data file records. The variable
names provided for MAILLIST.DOT are shown below:

```
.rv x, number, full-name, first, mi, last, Mr-Ms, title
.rv company, addr1, addr2, city, state, zip, country
.rv phone1, date, Jr-MD
.rv user1, phone2, user2, x, user3, remark1, remark2, remark3, ymd
```

where the *full-name* field is from the individual First Name, Middle Initial, and
Last Name fields in the MailList data records. The last field named by .rv, *ymd*,
is also supplied by MailList; it's the date from the record, in a format that can
be used for sorting—for example, March 23, 1992, would be 920323. The two
x fields are for internal use by MailList.

Insertion Points (&)

Within the merge print file, a pair of ampersands (&) is used to indicate
where data from the data file should be inserted into a printed document.

Enclosed within each pair of ampersands is one of the variable names from the .rv command line, or one of the predefined variables explained below.

Using Predefined Variables

On the Insert menu, the Variable option offers you eight predefined variables for merge printing. They perform the same functions as the eight macro inserts on the Macro menu. The difference is that the macro puts the function into a file being edited, whereas Merge Print puts the function into a file being printed.

Following is the submenu of the eight predefined variables you can access:

Notice that all of the symbols between the ampersands (@, !, and so on) are the same as those on the Macro menu for these functions.

For example, &@& places the date at the position of the variable when the file is printed. You can use the date variable with a memo heading, as shown in the following example. It automatically prints the correct date in place of the variable &@&.

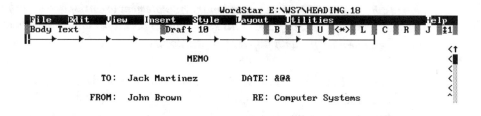

Note

The predefined variables can be used in any document. However, only the Merge Print operation inserts data from another file or data entered from the keyboard while printing.

Omit Blank Lines (/O)

The characters /O tell Merge Print not to leave a blank line if there is no data for this item. The /O must appear within the ampersand insertion characters for that variable. An example of the output with and without the /O characters is shown here:

```
&first& &last&           Kat Ballew
&addr1&                  6880 Walnut Blvd.
&addr2&
&city& &state& &zip&     Walnut Creek, CA 94598


&first& &last&           Kat Ballew
&addr1&                  6880 Walnut Blvd.
&addr2/O&                Walnut Creek, CA 94598
&city& &state& &zip&
```

What Merge Print Does

You have seen how variable names correspond to the data in each field of the data record in the data file. When a document is printed, Merge Print inserts into the master document the information from the corresponding data field in place of the variable name.

Note

In the printed document, you don't have to use the data from every field. However, you must have a variable name entered in the .rv statement to correspond to each field of data in the data file being used. This keeps data in the proper order and allows you to use the same data file with different master documents.

When the first letter is printed, the data from the fields in the first record of the data file will be substituted for the corresponding variables. When the second document is printed, the data from the fields of the second record will be substituted, and so on. The number of records in a data file is limited only by disk space.

Other Merge Print Applications: Data Reports and Envelopes

Now that you have a Merge Print application under your belt, let's try two more—a data report and envelopes—both of which come with MailList. We'll examine the data files and master documents that produce these applications.

Working with Data Reports

For the data report, we will use one of WordStar's master documents to print preformatted lists. This document, PROOF.LST, is on the Options directory with the other MailList programs. Technically, *data reports* are master documents. They are, however, different in the sense that they provide lists of information. The only text included is the text in the data file or in the dot commands. All files of this type supplied with MailList have the extension .LST, for list.

First let's print a *proof list* of your data file WSLIST.DTA. This prints out all the data in your file. WordStar supplies the master document, PROOF.LST. As before, let's print to the disk and review the output file on screen with WordStar. Since the master document is provided, follow these steps:

1. Transfer to the Options directory.
2. From the Opening screen, open the File menu and select **P** for Print.
3. Select the file PROOF.LST.
4. In the Printer field, select ASCII.
5. Press F10.

Examine the file ASCII.WS using WordStar.

Now let's examine the commands in the file PROOF.LST. Open PROOF.LST as a document file.

```
.df wslist.dta
.pl 11.00"
.mt  1.17"
.mb   .83"
.hm   .00"
.poo  .20"
.poe  .20"
.rm  7.60"
.ul on
.oc on
.h1 ^BMailing List Proof Report^B
.h2 ^S&@&^S
.f1 &#&
.oc off
.rv x, number, full-name, first, mi, last, Mr-Ms, title
.rv company, addr1, addr2, city, state, zip, country
.rv phone1, date, Jr-MD, user1, phone2, user2, x, user3
.rv remark1, remark2, remark3, ymd
.sv 1=RRRRRRRRR
.cp 13

.tb 4.10"
.rr————————————————————!————————————————————R
&number&                          &date&
.tb .20" 4.10" 6.50"
 &full-name&                      &Mr-Ms&          &Jr-MD/1&
 &company&                        &title&
 &addr1&
 &addr2&
 &city& &state& &zip&             &country&
 &phone1&                         &phone2&
User Fields:
.tb .30" 2.00"
1: &user1&            &remark1&
2: &user2&            &remark2&
3: &user3&            &remark3&
```

The dot commands at the top of this file are WordStar commands you have used previously. They change the default page layout to a suitable format for this report. Note also that .oc is used to center the output in the header and footer.

Next are the .rv commands required with WSLIST.DTA. There is only one new merge print command, .sv, which we'll discuss shortly. The last section formats the printout. Before going over the .sv command, let's print one more example.

Addressing Envelopes

The next project is to address envelopes. As we did previously, we'll go through the process and then look at the dot commands.

1. Change to the Options directory.
2. At the Opening screen, open the File menu and press **P** to select Print.
3. Select the file **ENVELOPE.LST**.
4. Change the Printer field to ASCII and press F10. A beep sounds.
5. Press ENTER and choose **Print**.
6. On the screen you see

   ```
   Ready envelope and press ↵
   ```

Note

Even though you're printing to the disk, the program acts as if you were at the printer. Press ENTER *each time the "Ready envelope..." message appears. Although you don't see it now, an envelope will be addressed. You can interrupt the process by pressing* ESC, *or continue through the ten names in the list.*

7. When you are finished, display the file ASCII.WS to check the address format.

Now let's examine the dot commands in the file ENVELOPE.LST. Open the file in Document mode.

```
.df wslist.dta
.op
.pl  4.17"
.mt  2.33"
```

18

```
.mb   .50"
.hm   .00"
.fm   .00"
.poo 4.20"
.poe 4.20"
.rm  9.50"
.rv x, number, full-name, first, mi, last, Mr-Ms, title
.rv company, addr1, addr2, city, state, zip, country
.rv phone1, date, Jr-MD, user1, phone2, user2, x, user3
.rv remark1, remark2, remark3, ymd
.sv A=LLLL
.if &Mr-Ms&=
.sv name, &first& &mi& &last&
.el
.sv Mr-Ms1 = &Mr-Ms/A&
.sv name, &Mr-Ms1& &first& &last&
.ei
.if &city&=
.sv CSZ, &state& &zip&
.el
.sv CSZ, &city&, &state& &zip&
.ei
.av "Ready envelope and press ↵ .",any-key
&name/O&
&title/O&
&company/O&
&addr1/O&
&addr2/O&
&CSZ/O&
&country/O&
.pa
```

At the top are dot commands used to set the page layout to fit the envelope by changing the default margins, headers, and footers. The format is for the standard business envelope, 4 1/8" by 9 1/2". If you use a different size envelope, you can adjust the layout settings. Page offset commands (.poo, .poe) are used to start the printing at the appropriate distance from the left margin. The next four lines define the read variable (.rv) commands that are standard with WSLIST.DTA. The commands .sv and .av are defined in the section just below, "Merge Print with Keyboard Data Entry." The remaining three new commands, .if, .el, and .ei, are defined later in "Conditional

Commands." Finally, at the bottom are the possible variables from WS-LIST.DTA that can be used in an address.

Note

WordStar provides special merge print files for LaserJet or compatible printers: HP-ENVMM.LST for LaserJet or LaserJet Plus; HP2-ENVM.LST for LaserJet Series II (manual); and HP2-ENVE.LST for LaserJet Series II (automatic envelope feed).

Merge Print with Keyboard Data Entry

In this section, you will see how to enter variable data into form letters directly from the keyboard while the letters are being printed. A variation of this process allows you to print directly from the keyboard. This is referred to as *Typewriter mode* and is discussed later.

To accomplish keyboard data entry during merge printing you will use the following dot commands:

Command	Function
.av	Asks for variable
.cs	Clears screen
.dm	Displays message
.sv	Sets variable

Keyboard Data Entry

To enter data from the keyboard while merge printing a document, you will find it most convenient to enter the series of commands discussed below. In effect, these commands tell WordStar to take data from the keyboard rather than from the data file.

Note

You can enter data from the keyboard and get data from a data file in the same merge print operation.

Let's return to the POLIT1.MRG file used earlier. Suppose you want to vary the contribution requested in the letter, from $25 to another value based

18

on the person's profession, past contributions, or some other factor. At the beginning of the file, just after the last .rv command, enter the following:

```
.cs
.dm Contribution request from: &Last&—profession: &user1&
.av "Amount of contribution?", Amount
```

Let's look at each of these commands in turn.

Clear Screen (.cs)

Generally, it is appropriate to use Merge Print's Clear Screen command (.cs) prior to using the .av command (discussed shortly). When .cs precedes .av, then each time Merge Print asks for data to be entered (via the .av prompt), the prompt will appear on a clear screen. This is particularly useful when there are several keyboard entries for each letter you are producing.

The Clear Screen command is used to help you recall what information is required. You can also specify a message after the .cs command, as in the command

```
.cs
```

Enter data as requested.

Display Message (.dm)

Generally, after you clear the screen you use the .dm command to display a message. This message may include variable names from the .rv command line. In the example of .dm presented just above, the insertion variable &last& is used to display the last name, and &user1& is used to show the profession of the individual from whom you are requesting the contribution.

Ask for Variable (.av)

The .av command specifies the variable to be entered from the keyboard. Just as when you use a data file, when Merge Print encounters the .av variable name, it replaces that variable name with actual data. The difference is that you must enter that data from the keyboard rather than have it automatically entered from the data file.

In the .av line presented just above, we entered the variable name, Amount. This variable must also be entered in the document file, bracketed by & characters to identify it as an insertion variable. Do this now; in the text of the master document, in place of the 25, type **&amount&**.

When you print this file, Merge Print will know that *amount* is a variable and that it should ask for that data. Merge Print does this by printing a message on the screen, prompting you to enter the data. The message it prints is the message you typed following the .av command—in this case, "Amount of contribution?" The message you enter after the .av command must be enclosed in quotation marks and have a comma separating it from the variable name. When you enter the variable's requested data, you are limited to the number of characters that will take you to the end of the line on your screen.

To run this merge print letter, select Print from the Opening screen File menu. Select POLIT1.MRG. When the beep sounds, press **P** and the screen message will appear. Enter appropriate values when requested.

Note

Depending on the characteristics of your printer, the point in your file where the printer is stopped may not appear to coincide with the data you are entering. Go ahead and enter data according to the prompt messages; WordStar will print the document as formatted in the master document. If you have more than one variable to ask for in a letter, each variable should be entered on a separate .av command line.

For example, if you use the commands

```
.av Name
.av Profession
```

you will respond during the merge print by entering data on the screen as follows, pressing ENTER after each line (the program prompts you with the variable name):

```
Name? Jennifer
Profession? TEACHER
```

18

Set Variable (.sv)

Another useful Merge Print command is .sv, for Set Variable. It has two functions: it specifies a variable to hold a constant value during merge printing, and it controls formatting.

In the current example, POLIT1.MRG, the name and address are changed for each letter. But there are other situations where a variable will be the same for several letters, or when the same variable might change several times in the same letter. For instance, take a look at Example 18D. It's a portion of the will used as Example 10 in Chapter 10. In a will, the same names normally occur several times. In place of the actual names, the variables *name1*, *name2*, and so forth, can be substituted in this will. The .sv command is used at the beginning of the file to identify the actual name that should replace each variable in the text. You can then type the names once, and they will be changed throughout the document. Each variable must be entered with a separate .sv command.

Note

Whenever something is centered in a merge print document, as is the name in the will heading in Example 10, you can use the centering format variable, .sv C, discussed in the next section.

While merge printing, you can automatically format both text and numeric data. To set up either text or numeric format strings, use the dot command .sv as explained in the following paragraphs. This is the way .sv was used in both PROOF.LST and ENVELOPE.LST.

Formatting Text with .sv

You can left-justify, right-justify, or center text using the letters L, R, and C, respectively, with the .sv command. The first step is to define the format field with .sv. For example,

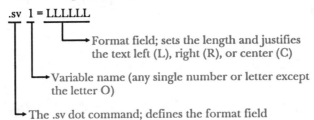

.sv 1 = LLLLLL

Format field; sets the length and justifies the text left (L), right (R), or center (C)

Variable name (any single number or letter except the letter O)

The .sv dot command; defines the format field

Text formatting follows these rules:

- In the first position of the format field, enter **R** to right-justify, **L** to left-justify, or **C** to center text within the format field.

- Any other characters, including spaces, will print in the position they appear.
- The number of characters in the format field determines the number of spaces available for the variable.
- Excess characters—those on the right for left-justification and those on the left for right-justification—will be cut off.
- Other characters or spaces add to the field length and will print literally, even if there are characters for that position. (An example of this is shown below in master document TEXT.MRG with the dot command .sv 1.)

In the following example, the format strings are labeled A, B, C, and 1. Format strings A and B are too short to hold the name *George Washington*; notice how it is shortened in each case. Format string C is the same length as the ruler line, 65 characters, and will center the text on a ruler line of that length. Format string 1 is presented to illustrate the masking effect of the characters other than L, R, and C in the format field.

Enter and print the following master document and data file to verify the results. The master document follows:

```
.he TEXT.MRG
.op
.df TEXT.DTA
.rv var1,var2
.sv A = LLLLLLLLLLLLL
.sv B = RRRRRRRRRRRRRR
.sv C = CCCCCCCCCCCCCCCCCCCCCCCCCCCCCCCCCCCCCCCCCCCCCCCCCCCCCCCCCCCCCCC
.sv 1 = LLABLL

&var1/A&
&var1/B&
&var1/C&
&var2/1&
------------------------------------------------------------------
```

When you enter a data file directly into WordStar without the aid of MailList or another database program, open a nondocument file and enter data with commas separating the entries.

The data file should look like this:

```
TEXT.DTA data:
George Washington,123456
```

The printout produced by **TEXT.MRG** is shown below:

```
George Washing
rge Washington
                            George Washington

12AB56
```

Formatting Numbers with .sv

Numbers are always right-justified when printed, but a variety of formatting options are available to control various characters that are printed with numbers. They can be used individually or in combination. Table 18-1 shows the format symbols available.

Following are a master document, the data file used by that document, and the output of the merged files. Experiment with these files to be sure your format strings behave the way you expect them to. Here is the master document:

```
FORMAT.MRG
.op
Format examples:
.sv1= 9999999.99
.sv2= ZZZZZZ.ZZ
.sv4= -$*****.**
.sv5= 999,999.99
.sv6= ($$$$$.99)
.df FORMAT.DTA
.rv DATA1,DATA2,DATA3
    &DATA1&               &DATA2&               &DATA3&
    ----------------------------------------------------------------
    &DATA1/1&             &DATA2/1&             &DATA3/1&
    &DATA1/2&             &DATA2/2&             &DATA3/2&
    &DATA1/3&             &DATA2/3&             &DATA3/3&
    &DATA1/4&             &DATA2/4&             &DATA3/4&
    &DATA1/5&             &DATA2/5&             &DATA3/5&
    &DATA1/6&             &DATA2/6&             &DATA3/6&
```

Table 18-1. *Numeric Formatting Options Used with .sv Command*

Format Symbol	Function
9	Substitutes a digit in place of each 9. If no digit is available, a zero is substituted. If you use the format string 99999.99, the number 231.40 will be displayed as 00231.40.
Z	Substitutes a digit in place of each Z. If there is no digit, a space is substituted. If you use the format string ZZZZZ.ZZ, the number 231.40 will be displayed as (two spaces)231.40.
*	Substitutes a digit in place of each asterisk. If no digit is available, an asterisk is substituted. After a decimal point, a zero is substituted. If you use the format string *****.**, the number 231.40 will be displayed as **231.40, and the number 231 will be displayed as **231.00.
$	Substitutes a digit in place of each $, if the first place is not a zero. Places a $ to the left of the first digit. If you use the format string $$$$$$.99, the number 231.40 will be displayed as (two spaces)$231.40.
–	Places a minus sign before the leading digit of a negative number. (See example .sv 4 in the FORMAT.MRG file.)
.	Places a decimal point in the position shown. If you use the format string 99999.999, the number 231.40 will be displayed as 231.400.
,	Places a comma in the position shown. If you use the format string 99,999.99, the number 1231.40 will be displayed as (one space)1,231.40.
( )	Places parentheses around negative numbers. If you use the format string ($$$$.99), the number –231.40 will be displayed as ($231.40).

18

Next is the data file used by the master document—the three numbers shown below:

```
FORMAT.DTA data: 231.40,2165.5678,-7954.12
```

Finally, here is the output produced by the master document:

```
Format examples:

      231.40                  2165.5678              -7954.12
-------------------------------------------------------------------
0000231.40                0002165.56             0007954.12
      231.40                  2165.56                7954.12
$000231.40                $002165.56             $007954.12
***$231.40                **$2165.56             *-$7954.12
000 231.40                002,165.56             007,954.12
    $231.40                  $2165.56             ($7954.12)
```

Conditional Commands

The conditional commands are powerful additions to WordStar's merge printing capabilities. These commands let you use the same master document to print a variety of material, depending on the conditions you set. For example, you can send a letter to only those individuals on your mailing list whose zip codes fall within a particular range.

The conditional commands have a wide variety of applications. After the following descriptions of the four conditional commands, an example will show how some of them are used.

The If Condition (.if)

The dot command .if is generally used to compare two items: when the comparison evaluates to true, then one operation is performed; when the comparison evaluates to false, then another operation is performed. To compare two items, you need an operator such as an equal sign. The operators recognized by the .if command are divided into two categories: text operators and numeric operators, as shown in Table 18-2.

You can use these operators to compare two variables or a variable and a constant. Here are two examples:

```
.if &purchase1& > &purchase2&

.if &purchase1& #> 500
```

Table 18-2.   Text and Numerical Operators Used with .if Command

Text Operators:

Operator	Meaning
=	Is the same as (alphabetically)
<	Comes before (alphabetically)
>	Comes after (alphabetically)
<=	Comes before or is the same as (alphabetically)
>=	Comes after or is the same as (alphabetically)
<>	Is not the same as (alphabetically)

Numerical Operators:

Operator	Meaning
#=	Is equal to (numerically)
#>	Is greater than (numerically)
#<	Is less than (numerically)
#>=	Is greater than or equal to (numerically)
#<=	Is less than or equal to (numerically)
#<>	Is not equal to (numerically)

18

The Else Condition (.el)

The dot command .el in the example below makes a decision, based on a given condition, on which path to follow.

```
.if &JOB& = D
Text of letter sent to doctors
.el
Text of letter sent to lawyers
.ei
```

In this example, the data file contains a field to identify whether the record holds the data for a doctor or a lawyer. When the record contains data for a doctor, signified by the letter *D*, the letter directed to doctors is printed. When the record contains data for a lawyer (anything except a *D* is in the field), a letter to lawyers is sent.

The End If Condition (.ei)

The .if command is normally followed by the text to be printed when the condition evaluates to true. When the condition evaluates to false, control proceeds to the next dot command—which may be another .if command or, more likely, is the .ei command. When all the .if conditions have been tested, an .ei command must end the process. An example of using the .ei command is shown in the last section, where the decision is made to send a letter based on profession.

The Go Command (.go)

The Go (.go) command allows you to bypass a portion of the text in the master document if a condition is met. In this example,

```
.if &INCOME&< 4000
.go bottom
.ei
```

when the .if condition evaluates to true, control passes to the end of the file, bypassing a section of text. When the .if condition evaluates to false, that section of text will be printed.

Entering **.go t** or **.go T** is the same as entering **.go TOP**. Entering **.go b** or **.go B** is the same as entering **.go BOTTOM**.

Using the Conditional Commands

Let's try some of the conditional commands in a master document. The following document, CONDIT.MRG, directs different letters depending on the town in which the addressee resides:

```
.op
.df wslist.dta
.rv x, number, full-name, first, mi, last, Mr-Ms, title
.rv company, addr1, addr2, city, state, zip, country
.rv phone1, date, Jr-MD
.rv user1, phone2, user2, x, user3, remark1, remark2, remark3, ymd
.if &zip& #=94553
As a resident of Martinez ..... &Mr-Ms& &last&
.ei
.if &zip& #=94598
As a resident of Walnut Creek..... &Mr-Ms& &last&
.ei
.if &zip& #=94520
As a resident of Pleasant Hill..... &Mr-Ms& &last&
.ei
```

If you use this document with WSLIST.DTA, here is an example of output from these files (the actual printout will depend on your data):

```
As a resident of Pleasant Hill..... Mr. Rath
As a resident of Martinez..... Ms. Carlson
As a resident of Pleasant Hill..... Mr. Carlson
As a resident of Martinez ..... Mr. Godfrey
```

Using Typewriter Mode

Next, let's consider a feature that allows you to use your printer like a typewriter. This feature is most commonly used to fill in forms or address envelopes.

18

Creating a Template File

To use Typewriter mode, you first create a *template file*, which is a regular WordStar file created in document mode. Its purpose is the same as a master document. It controls printing the data, but in this case the data comes exclusively from the keyboard, rather than from a combination of a data file and keyboard entry. The template consists basically of a series of dot commands—the merge commands introduced in this chapter, as well as other dot commands that define headers, footers, margins, and other aspects of page layout. You can also introduce font tags in your template file to allow use of any of the available fonts that your printer is capable of handling.

Table 18-3.   *WordStar Commands and Functions for Addressing Envelopes*

Command	Function
.he templt.mrg	File title
.rp 6500	Allow for multiple entries
.mt 0	Set margins
.mb 0	Set margins
.lm 20	Set margins
.op	Omit page number
.cs	Clear screen
.dm Enter name	Display screen instruction
.av "",name	Store entry
&name&	Print entry
.dm Enter address	Display screen instruction
.av "",address	Store entry
&address&	Print entry
.dm Enter city/state/zip	Display screen instruction
.av "",csz	Store entry
&csz&	Print entry
.pa	Advance to new page

The Table 18-3 describes several WordStar commands that can be used to address envelopes.

Note

Setting the repeat command (.rp) to its maximum value (65,000) allows you to enter as many names as you wish. You can, of course, terminate your keyboard entry after any number of envelopes.

When you enter a file of this type, use Margin Release, ^OX, for any entry other than dot commands so those entries won't move over to the left margin. To run this file, use Typewriter mode as discussed below.

If your template is designed to fill in a form, it will most likely need to advance the paper between entries on the form. This is accomplished by entering in the template file the necessary number of carriage returns between the appropriate print commands. Note the .pa command at the end of the template file; this is necessary in all your template files to advance the paper from one form to the next.

Selecting Typewriter Mode

You can select Typewriter mode, also referred to as Keyboard mode, from the Opening menu. To select Keyboard mode, display the File pull-down menu and choose **K.** When Typewriter mode is selected, the Print from Keyboard window shown here is displayed:

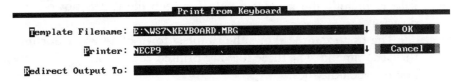

By default, the template file KEYBOARD.MRG supplied with WordStar 7.0 is selected. You may change this selection by selecting another file.

Tip

If you wish, you can open KEYBOARD.MRG as a document file and modify it any way you choose. In general, its purpose is to prompt you for an appropriate response, then print that response in the proper location.

When you have chosen the file you want, press F10. You are now ready to begin your keyboard entry. Whether or not your printer prints immediately when you press ENTER depends on its characteristics. It may be that your last entries will not print until you indicate you are finished by pressing ESC. Any data still in the printer's buffer at this time will print in the proper position. Pressing ESC also returns you to the Opening menu.

File Insert (.fi)

At times you will create a master document to direct printing from a data file, a document file, or both. This section introduces the .fi command that allows this operation. Then, in the next section, you'll learn about the .pf command for controlling print-time formatting.

The File Insert command (.fi) is used to perform two functions: *chaining* and *nesting*. You can create a master document using a series of .fi commands to select a series of files to print; this is called *chaining*. You can also use the .fi command to insert the text of one file into the text of another; this is called *nesting*.

Two examples of chaining are shown here. Each example shows how the master document file appears on the screen. Pay particular attention to the symbols in the flag column. Notice that ENTER is pressed twice to separate each .fi command, and a final ENTER follows the last .fi command. Also, be sure to include the necessary path for each file if it is not on the current directory.

The first example shows the simplest form of a master document using the .fi command. The three files are printed continuously, with only a single line between the files.

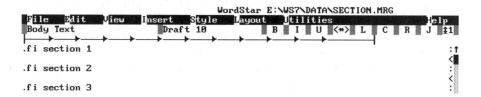

In the second example, notice that .pa is placed between the .fi commands so that each section will begin on a new page.

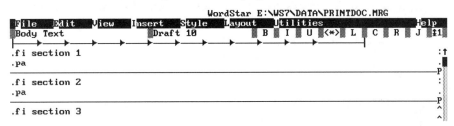

Suppose you are planning a joint class reunion for the classes of 1981 and 1982 and have a different letter to be sent to the members of each class. This can be accomplished by using the nesting function, as shown below, which prepares the appropriate letter for the members of each class.

```
.if &user1&= CLASS of 81
.fi CLASS81.DOC
.el
.if &user1&= Class of 82
.fi CLASS82.DOC
.ei
.ei
```

Note

Be sure that for each .if command there is a corresponding .ei command. It is not necessary, however, that each .if command have an .el command.

Chaining and nesting are performed by selecting Print in the usual manner.

18

Print Formatting (.pf)

When you use Merge Print, the data read for a particular variable will generally vary in length in different files. The Print Formatting command, .pf, is used to reformat the paragraphs as data is inserted.

The .pf command can have any one of three settings: on, off, or dis (discretionary). If you use .pf on, formatting is performed throughout the file unless a section is specifically turned off with the .aw command. If you use .pf off, formatting is not performed. If you use the dis option, formatting is performed only where merge printing variables are introduced.

Calculating While Merge Printing (.ma)

WordStar lets you solve mathematical problems while merge printing by using the .ma command. This dot command allows you access to all the math functions available in calculator mode. The format for the math dot command (.ma) is

.ma *variable = equation*

With a simple equation, the command looks like this:

```
.ma SUM = &purchase1& + &purchase2& + &purchase3&
```

A comma may be used in place of the equal sign, as shown here:

```
.ma SUM,&purchase1& + &purchase2& + &purchase3&
```

Note that the variables to the right of the equal sign (or comma) are enclosed by ampersands (&), and the variable to the left is not. The variables on the right need data substituted into them and therefore require ampersands. When you merge print, the data file is read, information is substituted for the variables, calculations are performed, and the result is printed in your text in place of the variable &SUM&.

A sample master document and data file using the .ma command are shown here:

```
.he PURCHASE.MRG
.op
.oj on
.df purchase.dta
.pf on
```

```
.rv purchase1, purchase2, purchase3
.ma sum=&purchase1&+&purchase2&+&purchase3&
.ma total= .075*&sum&+&sum&
.sv1=$*****.**
Mr. John Smith
789 Pine Street
Martinez, CA 94553

Dear Mr. Smith:

Your purchases for May were &purchase1&, &purchase2&, and
&purchase3&. The total of your purchases was &sum&. With tax your
bill comes to &total/1&.

Sincerely,


Jack Super
```

Here's the data file:

```
PURCHASE.DTA data

19.31,33.14,21.56
```

The printout using these two files is shown in **Figure 18-8.**

Figure 18-8.   *A merge printed letter containing calculation results*

```
Mr. John Smith
789 Pine Street
Martinez, CA 94553

Dear Mr. Smith:

Your purchases for May were 19.31, 33.14, and 21.56.
The total of your purchases was 74.01. With tax your
bill comes to ***$79.56.

Sincerely,

Jack Super
```

18

Exercises

1. Add the data for three more people to the WSLIST.DTA file. Sort them by state in reverse alphabetical order.

2. Print the political contribution letters set up in this chapter, entering the contribution amount from the keyboard and setting the date using the predefined date variable. Use the .sv command to define the appropriate format string for the contribution.

3. Print the political contribution letters again, but this time enter names and addresses from the keyboard instead of from a data file.

4. Print the will from Chapter 10, entering the name of the testator and friend only once. Example 18D shows the dot commands and three sections of the document file.

5. Add a section to the template file for addressing envelopes, to make it also print the return address.

6. Reprint the list of contributors, using the conditional commands to limit the list to people in the medical profession.

7. Create a master document to print four of your existing files in succession.

8. Redo the mailing label example to suit the format of the mailing labels you use.

9. Use the file ROLODEX.LST supplied with WordStar to print Rolodex cards. Print cards to disk and to your printer. Open the file ROLODEX.LST and notice the use of chaining. Open both files used in ROLODEX and examine the commands.

10. If you will have need for the inventory data file, enter five or more items into the file. Try sorting, adding, and deleting with this form.

Example 18A

```
Mr. Henry Rath          123 Sack Street      Apt. 6  Pleasant Hill  CA  94520  (510)229-6251  legal
Mr. Kat Ballew          6880 Walnut Blvd.            Eugene         OR  97401  (503)698-3220  medical
Ms. Effie Carlson       214 Midhill Dr.              Martinez       CA  94553  (510)228-3006  teaching
Mr. Frank M. Terry      2214 Richmond Blvd.          Eugene         OR  94701  (503)235-5252  commercial
Mr. Ralph Knight        370 Main St.                 Portland       OR  94207  (503)378-5567  teaching
Mr. Carl Carlson        989 Peach Blvd.              Concord        CA  94520  (510)636-2459  medical
Mr. George Godfrey      1891 Alhambra Ave.           Martinez       CA  94553  (510)372-6483  legal
Mr. David Perez         2922 Laguna Court            Portland       OR  94207  (503)398-3515  medical
Mr. Steve A. Quinn      293 Bovet Road       5th Fl. San Mateo      CA  94402  (415)451-3159  medical
Ms. Elizabeth Mitchell 1807 Highland Dr.             Agoura Hills   CA  91301  (818)991-8143  teaching
```

18

Example 18B

```
          DESERT SPRINGS COUNTY SUPERVISOR'S OFFICE
               COUNTY BUILDING - SUITE 3001A
                   2105 WEST ACACIA BLVD.
             DESERT SPRINGS, CALIFORNIA  94562

                           &@&


&Mr-Ms& &first& &last&
&addr1/O&
&addr2/O&
&city& &state& &zip&

Dear &Mr-Ms& &last&:

In my three terms serving as your County Supervisor,
I hope my honest support of the &user1& profession
has earned your trust and your vote. More than that,
&Mr-Ms& &last&, I hope you can see your way clear to
the modest campaign contribution of 25 tax deductible
dollars.

Sincerely,


Jerome P. Hunnycutt
County Supervisor

JH:sb
```

Example 18C

```
        DESERT SPRINGS COUNTY SUPERVISOR'S OFFICE
             COUNTY BUILDING - SUITE 3001A
                2105 WEST ACACIA BLVD.
           DESERT SPRINGS, CALIFORNIA  94562



March 23, 1992

Mr. Kat Ballew
6880 Walnut Blvd.
Walnut Creek, CA 94598

Dear Mr. Ballew:

In my three terms serving as your County Supervisor,
I hope my honest support of the medical profession
has earned your trust and your vote. More than that,
Mr. Ballew, I hope you can see your way clear to the
modest campaign contribution of 25 tax deductible
dollars.

Sincerely,


Jerome P. Hunnycutt
County Supervisor

JH:sb
```

18

Example 18D

```
.pn

.SV NAME1, JOHN PHILIP SMITH

.SV NAME2, MARCY SIMMONS

              LAST WILL AND TESTAMENT

                       OF

                 JOHN PHILIP SMITH
    I, &NAME1&, presently residing in the City of
Walnut Creek, Contra Costa County, California, being
of sound and disposing mind and memory, and not acting
under duress, menace, or undue influence of any kind
or person whatsoever, do hereby make, publish, and
declare this to be my Last Will and Testament in the
following manner:

                    ARTICLE V

    I give, devise and bequeath one-half (1/2) of the
residue of my estate, real, personal, or mixed, of
whatever kind and wheresoever situated, to my very
good friend, &NAME2&, and then to her issue by right
of representation. If &NAME2& shall predecease me,
this gift shall lapse.

                   ARTICLE VII

    I hereby nominate and request the court to appoint
my friend, &NAME2&, as Executrix of this will, to
serve without bond. Should &NAME2& serve as Executrix,
I authorize her to sell, lease, convey, transfer,
encumber, hypothecate, or otherwise deal with the
whole or any portion of my estate, either by public
or private sale, with or without notice, and without
securing any prior order of the court therefor.
```

19

Inset

The Inset companion program was a major addition to WordStar version 5.5. With Inset you can incorporate a chart or picture into a WordStar file to enhance your document. For example, you can

- Use Lotus 1-2-3 graphics displays in your Wordstar files
- Create your own charts or other artwork, using programs such as PC Paintbrush
- Use displays from clip art libraries such as those included in Inset
- Use Inset to create original free-form art

Getting Started with Inset

You can use Inset as a stand-alone program or in conjunction with WordStar and other commercial programs. As a stand-alone program, Inset is used to capture, edit, or create a screen image. (*Capture* means to save the image you see on your computer screen.) After capturing an image, you can use Inset to put it into the form you need. Before an image can be edited using Inset, the image must be in *graphic* format; let's consider what the terms *graphic* and *graphics* mean as used with Inset and WordStar.

ASCII Displays Versus Graphic Images

All of the screen displays seen so far in this book were made up using the ASCII or extended character set. These characters include letters and numbers, as well as all the lines and bars that make up a WordStar dialog box or menu. The complete list of the ASCII and extended characters is shown in Table B-3 of Appendix B.

In this chapter you will work primarily with another type of screen display—the graphics display. You have a great deal more control over a graphics display (provided you have the right software) than you do over an ASCII display. First, you can create any kind of image on the graphics display; you aren't limited to just the ASCII and extended character sets. Second, you can manipulate the graphics display to a much greater extent. For example, you can increase or decrease the size of a graphic image, change its scale, and rotate the display. If the screens you work with are made up of ASCII characters, with Inset you can convert them to graphics displays and edit them.

Note

All the Inset files, as you'll see shortly, have the filename extension .PIX to indicate they are graphics files. All screen displays, graphics or ASCII, are made up of pixels. A pixel is the smallest unit that can be displayed on the screen.

Installing Inset

To install Inset, change to the Inset directory, C:\WS\INSET, and then type **INSET**. Run Inset's Setup program to configure the Inset software for your hardware—monitor, graphics board, printer, and so on. Inset used in conjunction with WordStar requires 640K of memory. If you change any of WordStar's default memory settings, you may receive a message indicating there is insufficient memory for some Inset operations. In that case, go back to the default settings.

Loading Inset

To load Inset, you must be logged into the Inset subdirectory, \WS\INSET. If you aren't already in that subdirectory, type **CD\WS\INSET** and press ENTER. Then type **INSET** and press ENTER. Inset loads into memory, but it is not ready to use until it is activated—which you can do from any subdirectory. You're going to start by looking through Inset's clip art library, so stay in the Inset subdirectory.

Using Inset

Let's activate Inset and try some of its more commonly used operations. To activate Inset, press ^SHIFT. (The SHIFT key pressed with CTRL must be the SHIFT key on the *left* side of the keyboard. Either the left or right CTRL key can be used.) Inset's main menu appears at the bottom of the screen; it looks like this:

<VIEW> SAVE MODIFY EDIT PRINT OUTPUT HELP ◄—— Menu line
LOAD IMAGE FOR VIEWING AND MODIFICATION ◄—— Description line

In this chapter, you will work mostly with two of Inset's commands—Modify and Edit—along with the options associated with each of these commands. The Modify options only affect what is printed; they have no effect on the screen display. For example, if you use the Modify command to enlarge an image to three times its original size, there will be no visual effect on screen. But when printed, the effect will be obvious. On the other hand, the Edit command options do affect the screen image, as well as printed material.

Cursor Control: Numeric Keypad or Mouse?

Because Inset is used to create and edit graphic images, you'll be moving the cursor frequently and extensively. One way to quickly place the cursor

19

where you want it is to use the keys on the numeric keypad; with Inset, they work as shown here:

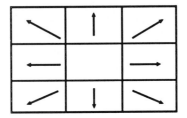

Pressing a key and holding it down moves the cursor in the direction of the arrows shown in the illustration. This applies, where appropriate, to both Modify and Edit options.

Inset has its own mouse control system. You can use the mouse for selecting a menu, placing the cursor, and drawing. To select menu items, slide the mouse back and forth to highlight the various menu options. Pressing the left mouse button selects the highlighted item. Pressing the right mouse button moves you backward through the command process (as does pressing the ESC key). The mouse is most useful when you are drawing. It lets you place the cursor and move and/or drag objects easily around the screen. The best way to get accustomed to how the mouse works with Inset is to practice and experiment.

You will find that, even if you use the mouse frequently, there are some operations for which the cursor keys are better suited, as in the graph example used later in this chapter (in "Creating a Bar Graph"). The instructions given in this chapter tell you what keys to press, but if you have a mouse, try doing each procedure using both the mouse and the keypad.

Note

If you activate the mouse before you start Inset, Inset will automatically detect it.

While working with the examples presented in this chapter, it's likely you will try some experiments. Therefore, keep these points in mind:

- Pressing ESC or the right mouse button moves you backward through the command process one step at a time.

- If you are at the main menu and you press ESC, you exit Inset. Just press ^SHIFT to return to Inset.

- To clear graphics material from the screen without saving, select Edit, then Options, then Clear. With the screen clear, press ESC until you return to the desired menu.

- To clear text material from the screen, select Edit and then Blank.

Note

As these last two points show, the same command can present different options, depending on the state of the screen when the command is selected. For example, Edit presents certain options with text screens and other options with graphics screens.

Working with Inset's Menus

Inset's menu operations may be familiar to you, since they work similarly to some other computer programs, for instance, Lotus 1-2-3. The first of Inset's menu lines is the main menu line, showing the available choices. To change your selection on the menu line, use the LEFT ARROW or RIGHT ARROW. As you highlight various choices, the description line (below the menu line) changes. It will either indicate what will happen if the highlighted choice is selected, or provide you with a list of additional options available for that choice. When the option you want is highlighted, press ENTER.

Another method of making a menu selection is to press the first letter of an option. This method will be most useful after you are familiar with Inset; it selects the option immediately, without displaying the description line.

Note

As you work with the menu and description lines, frequently one menu selection will display a new set of options. As you gain experience, you will soon recognize which command the displayed options refer to.

Remember

Pressing ESC always moves you to the previous step. Press ESC at the main menu, and you exit Inset. If you exit in error, press ^SHIFT to reactivate Inset. Then return to the desired activity.

19

Selecting a File with the View Command

As you see in the description line of the main menu shown previously, the View command is used to select an image file. Highlight View and press ENTER. On the second line from the bottom of the screen is the field used to enter your selection. Below that is the list of the graphics files supplied with Inset, as shown below.

The list will show only .PIX files, though the extension itself does not show. Since the area that displays filenames is limited, you will find it helpful to use the wildcards * and ? to choose files. For example, to see .PIX files that start with the letter *L*, type **L*** in the Name field and press ENTER.

Use the LEFT ARROW or RIGHT ARROW to highlight the name of the file you want, and press ENTER to load the file. For this exercise, highlight LOGOS1 and press ENTER; you'll see a display of symbols like those shown in Figure 19-1 on your screen.

Figure 19-1.   Inset screen display of LOGOS1 file

Note

When you load certain files, you may see the message, "Screen conversion required, proceed?" and a suggested option. This message occurs when there is a difference between the type of graphics display used to save the file and your current graphics display. You can still display the file, but some detail may be lost. Pressing ENTER to proceed displays the further message: "Half or full page?" Press ENTER to select the default (highlighted) selection.

Browsing Through the Clip Art Library

With LOGOS1 displayed, the main menu is still present at the bottom of the screen, though the screen is now in Graphics mode and may have a different appearance depending on your graphics board and monitor. Let's select another file from Inset's clip art library. With View highlighted, press ENTER. The file selection line appears again, with the name LOGOS1 displayed there. Press the SPACEBAR to erase LOGOS1, and press ENTER. The list of .PIX files reappears; highlight a new filename and press ENTER to display its contents.

Go ahead now and browse through the library of .PIX files supplied with Inset. When you're ready to continue, the next section helps you select and modify a portion of one of these files.

Capture/Clip/Edit an Image

Select View and display the SYMBOLS file. (Either type the filename or scroll through the list of filenames, highlight SYMBOLS, and press ENTER.) Use RIGHT ARROW to highlight the Modify command in the main menu. Notice that the option that appears at the far left of the description line is Clip. The Modify, Clip option is used to select, or *clip*, a symbol from the screen display. With Modify still highlighted, press ENTER. Select Clip (it is already highlighted), and press ENTER again. A large rectangle surrounds the screen display.

In the cursor movement instructions that follow, be sure to use the numeric keypad.

Remember

19

Let's select the ship symbol that appears near the lower-right corner of the screen, by moving the sides of the rectangle so it encloses just the portion of the screen that contains the ship. To begin, press the PGDN key on the numeric keypad. The lines at the top and left of the screen move down and to the right. Press and hold PGDN until the top line is just above the ship. (If the line moves down too far, use PGUP to move it back up.) Now press and hold RIGHT ARROW to bring the left side of the rectangle over to the ship. When the top and left sides of the rectangle are in position close to the ship, press ENTER to accept these positions.

Now move the bottom and right sides of the rectangle closer to the ship. Start by pressing HOME, and then press UP ARROW. Use DOWN ARROW and RIGHT ARROW to make any final adjustments to the lines. When they're in the correct position next to the ship, press ENTER. Now the lines disappear, and the screen is the same as when you first loaded SYMBOLS. In a moment, however, you'll see a change.

Tip

While you are moving the bottom and right sides of the rectangle, you can press ESC *to move the cursor to the upper-left of the rectangle if you need to reposition the top and left sides.*

Saving an Image

Save the ship image you just clipped from SYMBOLS. Press ESC to return to the main menu, select Save, and press ENTER. By default, SYMBOLS is in the Name field.

Caution

Don't use this name–it would replace the entire SYMBOLS file with the ship!

Enter the name **SHIP** as the filename for this image. (Don't enter the extension .PIX; that is automatically supplied by Inset.) Press ENTER.

Importing an Image

Let's use the ship you just clipped from SYMBOLS to create a letterhead. To do this, you'll clear the screen, *import* the image, and position it on the screen.

Start with the SHIP image file displayed on the screen. From the main menu, select Edit; from the Edit choices, select Options. Finally, from the Options choices, select Clear to clear the screen. Inset now suggests a graphics mode option for your screen. Press ENTER to accept the suggested, highlighted value.

Note

In the rest of this chapter, we will use the following format to express a series of command and option selections (like the one in the preceding paragraph): Edit, Options, Clear.

Press ESC to return to the Edit menu, and choose Block, Import. At the request for a filename, press RIGHT ARROW until SHIP is highlighted, and press ENTER. (Or type **SHIP** in the name field.) A rectangle appears on the screen. The cursor, now in the shape of a large plus sign (+), is in the upper-left corner of the rectangle. Use the keypad to move the rectangle to the upper-left corner of the screen. Keep the rectangle a little away from the edges. When the rectangle is positioned to your liking, press ENTER to import the ship image into the screen.

Adding Text to an Image

Now add some text to your letterhead. The letterhead will eventually look like the following:

World Wide Moving
624 Las Juntas Ave.   Martinez, CA 94553
(510) 228 2214

19

The appearance of the text on your screen may not exactly match the illustration, since your graphics board and monitor may be different from ours. However, your screen should be similar.

Press ESC until you are at the main menu, and select Edit, Text. As you can see, you have a variety of options at this point. You're going to enter text, but first let's pick a font. Select Font, and then Load. A list of fonts appears below the entry field. For this example, choose Roman. (In this example, text width and height are 1X.)

Now use the keypad to place the cursor so you can enter the text shown in the letterhead illustration. (Don't worry about placing the text in exactly the right position; you can easily adjust your entries later.) Use the keyboard letter keys to enter the text for the top line, **World Wide Moving**, and press ENTER to end text entry. If necessary, use the keypad keys now to adjust the position of the text. With the first line of text in the proper position, press the ESC key to get to the Text options. Select Accept to accept the text as displayed; it can no longer be edited. (You can, however, erase it and start over.)

To add the remaining text, select the Enter option and type the second line of the letterhead. When the text is in the proper position, press the ESC key to return to the options line, and choose Accept again to make the text permanent. Finally, return to the Text options and select Italic. Then enter the phone number, as shown in the illustration. Make sure the text is in the correct position, press ESC, and select Accept.

Here is a summary of the text entry features you've used up to now:

- Use standard procedures to enter upper- and lowercase letters.

- At any point during text entry (before using Accept), you can use the keypad to move an entire entry to the position you want.

- Press ESC to go to the menu lines. Before you select Text, Accept, you can use the Font, Height, Width, and Direction options to change the text's appearance, or select Undo and start over.

- Select Text, Accept to accept a text entry as displayed. Then you can select Enter to add additional text.

With the text lines of the letterhead entered, you're ready to add the long rule that sets off the letterhead (text and ship logo) from the rest of the page.

Looking at the illustration, you can see that this rule is wider than a standard line drawn on the screen. Here's how to draw a line and set the width: From the main menu, select Edit, Options, Width. From the Width options, choose 3 (for three times standard width) and press ENTER. Press ESC to return to the Edit options and choose Line. Move the cursor to the position where your line will begin and press ENTER. Press and hold down RIGHT ARROW to draw the line (at this point, it's still narrow). Press ENTER to end the line, and it will then change to the width you specified. At this point, you can move the cursor to a new position, press ENTER, and begin drawing another line.

Tip

Lines do not have to be only horizontal or vertical. After you press ENTER to set a starting point, you can move the cursor to any point on the screen, and the line always connects the starting point with the cursor. Pressing ENTER a second time determines the other end-point of the line. When your lines are complete, press ESC. This accepts the lines and returns you to the Text options.

After drawing the rule, press ESC to return to the main menu. Your letterhead is now complete. Select Save, choose the filename SHIP, and press ENTER to accept the default option, Replace. If you want to keep the SHIP file for future use as it is, enter a new name such as LTRHEAD for the letterhead just created.

Printing an Image

Now you will print the letterhead. With the letterhead displayed, select Print from the main menu. The Print options are displayed. Adjust your paper appropriately, using the options provided. Once everything is set, select Go to begin printing. When printing is complete, select Print again, and choose the Formfeed option to advance the paper to the beginning of the next page.

Note

If a border is printed around the letterhead, use the Modify, Border option to toggle the border off, as explained in the later section about Inset's Modify commands.

19

Creating a Bar Graph

To gain experience with a few more of Inset's commands, let's create a simple bar graph. First, using the procedure described earlier, save whatever image you have on the screen (if necessary). Then, start from the main menu and select Edit, Options, Clear and press ENTER. A list of graphics modes is displayed. Press ENTER to select the suggested, highlighted mode, and then ESC to return to the main menu.

Here is the bar chart you'll create:

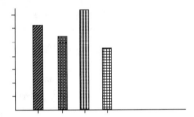

The first step is to create the horizontal and vertical axes. Start by resetting the line width to 1; select Edit, Options, Width and choose 1. Return to the Edit options and select Line. Move the cursor to the position on your screen for the beginning of the vertical axis and press ENTER. Using DOWN ARROW, draw a line for the vertical axis. End the line by pressing ENTER. Since the horizontal axis starts at the same point, press ENTER again without moving the cursor. Then use RIGHT ARROW to draw the horizontal axis and press ENTER when the line is the length you want.

Now you can add the tall rectangles that represent the vertical bars for the graph. Press ESC to return to the Edit menu. Display the Edit options and select Rect. You are asked if you wish to fill in a pattern; select Yes. You now see a choice of 16 patterns to fill the rectangle. As you highlight the choices, a description below the menu gives the name of the pattern or shows the symbols that will be used to make the pattern. Choose a pattern and press ENTER. (Don't worry about trying to match the fill pattern in the illustration.)

Next, you are asked to choose the primary fill color; select the default value 1 and press ENTER. Then select 0 for the background fill color. You are now back in the screen, ready to create the rectangle. Move the cursor to a position on the horizontal axis where you want to start the first bar, and press ENTER. Using PGUP and RIGHT ARROW, draw the rectangle. Press ENTER and the rectangle fills with the pattern and colors you selected.

Press ESC to return to the Edit menu, and follow the procedure you just used to select a new pattern or color. Return to the screen and draw the next bar. Repeat the procedure until all four bars are in place.

Next, using the Line option, draw the scale marks on the vertical axis. Don't worry about making them exactly the same length; just make sure they're all about the same length and that they occur at even intervals. Then try this technique for making even-length lines: Press ESC to return to the Edit options, and select Erase. Using the Erase option is much the same as drawing a rectangle. Position the cursor, press ENTER, and draw a long rectangle so that it cuts through the scale bars, like this:

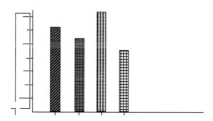

As soon as you press ENTER after drawing the rectangle, everything inside it is erased, leaving the scale marks all the same length. Use this same trick to enter and even up the scale marks on the horizontal axis.

Tip

Experiment with the various options on the Edit menu—use some new ones as well as some you've already tried. You can create circles and ovals and fill them with patterns just as you did the rectangles on the bar chart. If you do detailed drawings, you'll find the Edit, Magnify option useful. And if you have a color monitor, practice with the color options until you are used to how they work.

Converting from ASCII to Graphics

All of the work in this chapter so far has been with graphic images. As stated earlier, an image in ASCII format can be manipulated only after it has been converted to a graphic image. The process is as follows: display the ASCII image, activate Inset by pressing ^SHIFT, and select Edit, Convert. When the conversion to graphics is complete—a few seconds—press ESC, and when asked to save the image, give it a new name. You can then work with the image as you did with the other graphics in this chapter. To try this, leave Inset now and load WordStar; display the CHART file located on the Inset directory, or use a paragraph from one of your WordStar files. Then convert it to a graphics file as outlined in this paragraph.

Using Inset from Within WordStar

Inset is included with WordStar so you can use Inset's graphics capabilities to create images and incorporate them into WordStar files. To illustrate this process, let's use the letterhead you created earlier in Inset. Bringing an Inset file into WordStar works the same, whatever files you use—once you've used Inset to create and edit the image in the required format, you can use WordStar to change the size of the image to suit your file.

Before you bring material into WordStar, it's a good practice to use Inset's Status command (explained later in this chapter) to check the clip lines and other styles you expect. (As an example, see Figure 19-3 later in this chapter.)

Note

Adding an Image to a WordStar File (^P*)

To add an Inset image to a WordStar file, first load the WordStar file. For this example, open a new file and call it LETTER.HED. Position the cursor in the file at the point where you want to place the upper-left corner of the image, and press ^P*. As shown in Figure 19-2, the Insert Graphic dialog box and a directory of the .PIX files are displayed. (This is the directory you assigned to hold graphics files during the Inset installation process.)

To select the file SHIP.PIX, highlight that filename, and with the name in the Filename field, press ENTER. In your file at the position of the cursor, a tag appears showing the path and the name of the .PIX file. (To select a .PIX file from a directory other than the one shown in Figure 19-2, enter the path and the filename in the Filename field.)

Figure 19-2.   *WordStar's Insert Graphic dialog box with listing of .PIX*
                         filenames

```
                              Insert Graphic
                                                                    OK
 Filename:
                                                                   Cancel

 Filenames:          Path: E:\WS7\INSET   9.2M free
    ..            \ | BORDERS.PIX   10k | CAPMSG.TXT    .5k | CHART         .6k
 DINGBATS.PIX 7.5k | DRIVER.LST    6.3k | EGACHART.PIX  34k | EGALOGOS.PIX  38k
 GRAPH.PIX     28k | GRAPH2.PIX     28k | GRAPHICS.DOC 1.5k | IN.SET        .7k
 INSEDIT.TXT  8.7k | INSET.HLP      30k | INSLOAD.TXT  2.0k | LEISURE.PIX  6.4k
 LETTER.BAK    .3k | LETTER.HED     .3k | LOGOS1.PIX   6.6k | LOGOS2.PIX   6.7k
 MAN.PIX      5.4k | PC.PIX        4.6k | PCMAN.PIX    7.2k | PIES.PIX     5.4k
 SHIP.PIX      33k | SHIP.WSG       17k | SPORTS.PIX    11k | SYMBOLS.PIX  5.4k
 TEST.PIX     9.6k | WSILOGO.PCX    37k |
```

Loading Inset from WordStar (^P&)

Before you can view or change the size of the image, you must load Inset.
To do this from within WordStar, press **^P&**. Inset's main menu, the same
one you worked with previously, is displayed at the bottom of the WordStar
screen.

Note

*To work with Inset from within WordStar, you should always use ^P&. If you load
Inset with this command, Inset will automatically be removed from memory when you
press* ESC *to leave Inset. If you are working with Inset outside of WordStar, you should
remove Inset from memory before loading WordStar. To remove Inset from memory,
from the DOS command line type **RI** (for remove Inset) and press* ENTER.

Changing the Size of the Image

When you press **^P&** to load Inset within WordStar, a rectangle appears
on the screen in your WordStar file showing the size and location of your
graphic image. Notice that in the top border of the rectangle, the image size
is indicated in rows and columns.

To change the image size, select Modify and press ENTER. Three options
appear: Image, ReSize, and PreView. Select ReSize and press ENTER. The two
ReSize options are Natural and Scale. Natural allows the size to be changed

19

only in multiples of the current size; Scale lets you change length and width independently. This gives you more flexibility but can cause distortion in the image. For this example, select Scale. Your screen now looks like this:

```
                              WordStar E:\WS7\INSET\LETTER.HED
File    Edit    View    Insert    Style    Layout    Utilities            Help
Body Text                    Draft 10              B   I   U  <*>  L   C   R   J  ‡1



[E:\WS7\INSET\SHIP.PIX] R6 C75                                              ^↑

```

You can use the gray + and – keys on the numeric keypad to make the image as a whole either larger or smaller, or you can use the arrow keys to adjust the length row by row, and the width column by column. Note that the latter process changes the proportions of the image. When the image size is correct, press ENTER to accept the screen display. Or you can press ESC to get back to the main menu and return the image to its original size.

Displaying the Image

There are two ways to view an Inset image in a WordStar file. One way is to select Modify, PreView from the Inset menu at the bottom of the screen. PreView displays the image along with whatever text is on the screen. This lets you check the image and see how any changes you made in its scale affected its appearance. When you are through, press ESC to return to the main menu. The illustration below shows the LETTER.HED file using PreView:

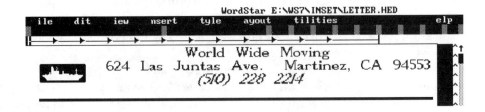

Another method of seeing the image within the file is to exit Inset and use WordStar's Preview feature (^OP). With this method, you will be able to see the image and its position on the page.

Printing a WordStar File with a Graphic Image

After you have previewed your file and the inserted image and are satisfied with its appearance, you can print the file from WordStar just as you print any other WordStar file.

Inset Commands

The rest of this chapter provides descriptions of the commands on Inset's main menu, and most of the command options. With a little experience, you will find Inset a powerful addition to WordStar.

<VIEW> SAVE MODIFY EDIT PRINT OUTPUT HELP
Load Image for Viewing and Modification

Select View to load a graphic image for viewing or modification. You can type a filename or use the arrow keys to select one of the files listed below the file entry line. You can use the wildcards * and ? to limit the files displayed. The indicated path to the .PIX files is the one entered during Inset Setup; the default path is WS\INSET. Notice that you do not have to type the extension .PIX; it is automatically provided by Inset.

VIEW <SAVE> MODIFY EDIT PRINT OUTPUT HELP
Save Screen Image and Modifications

Use Save to save the image on the screen, either initially or after modification. The file is automatically saved in the subdirectory you indicated during Setup (default is WS\INSET), unless you specify another path. When you save a file, the name supplied by default will be the name of the last file you worked with. *Frequently this won't be what you want, so be sure to change the name before you execute the save.* Each time you make modifications to an existing file and choose Save, you will be asked if you wish to replace the existing file. At that time, you can give the file a new name or replace the old file.

19

VIEW SAVE <MODIFY> EDIT PRINT OUTPUT HELP
Clip, Rotate, Expand, Ink, Pass, Border, Status, NoMenu

Any modifications you make to a file using the Modify command affect only the printed output—they cannot be seen on the screen. (Screen changes are discussed in the next section about the Edit command.)

The description line for the Modify command offers the command options, separated by commas. This format lets you know that each option (Clip, Rotate, and so on) has its own set of additional options. Here are brief descriptions of each option:

Clip
Modify Printed Image Bounds

Clip is used to select, or clip, a rectangular section of the screen image.

Rotate
Rotation: Left, Horizontal, Right

Rotate lets you rotate an image 90 degrees left or right. The Horizontal option means standard (portrait) orientation.

Expand
Expansion Sizes: 1x, 2x, 3x, 4x, 5x, 6x, Cols, Inches

Expand lets you change the size of your picture when it is printed. You can expand it from one to six times its size, or set the dimensions in columns and rows, or set the width and height in inches.

Ink
Ink: Standard, Invert, B&W, Table

The Ink option lets you select colors or shades of gray, depending on your printer. Invert is a toggle that switches the background (screen) and text colors—for example, white text on a black background becomes black text on a white background. Table is the option that selects the color intensity for a color printer or shades of gray for a black/white printer.

Pass
Single, Double Printer Graphic Pass

Pass determines how many times, once (Single) or twice (Double), the printer passes over the image. For final images you will most likely use Double for a darker result. For preliminary output, Single prints more quickly.

Border
Border Print Control: Yes, No

Selecting Yes for the Border option places a rectangle around the image.

Status
View Status of Modifications

Selecting Status provides some statistical data about the image, as well as shows the clip lines for the picture. This is very useful for previewing files. Sample status information for SHIP is shown in Figure 19-3.

NoMenu
No Menu Until Next Key

Selecting NoMenu is useful for viewing a full-screen image. The menu and description lines are eliminated from the screen to allow more room for the image. The menu lines return when you press any key.

Figure 19-3.   *Screen display from Inset's Modify, Status option, showing clip lines*

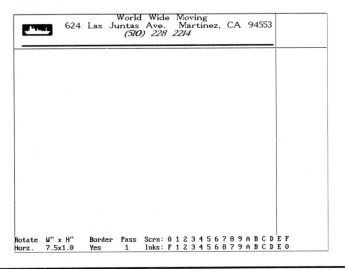

19

VIEW SAVE MODIFY <EDIT> PRINT OUTPUT HELP
Line, Rect, Circle, Dots, Magnify, Text, Block, Fill, Erase, Options

Edit is used to create original artwork, as well as to edit or enhance clip art. As with Modify, Edit provides you with a series of options.

Line, Rect, Circle, Dots
Draw Line, Rectangle, Circle/Oval, Dots - Freehand

The Line, Rectangle, Circle, and Dots options are used to create free-hand charts, graphs, or any type of drawing you want. Using Dots, you can create very detailed drawings.

Magnify
Magnify for Close-up Work

Using Magnify, you can enlarge a section of your artwork to do very detailed work. This option is generally used to add or delete individual dots.

Text
Text, Dir, Height, Width, Italic, Font

With Edit, Text you can add text to an existing clip art file or to one that you create. Text also provides several font options. Either before or after entering the text, but before accepting it, you can select one of the Text options from the description line and see what effect it has on the image.

Block
Copy, Move, Import

Edit, Block allows you to import a section of one file and place it in another. With the Block options you can mark a section of a screen and move it or copy it to another part of the screen. Selecting Import displays the same option line at the bottom of the screen as View. Select the second image you want displayed on the screen and press ENTER. You can now create a new image by modifying the two images on the screen.

Fill
Fill Enclosed Area with Color

Using Fill you can fill rectangles, circles, or ovals with a variety of patterns and colors.

Erase
Erase Dots

Erase allows you to quickly erase complete sections or individual dots of an image.

Options
Draw_Clr, Eras_Clr, Palette, Width, Clear

The Edit, Options choices let you set line width, change colors, and change the mode for your drawings (mode refers to the type of graphics adapter). The Clear option erases a graphics screen in preparation for the next drawing.

VIEW SAVE MODIFY EDIT <PRINT> OUTPUT HELP
Go, Margin, Formfeed, Down, Up, TOF

With the options of the Print command, you can position your paper before printing. You can set the left margin; move the paper down and up (the Up option produces reverse line feed, if that is supported by your printer); or move to the top of the next form (TOF). When the paper is properly positioned, select Go to begin printing.

VIEW SAVE MODIFY EDIT PRINT <OUTPUT> HELP
Offset, Pitch, Quality, Driver, Fast

The Output command is used to set print options when you are printing from Inset rather than WordStar. It presents several options.

Offset
Relative Column Offset of .PIX tags

Offset allows you to set the distance between images printed on the same piece of paper. If you are working in WordStar, you accomplish this by positioning a graphics tag. From within Inset, you use the Offset command to position files printed on the same page.

19

Pitch
Printer Pitch

Pitch allows you to change the printer pitch, or type size.

Quality
Draft/Letter Quality Graphics

The Quality option lets you change the output quality (to either draft or letter quality) from the default value you entered in Setup.

Driver
Modify Printer Driver

If you have more than one printer available, the Driver option allows you to change from the default printer.

Fast
Automatically Create .FST Files: Yes No

Fast lets you turn on or off the creation of .FST files. These files are created when an image is printed; they make subsequent printings of the same file two to ten times faster. If modifications are made to an image, the .FST file is not used.

Note

The .FST files take up considerable space; if that is a consideration on your disk, you can turn off the creation of these files here. (You can also set the .FST option in Setup to No.)

VIEW SAVE MODIFY EDIT PRINT OUTPUT <HELP>
Help-Overview

The Help command allows you to get help on any of Inset's commands, by highlighting the command and pressing F1. Help gives you additional information on each command that is displayed.

Exercises

1. Select an image from one of Inset's clip art files and create a personal logo. Use the Modify, Border option to place a border around the heading.

2. Use Inset to erase the text from the LETTER.HED file. Then experiment with entering the letterhead text using different fonts.

3. Use Inset to convert and save to a graphics file the table of function keys you created in Exercise 2 of Chapter 16.

4. Load the file from Exercise 3 into WordStar. Change the image size, first by using the gray + and – keys and then by using arrow keys. View the image from both Inset and WordStar Preview.

5. Label the bar chart you created in this chapter "Widget Sales by Region." Enter units from 0 to 50 on the vertical axis, and regions A, B, C, and D on the horizontal axis. Experiment with using different fonts and different type sizes for the labels.

6. Design a graphical pie chart and incorporate it into a report printed using newspaper-style columns.

20

ProFinder

The ProFinder feature was introduced with WordStar 5. ProFinder makes it easy to organize and work with the files on your hard disk—not just WordStar files, but any files. ProFinder performs functions you've probably wished DOS would do and wondered why it doesn't. With ProFinder you can

- Select groups of files to copy, move, or delete
- Sort files on a directory by filename, extension, time/date, or size
- Search all files in a subdirectory for specified text or title
- View the contents of a WordStar or ASCII file
- Create your own menu

ProFinder can be used with floppy disks, but its primary function is to organize your hard disk files.

Getting Started with ProFinder

ProFinder is automatically initialized when it is installed using WordStar's WSSETUP program. If you move ProFinder to another directory, run the ProFinder installation program PFINST.EXE and enter the name of the new directory. At any rate, be sure ProFinder is on a directory that is included in your PATH statement, so you can load it from anywhere on your hard disk. (A discussion on paths is in Appendix D.)

To run ProFinder, type **PF** and press ENTER. (If you placed the PF files on a subdirectory other than WS, the first time you type **PF**, a screen message will ask you where the PF files are located. Enter the subdirectory name in the dialog box provided and press ENTER.) The screen displays the current directory along with some other information, as shown in Figure 20-1.

Figure 20-1.   The ProFinder screen

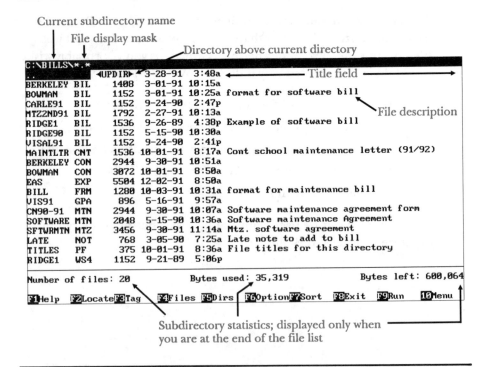

Notice the display of each function key's role, listed at the bottom of the screen. You will learn about each of these operations later in the chapter. With your experience in WordStar, you will find ProFinder easy to use. Both use the same commands to perform the same functions.

Note

The mouse cannot be used with ProFinder.

Moving About the File List

Once you open ProFinder, the screen displays the files on the current directory. In Figure 20-1 you can see the cursor positioned at the ▶UPDIR◀ selection (beside the .., which signifies the UP directory) near the top of the screen, waiting for your command. As you might expect, you use the standard WordStar commands for moving about the file list. Table 20-1 summarizes the keypad and WordStar commands used for cursor movement in ProFinder.

Table 20-1.   *Keypad and WordStar Commands for Cursor Movement in ProFinder*

Keypad Command	WordStar Command	Function in ProFinder
UP ARROW	^E	Scrolls up one filename
DOWN ARROW	^X	Scrolls down one filename
PGUP	^R	Scrolls up one screen
PGDN	^C	Scrolls down one screen
HOME	^QE	Moves the highlight to the top of the screen
END	^QX	Moves the highlight to the bottom of the screen
CTRL-HOME	^QR	Moves the highlight to the beginning of the list
CTRL-END	^QC	Moves the highlight to the end of the list
	^Z	Scrolls the screen up one filename
	^W	Scrolls the screen down one filename

20

Table 20-2 lists additional key commands for working in the ProFinder screen.

Table 20-2.   *Key Commands in the ProFinder File List Screen*

Key	Command Description
ENTER	Pressing ENTER with a directory name highlighted displays the file list for that directory. Pressing ENTER with a filename highlighted displays that file.
. (period)	Moves you to the directory above the current directory (this is UPDIR).
A Z	Pressing a single letter key moves the cursor to the next filename starting with that letter.
SHIFT-A Z	SHIFT plus a letter key moves the cursor back to the last filename starting with that letter.
RIGHT-ARROW	Moves the cursor to the title field.
F1 F10	Pressing a function (F) key selects the ProFinder function associated with that key.
TAB	Toggles the cursor between the file list and the title field.
ESC	In general, moves the cursor to your previous command position. From the file list, ESC exits to DOS in the directory you were in when ProFinder was loaded. If the cursor is in a dialog box, ESC returns it to the previous dialog box.
\	Presents a dialog box for you to enter a path and lets you restrict which filenames are displayed in the file list. For example, *.DOC displays only files with the extension .DOC in the current directory.
* (asterisk)	Lists all files on the current directory (and ends the restrictions entered with \).
: (colon)	Displays a dialog box showing the current disk drive and lets you enter the appropriate letter for a new drive.

Using the Title Field

An eight-character filename plus a three-character extension doesn't say very much about the contents of a file. Therefore, ProFinder's file list has a *title field* in which you can enter a file description (sometimes called a *file title*) up to 39 characters; some examples appear in Figure 20-1.

Follow these guidelines for using the title field:

- Move to the title field by pressing TAB or RIGHT ARROW.
- Type your entry using the standard WordStar editing features.
- Use the INS key to toggle between insert and overtype modes, just as you do in WordStar. Try it now, and notice that in insert mode, the shape of the cursor changes.
- To move from the title field back to the filename column, press ENTER, ESC, or TAB.

Using the Hot Keys (Gray + and – on the Keypad)

A *hot key* is a key that takes immediate action when you press it. There are two hot keys in ProFinder—Flip and Copy, the gray + and – keys, respectively, at the right side of the numeric keypad. Flip switches between WordStar and ProFinder. Copy writes a selected block of information from a file in Pro-Finder to a file in WordStar.

Flip (Gray + Key)

To use the Flip (gray +) hot key, use the ProFinder functions (you'll be learning these shortly) to locate the file you want to edit with WordStar. Highlight the filename in the file list and press the gray + key. WordStar is then loaded, along with the selected file, with the cursor at the beginning of the file where you can proceed with the editing. At any time, you can switch back to ProFinder by pressing the Flip key again.

If you use this Flip method to enter WordStar while in ProFinder, keep in mind the following save/exit rules:

- Pressing the Flip key toggles you back and forth between WordStar and ProFinder.

20

- If you save a file and exit WordStar, you return to ProFinder.
- To exit ProFinder, you must first close and exit WordStar—not just close the file and return to the WordStar Opening screen.
- To open a new file using the Flip key, you must close the current file and exit WordStar. You will be back in ProFinder, where you can highlight a file and then flip to WordStar.

Copy (Gray – Key)

The Copy (gray –) hot key is used to copy files or blocks of data from a file in ProFinder into the file you are editing with WordStar. While in ProFinder you can block a portion of a file, flip back to WordStar with the gray + key, and then press the gray – key to transfer the blocked material into your WordStar file. Here are the steps:

1. Open a file in WordStar using the Flip hot key.
2. Flip to ProFinder, view the file, and block the material to be transferred (you'll learn how to do this shortly).
3. Flip back to WordStar.
4. Position the cursor where you want the block copied, and press the gray – key to copy the block.

You can also use the Copy hot key to copy an entire file into the WordStar file being edited, as follows:

1. To copy an entire file, in ProFinder highlight the filename to be copied.
2. Return to WordStar and press ^KR. Then press the Copy hot key; the highlighted filename is placed in the Insert File window.
3. Press ENTER and the file is copied.

Working with ProFinder Functions

With many of ProFinder's functions, an option window or dialog box is displayed, listing choices or requesting information. Keep the following in mind as you make selections from the option windows:

- To select an option, type the first letter of its description, or use UP ARROW and DOWN ARROW to highlight the option and press ENTER to accept it.

- If the option is a toggle (offers yes or no), press the first letter of the option to toggle between yes and no. You can also use UP ARROW or DOWN ARROW to highlight the option and then press ENTER to toggle between yes and no.

- In some cases, selecting an option will open another option window (there may be several). The guidelines offered here apply to all the option windows.

- You can make a selection only from the last option window opened.

- Selecting an option in the most recent option window or pressing ESC in any option window returns you to the previous window.

Now let's look at each of ProFinder's functions.

View (ENTER)

With the View function you can call up any file in WordStar or ASCII format. To view a file, highlight the filename in the ProFinder file list and press ENTER. Your screen will look similar to Figure 20-2.

View allows you to display a WordStar or other file quickly, and perform a variety of functions, such as

- Move blocks of text to other files
- Write blocks of text to the disk
- View up to three files at a time
- Locate specific text in a file

With a file displayed, press F1 to display the Help window. This window, as shown in Figure 20-3, shows the WordStar commands that are available to review the displayed file.

20

Figure 20-2.   *The file display in ProFinder*

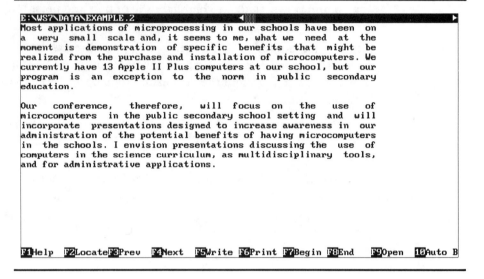

```
E:\WS7\DATA\EXAMPLE.2                      ◄█        ►
Most applications of microprocessing in our schools have been  on
a  very  small  scale and, it seems to me, what we  need  at  the
moment  is  demonstration  of  specific  benefits  that  might  be
realized from the purchase and installation of microcomputers. We
currently have 13 Apple II Plus computers at our school, but  our
program  is  an  exception  to  the  norm  in  public   secondary
education.

Our   conference,   therefore,   will  focus  on  the   use   of
microcomputers  in the public secondary school setting  and  will
incorporate  presentations designed to increase awareness in  our
administration of the potential benefits of having microcomputers
in  the schools. I envision presentations discussing the  use  of
computers in the science curriculum, as multidisciplinary  tools,
and for administrative applications.
```

`F1`Help `F2`Locate`F3`Prev `F4`Next `F5`Write `F6`Print `F7`Begin `F8`End   `F9`Open `10`Auto B

Figure 20-3.   *ProFinder's Help menu while viewing a file*

```
┌──────────────────────── Help ────────────────────────┐
│ You can use these keys while you are viewing the file:│
│                                                        │
│ ←  or ^S  - Previous char  ║ F1 or ^J  - Help          │
│ →  or ^D  - Next char      ║ F2 or ^QF - Find text      │
│ ^← or ^A  - Previous word  ║ F3 or ^QV - Find previous  │
│ ^→ or ^F  - Next word      ║ F4 or ^L  - Find next      │
│ ↑  or ^E  - Previous line  ║ F5 or ^KW - Write block    │
│ ↓  or ^X  - Next line      ║ F6 or ^KP - Print block    │
│ ^QS       - Begin of line  ║ F7 or ^KB - Mark begin block│
│ ^QD       - End of line    ║ F8 or ^KK - Mark end block │
│ ^Home     - Begin of file  ║ F9 or ^OK - Open another file│
│ ^End      - End of file    ║ F10       - Auto block     │
│ PgUp      - Previous page  ║ ^KH - Hide block           │
│ PgDn      - Next page      ║ ^QR - Begin of file        │
│ Home      - Begin of screen║ ^QC - End of file          │
│ End       - End of screen  ║ ^QG - Toggle file format   │
│ Space     - Next char      ║                            │
│ Backspace - Previous char  ║ ^W - Scroll down           │
│ Tab or ^I - Tab            ║ ^Z - Scroll up             │
└──────────────── Press any key to continue ─────────────┘
```

When you are viewing a file, the function keys are redefined to do the following:

F1 Help	Display available WordStar commands
F2 Locate	Find specified text
F3 Prev	Go to previous occurrence of located text
F4 Next	Go to next occurrence of located text
F5 Write	Write blocked material to disk
F6 Print	Print the file
F7 Begin	Mark beginning of a block
F8 End	Mark end of a block
F9 Open	Open a file (up to three may be opened)
F10 Auto B	Mark the line the cursor is on as a block

Viewing a Second or Third File

To open a second file, press F9. ProFinder prompts you to type a filename (of course, you may also indicate a path for the file). Follow the same steps to open a third file. As you open each additional file, it is automatically allocated to a portion of the screen. You cannot change the portion allocated to each file. Also, you can scroll only in the last file opened. To close the last file opened, press ESC. The cursor is then in the previously opened file, which you can scroll. When you press ESC in the first file opened, the cursor moves back to the file list.

File Format (^QG)

WordStar file format is the default. If you are viewing another type of file and a lot of strange characters appear, press ^QG to cycle the file format to ASCII, WordStar 2000, and back to WordStar. You can then select the best of these three formats. As you will see, WordStar also lets you change the default format.

Help (F1)

To see the help screen, press F1. The help screen lists the ten function keys, F1 through F10. You can select help for any of these function keys by highlighting it and pressing F1. For each function key help screen you select

20

(other than F8 Exit and F9 Run) you can press the F1 key to see additional help screens. Also, as you select the various options of a function, further help screens are available—always by pressing F1.

Locate (F2)

Locate allows you to search files or file titles (descriptions) for specific text. The search can include three strings, or text groups, with up to 20 characters in each group. Press F2 to see the first Locate dialog box:

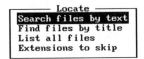

```
        ── Locate ──
  Search files by text
  Find files by title
  List all files
  Extensions to skip
```

Select either of the first two options, and the Text to Locate window is displayed:

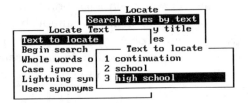

```
                    ── Locate ──
              Search files by text
  ── Locate Text ──    y title
  Text to locate       es
  Begin search    ── Text to locate ──
  Whole words o   1 continuation
  Case ignore     2 school
  Lightning syn   3 high school
  User synonyms
```

In the foregoing Text to Locate window, three different strings (text groups) have been entered; you'll see the result shortly. If you are searching file titles, you can use the whole file title or any portion of it for your search. After you enter the text to locate, press ESC to move to the next window, Locate Text:

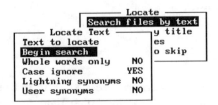

```
                ── Locate ──
          Search files by text
  ── Locate Text ──    y title
  Text to locate       es
  Begin search         o skip
  Whole words only    NO
  Case ignore         YES
  Lightning synonyms  NO
  User synonyms       NO
```

Here you have several toggle options; make your choices, select Begin search, and press ENTER. Your screen looks like Figure 20-4.

Notice that the three search strings appear at the top of the screen. An *x* is printed in the column designated for each string to indicate in which files the strings were found. At this point you can highlight a file and press ENTER to view it, or use the Flip hot key (gray +) to load it with WordStar. Press ESC to return to DOS.

Excluding Files to Search

Often when you do a search using Locate, you are interested only in files that contain data you entered. Therefore, the Locate dialog box offers the option, Extensions to skip. With this option you can limit the files that are searched by choosing filename extensions. Select this option and you'll see that 13 extensions are already listed; you can specify another two. To delete an entry, highlight it and press F3, Clear. To delete all the entries, press F4,

Figure 20-4.   *File list display after doing a search using the Locate function (F2)*

```
C:\LETTERS\CONF91.ANS                                    3 search items in effect
                    school
          continuation ⌐|⌐ high school
FRAME     LET    1664 xx   2-11-91  8:20p Potential buyer
MM-CONT          1152 xx   4-12-91 11:54a
MARK      1      2688 x   10-14-91 11:24a
LABEL     MM      384 x    4-13-91 12:58p
GREG2     LET    1408 x    7-30-91  4:55p
CARLE     LET    1152 xx   3-22-91 10:50a
ERIC      G      1920 x   11-04-91 11:07a
CALBERT3  LET    3712 x    1-13-91  8:06a Calif Dept of Ed
GREG      LET    1280 x   10-22-91 12:33p
BOUTWEL   SEL    2304 xxx  4-02-91 11:29a
YEAREND   LET    1408 x    7-30-91 11:50a End of year letter 89/90
DIGANGI   LET    2688 xx   4-02-91 11:32a
KANATZAR  LET    2432 xx   5-05-91 10:53a
CALDAREL  VNT    1920 xx   5-05-91 10:43a
CCEA      91     2048 xx   4-13-91 12:05p
CNLET     MM     2176 xx   4-16-91 11:35a Conference letter 91
TEMPLEMA  LET    2304 xxx  4-17-91 10:37a
MONTGMRY  LET     768 x    4-17-91 10:40a move letter
CONF91    ANS    1792 xxx  4-22-91  3:59p

Number of files: 69          Bytes used: 162,185          Bytes left: 608,256
F1Help   F2LocateF3Tag   F4Files F5Dirs  F6OptionF7Sort   F8Exit  F9Run   10Menu
```

Zap. You can replace any deleted extension with one of your choice. After using Zap, if you want to reset all the original extensions, press ESC to exit to DOS and then return to ProFinder.

To return to the opening file list, press F2 again and select List all files.

Tag (F3)

To *tag*, or select, a file or group of files, use the cursor keys to highlight the filename and press F3. On tagged files you can perform the file functions displayed when the Files key, F4, is pressed (discussed next). Figure 20-5 shows a sample display with tagged files.

If you tag a file in error, return the cursor to the filename and press F3 again. F3 acts as a toggle, tagging and untagging the highlighted file each time the function key is pressed.

Figure 20-5.   *Screen display showing tagged files*

```
C:\BILLS\*.*                        Copyright (c) 1990 WordStar International, Inc.
BERKELEY LTR     1536   9-30-91 10:48a
CARLE'   LTR     1536  10-01-91  5:18p
DELANO   LTR     1536  10-01-91  8:55a
LIDDELL  LTR     1280   3-17-91  1:49p
LIDEL2   LTR     1024   5-10-91 10:16a
VIS91    GPA      896   5-16-91  9:57a
RIDGEVIE LTR     1536  10-01-91  8:27a
VISMTN91          896   9-30-91  7:32p
EASINC   1-2     3456   8-27-91 12:53p
DELAN091 BIL     1152   9-24-90  2:43p
FREMONT4 BIL     1024   8-16-89  5:37p
LATON90  BIL     1280   5-10-91  9:13a
MTZ1ST91 BIL      896   9-30-91 11:12a
BOWMAN   LTR     1792  10-08-91  2:23a
BERKELEY CON     2944   9-30-91 10:51a
SEQUOIA  LTR     1536  10-01-91  9:00a
VALLEJO  LTR     1536   9-30-91 10:46a
SERVICE  SCH     1152   3-28-91  5:25a
VIS91    TRN     1024   5-16-91 10:01a
MAINTLTR CNT     1536  10-01-91  8:17a Cont school maintenance letter (91/92)
BOWMAN   CON     3072  10-01-91  8:50a

Number of files: 53          Bytes used: 89,975          Bytes left: 608,256
F1Help  F2Locate F3Tag  F4Files F5Dirs  F6Option F7Sort  F8Exit  F9Run  10Menu
```

Files (F4)

When you select F4, the following dialog box is displayed, showing the Files options available with ProFinder. Some of these commands are familiar from DOS. The rest are only available in ProFinder.

Copy and Move/Rename Files

Copy or Move copies or moves the tagged files to the subdirectory you select. It opens a dialog box, where you enter the directory to which you want to copy or move the files. Move copies the files to a new directory or disk and deletes them from the original directory in a single operation.

The Move/Rename command serves a double function. To rename a file, tag the file and press F4. Select Move/Rename. In the Move To window, enter the new filename and press ENTER. Use standard DOS naming rules.

Delete Files

Select Delete to delete all tagged files. If you have not tagged any files, you can still delete a file by entering its name in the Files to Delete window. You can also delete a file in another directory on another disk by indicating a path with the filename. When you select Delete and press ENTER, deleting begins immediately.

20

Time/Date Stamp

When you tag a file or files and select the Time/date stamp option, you'll see a window where you can enter the date and time. To use the current date and time (as set in DOS) press ENTER. All tagged files will receive the new date and time in all DOS ProFinder listings.

If you select Time/date stamp without tagging files first, a dialog box appears in which you can enter a filename, or use the ? and * wildcards to select groups of files to receive the new time/date stamp.

Print File List

Selecting Print file list prints the file list for all files on the current directory, with the directory summary at the end of the file list. Tagged files are marked with an asterisk (*).

Write Filenames

Selecting Write filenames creates a disk file with a list of the filenames on the current directory. If you tagged files, only tagged files are written to the file; otherwise all filenames in the current directory are included in the list.

When you select Write filenames, a window appears where you enter the filename to which the list will be written, and you can also enter a prefix and/or a suffix of up to 20 characters. You can enter any information you choose, but the primary purpose of the prefix or suffix is to use it with DOS commands that will be used in a batch file.

Go to DOS

Select Go to DOS to exit ProFinder and return to DOS. You can then use any of the DOS commands. Type **Exit** to return to ProFinder. Note that you cannot use Go to DOS if you have used Flip (gray +) to run WordStar.

Caution

When you use the Go to DOS option to return to DOS from ProFinder, do not start any memory-resident programs such as Inset.

Select Tagged Files

The Select tagged files option displays only the tagged files on the screen. To restore the full file list, select List all files.

List All Files

If the file list has been changed to display a particular selection of files, use List all files to restore the complete list.

File Tag by Wildcard

This option lets you use the standard DOS wildcards, * and ?, to tag groups of files. You can then apply any of the File options discussed here.

Retag/Untag All

After you tag files and perform an option on the Files window, the files are no longer tagged. To retag previously tagged files, choose Retag.

Use the Untag all option to remove tags from all files.

Dirs (F5)

F5 gives you a fast, easy way to manage directories. When you press F5, the menu below is displayed. Highlight the option you want and press ENTER.

Create

When you select Create, a window opens where you can enter the name of a directory you wish to create. Type the name and press ENTER.

Rename

When you select Rename, a window opens where you can type the directory whose name you wish to change. Press ENTER, and a second window opens where you type the new directory. Press ENTER and the name is changed.

Delete

When you select Delete, a window opens where you enter the name of the directory you wish to remove. If there are no files in the directory, it is immediately deleted. If there are files in the directory, you are warned the files will be deleted and asked if you wish to continue. Press **D** to delete the files and the directory.

Try all of these Directory command options by creating a directory called XYZ. Rename it to ZYX, then delete it. To see the confirmation process, copy some files to the directory before deleting it.

Options (F6)

The Options function offers several choices, as shown in its initial window display:

```
┌──── Options ────┐
│ Resume          .       │
│ Directory list          │
│ List all files          │
│ Programs only   NO      │
│ Subdirs only    NO      │
│ Titles          YES     │
│ Configure               │
└─────────────────┘
```

Selecting the top option, Resume, has the same effect as pressing ESC—it returns you from the Option menu to the ProFinder file list.

The next five Options selections allow you to determine what files and information are included in the file list. Directory list lets you list files from a different drive or directory, or use the * and ? wildcards to limit the file list. List all files shows all the files in the current directory. The next two toggle options let you list only programs or only subdirectories. The Titles option lets you turn on or off the display of the title field for each listed file. The final option, Configure, is discussed next.

Configure

Selecting Configure on the Options window presents this additional window; its choices are described in the paragraphs that follow.

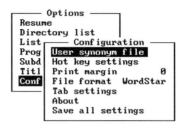

User Synonym File   With this option you can create a user synonym file to use with the ProFinder Locate function. (The default file is named USERSYN.PF.) When you use Locate to search a file for specific text, it will also search for the synonyms you enter in the user synonym file. For example, you might use the word *auto* as your search string. In your synonym file, you could add *car* and *automobile* as synonyms for *auto*.

To enter data into the user synonym file, open it in WordStar as a nondocument file. Then type the search string first, followed by the synonyms, separating the words with commas.

Hot Key Settings   Selecting the Hot key settings option displays a window where you can change the keys used as the Flip and Copy hot keys. The default settings are the gray + key for Flip, and the gray – key for Copy. These settings also include the WS to start WordStar, and "no delay" for the speed at which ProFinder copies blocks in response to the Copy hot key.

Print Margin   Selecting Print margin displays a dialog box where you can change the left margin, measured in columns, used when printing from the View function.

File Format   Selecting File format sets the file format for the View option (F5); the default is WordStar format. Another option is ASCII, which may be better for viewing files created with other programs. A third option is the WordStar 2000 format. Try each of them to see what works best with non-WordStar files.

20

Remember

When viewing a file in ProFinder, you can use ^QG to cycle among WordStar, WordStar 2000, and ASCII file formats.

Tab Settings   This option is primarily used to control the file list display for program files. When you select Tab settings, you see a dialog box showing the default tab settings for the ProFinder file list. You can indicate specific tab settings for lists containing files with three different extensions; the tab settings for .C and .H files are commonly used by programmers, and these are included by default. You can indicate whatever extensions and tabs you like. The tabs set with Others will be used for all files in your display that do not have one of the three specified extensions.

Save All Settings   With this option you can save the changes you made to all the default ProFinder settings you made using the Options, Configurations, or other ProFinder menus. When you select Save all settings, a message appears at the bottom of the screen, "Settings have been saved—Press any key."

Sort (F7)

The Sort function lets you sort the file list for a directory in a variety of ways. Pressing F7 displays the Sort and the Order windows as shown below:

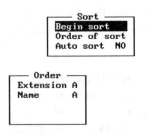

The Order window shows the order in which the file list will be sorted when you select Begin sort. The default order is first by filename extension and then by filename, both in ascending alphabetical order; this is probably the most commonly requested sort order. Highlight Begin sort and press ENTER, and the file list will be placed in that order. Try it.

To sort the filenames in a different order, select Order of sort from the Sort window and press ENTER. A second Order window is displayed.

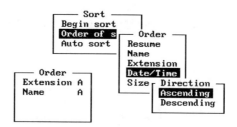

Select one of the five options there and press ENTER again; the Direction window is displayed. Choose Ascending (A to Z) or Descending (Z to A), press ENTER, and your selection is displayed in the Order window—in this example, "Date/Time A." Press ENTER two more times to select Resume in the Order window and Begin sort in the Sort window. In a fraction of a second, your filenames are displayed in ascending order by Date/Time.

Notice in the preceding illustration that the Sort window has the option, Auto sort. This is a Yes/No toggle that you can change by pressing ENTER or pressing **A**. If you choose Yes for this option, when you change subdirectories the filenames will be sorted according to the display in the Order window.

Tip

After you specify your sort options, you can select Options (F6), choose Configuration, and then choose Save all settings; then, whenever you load ProFinder in the future, your directory will be sorted according to the sort options you saved. Also, you can use the ProFinder installation program to change the default sort values.

Exit (F8)

Press F8 to exit from ProFinder to DOS in the current directory. (Press ESC to exit to DOS in the directory you were in when you started ProFinder.)

Note

If you started WordStar using the Flip hot key, you must close any open file and exit WordStar before exiting ProFinder.

20

Run (F9)

You cannot use the Run command if you started WordStar using the Flip hot key.

The Run command gives you two methods for running a program.

- To run an executable program (one with the extension .COM, .EXE, or .BAT) listed in the ProFinder file list, just highlight the program and press F9.
- To run a program with an extension listed in the ProFinder file called EXTLIST.PF, highlight the filename and press F9. The extensions included in EXTLIST.PF are .WKS and .DOC. If you select a .WKS file and press F9, Lotus 1-2-3 is loaded and the program is run. If you select a .DOC file and press F9, WordStar is loaded and the file is displayed, ready for editing.

Menu (F10)

The Menu option allows you to design your own menu. Let's start by looking at the Sample Menu that comes with ProFinder. Press F10 and the following menu is presented:

```
———— Sample Menu ————
Documents
——————— Inset ————————
Inset
Remove Inset
———— PC Outline ————
Normal version
Small version
——————— Other ————————
Lotus
Quit
```

ProFinder's menu option can be helpful to a WordStar user in a couple of ways. Besides WordStar and its companion programs, MailList and TelMerge, you might also use a database package, a spreadsheet, and other programs that are not necessarily associated with WordStar. The menu you

create here in Profinder will let you load and run any program. When you
have finished with the program selected from the menu, you can automatically return to ProFinder's menu if you wish. You can also use the menu to
transfer to a subdirectory and display the file list in a predetermined order.

Selecting from the Menu

To select one of the titles displayed in bold on the screen, press the first
letter of the title, or use the arrow keys to highlight the title and then press
ENTER.

Some programs, such as Inset, are designed to stay in memory when you
exit them. Having Inset in memory allows you to rapidly move back and forth
between Inset and other programs. Sometimes, though, all your memory is
required for a particular function. At such times you can remove Inset from
memory by selecting Remove Inset from the menu.

Understanding the Menu Program

Now let's look at the program file, USERMENU.PF, that produces the
menu. To display it on your screen, highlight it on ProFinder's file list and
press ENTER. Here is a printout of USERMENU.PF:

```
>Sample Menu
Documents,      /k=":c{enter}{F3}\doc{enter}{F7}{enter}"
<------ Inset -------
Inset,          c:
                cd \ws\inset
                inset
                pf ~d~p
Remove Inset,   c:
                cd \ws\inset
                ri
                pf ~d~p
<---- PC Outline ----
Normal version,c:
                cd \pco
                pco /r
                pf ~d~p
Small version,  c:
                cd \pco
                pco /r /m=20
                pf ~d~p
```

```
<------ Other -------
Lotus,          c:
                cd \lotus
                123
                pf ~d~p
Quit,           /m=quitmenu.pf
```

This program listing may look intimidating, but all you need to do to create your own version of the menu is to make a few easy substitutions. The program contains these two basic elements, which are explained in the paragraphs that follow:

- The display elements that show up on the screen
- The commands that tell ProFinder and/or DOS what to do when you make a selection

Menu Program Display Elements   First let's consider the part of the program that produces the menu display. Notice the symbols > (greater than) and < (less than) in column 1. The symbol > tells ProFinder that this is the menu title and it should be centered; this symbol must be in column 1. The symbol < denotes a section of the screen display. It is not displayed in boldface and cannot be selected. This symbol, too, must be in column 1.

Now consider the words on the menu, such as Inset, that are the items to be selected. These items, also, must have entries in the program starting in column 1. Items to be selected can be directory names, program names, functions, and so on. These selections require ProFinder or DOS commands, or both, to be executed.

Menu Program Commands   In the USERMENU.PF program you'll also find the ProFinder and DOS commands that are carried out when a menu selection is made. We'll begin with the ProFinder commands /k and /m:

- The command /k, in the second line of the program, closes the ProFinder menu and performs the functions specified after the /k command. The following illustration explains the action of /k, using the second line of the program as an example:

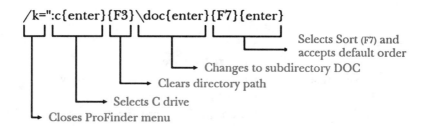

- The command /m, in the last line of the program, tells ProFinder to close the current menu and display the menu specified after the equal sign—in this case, the menu called QUITMENU.PF. (To see the effect of the /m command, press **Q** from the Sample Menu. You will see the Quit menu, called Exit to, on the screen.)

Note

If you want to examine the program for the Exit to menu, you can open the file called QUITMENU.PF in WordStar. Any time you open an executable program file, be sure to open it in Nondocument mode. If you make a mistake and open the program in Document mode, abandon it; don't save it.

Two additional ProFinder commands, ˜d and ˜p, are used in the USERMENU.PF program:

- The ˜d command represents the current drive letter and a colon.
- The ˜p command represents the current directory path.

The purpose of these two commands is to store the current drive and path. In this way, when you select an option that changes the current drive or path, ProFinder knows how to find its way back to the current directory when the operation you perform is complete.

Now let's look at the DOS commands that are involved in loading and running a program from the Sample Menu. Take another look at the listing of the USERMENU.PF program, and you'll see the command sequence is the

20

same for any program selection on the menu. Here is the command sequence for Inset:

Command	Function
c:	Change to drive C
cd\ws\inset	Change to the Inset subdirectory
inset	Load Inset
pf ~d~p	When finished with Inset, return to the ProFinder menu

For each of the other menu selections, the format is the same; only the directory name and the program name are changed.

Modifying the Sample Menu

Now let's go through the process of modifying the menu program to produce a useful menu; you can then use this procedure to create your own menu. In this example, called Walt's Menu, we'll add the following items so you can access them from the menu: WordStar; the database program Q & A; the Multiplan spreadsheet program; and the three subdirectories, Book, Games, and Letters. Here is the modified USERMENU.PF program, followed by the detailed steps to change it:

```
>Walt,s Menu
Book,          /k=":e{enter} {F3}\book{enter}{F7} {enter}"
Games,         /k=":c{enter} {F3}\games{enter}{F7} {enter}"
Letters,       /k=":c{enter} {F3}\letters{enter}{F7} {enter}"
<------- Inset ---------
Inset,         c:
               cd \ws\inset
               inset
               pf ~d~p
Remove Inset, c:
               cd \ws\inset
               ri
               pf ~d~p
<------ WordStar -------
WordStar,      c:
               cd \book
               ws
               pf ~d~p
```

```
<------ Multiplan ------
Plan,          c:
               cd\mp
               mp
               pf ~d~p
<-------- Q&A ----------
Q&A,           c:
               cd \QA
               QA
               pf ~d~p
<----- End Session -----
End,           /m=quitmenu.pf
```

The following steps were taken to change USERMENU.PF so it displays Walt's Menu. As you go through the steps, refer to the program listing above, and the illustration of Walt's Menu shown later in this section.

1. Open USERMENU.PF in WordStar as a nondocument.

2. Change the menu name, Sample, to the name you want for your menu (in this case, **Walt's**).

3. Insert a blank line and in that line enter the first directory's data, beginning with the Book directory.

4. To add additional directories (in this case, Games and Letters), make two copies of the line for Book that you just entered, and then edit the copies for the other directories' requirements.

5. For each program section, substitute new menu section names, program names, and paths. Block and copy one section to make additional sections, editing the material as necessary to include the appropriate names and commands.

6. Change the last section, Quit, to **End Session**. This keeps the first letter of each menu selection unique. (When multiple items on a menu begin with the same letter, the first of those items will be the one selected when you press that letter. So if you allowed both Q & A and Quit to be selections on the menu, pressing **Q** would always select Q & A. This is also the reason for using Plan as the menu selection for the Multiplan program.)

20

With these changes complete and ProFinder loaded, pressing F10 displays the
new Walt's Menu:

Here are some other things to remember about menu creation in Pro-
Finder:

- Each selection entry (those that appear bold on the screen—for
  example, Letters) must be separated from ProFinder or DOS commands by a comma.

- ProFinder and DOS commands can begin in any column except
  column 1. It is common to have them all start in the same column,
  as shown in the examples in this chapter.

- The strings of dashes used on either side of the menu section titles
  should be the same length, for an aesthetically pleasing menu.

Displaying the Menu from a Batch File

People use their computers and programs in a variety of ways. If you find
that ProFinder's Menu option works well for you, you might want to try
loading it with a batch file. The details of using a batch (.BAT) file are
discussed in your DOS manual, but here is a simple example.

Open a nondocument file with WordStar, and give it the name
MENU.BAT. In the file, enter **pf /m=usermenu.pf**, as in the following
illustration:

Place the file in a subdirectory that's in the PATH statement of your AUTOEXEC.BAT file. Now, whenever you are in DOS, you can type **MENU** and ProFinder will be loaded and the menu you created will be displayed. If you wish, you can place this command in your AUTOEXEC.BAT file, to load and display the menu each time you turn on the computer.

Exercises

1. Use the ProFinder Directory function (F5) to create a subdirectory on your hard disk named Exercise. Use the Tag function to tag the filename for each example from this book that you entered. Then, using Copy in the Files function, copy each example to the Exercise directory.

2. Again using the Files function, delete the example files from their original directory. Then use Move to move the files back to their original directory.

3. Sort the files on the WS subdirectory by extension only in descending alphabetical order.

4. Save the sort order from Exercise 3 and exit ProFinder. Return to ProFinder and check to see that the file list is as you expect. Return the sort order to the default value.

5. If you haven't done so already, modify the Sample menu to create a menu that lets you choose among the programs you work with.

20

A

New and Modified Commands and Mouse Support in Version 7.0

This appendix lists commands and topics in WordStar 7.0 that are new or have major modifications. These commands and topics are listed in the order in which they are introduced in this book. See Table A-1.

Also new with WordStar 7.0 is the mouse support. A summary of mouse scrolling techniques and mouse shortcuts is also included in this appendix.

WordStar 7.0 Mouse Support

The vertical scroll bar, located along the right side of the screen, is for using the mouse to move forward and backward in a document. The vertical scroll bar contains a slider box that indicates the relative position of the cursor in the file. Table A-2 lists the vertical scroll bar options.

Table A-1.   *New/Revised WordStar Commands and Functions*

New/Revised Command	Chapter	Function/Operation
	1	Operation of lists
	1	EMS support
^OB	3	Hiding dot commands and screen settings
^P	4	Print
.sb	6	Suppress blank lines
^KU		Mark previous block
^KW	7	Write block to an ASCII file
^K<	7	Unmark a block
^Q<	7	Go to next style
.bn n	8	Customized bin names
	9	Fax support
^K], ^K[	11	Copy to/from Windows Clipboard
^M	14	Macros
P (Opening screen)	18	Merge Print
K (Opening screen)	18	Print from Keyboard

Table A-2.   *Using the Mouse with the Vertical Scroll Bar (Courtesy WordStar® International, Inc.)*

Destination	Mouse Action in Vertical Scroll Bar
Previous line	Click ↑
Next line	Click ↓
Previous screen	Click above the slider box
Next screen	Click below the slider box
Beginning of document	Drag the slider box to the top
End of document	Drag the slider box to the bottom
Approximate position in document	Drag the slider box to the relative position in the file

WordStar Mouse Shortcuts

Table A-3 lists mouse shortcuts used to make menu selections.

Table A-3.   *Mouse Shortcuts (Courtesy WordStar® International, Inc.)*

Action	Mouse Shortcut
Change drive/directory at a filenames list	Double-click the directory.
Open a document	Double-click the document name.
Close a document	Double-click the Close File button in the title bar.
Go to a page	Click the page number in the status line. In the Go to Page box, insert a page number.
Go to a marker	Click the marker in the status line.
Go to beginning/end of a block	Click <B> or <K> codes to move cursor to beginning/end of block.
Switch windows	Click in the window.
Select a style bar setting	Click the button in the style bar.

B

WordStar Reference Codes

This appendix lists various reference codes used in WordStar: flag characters (Table B-1), status line messages (Table B-2), and codes for both the standard and extended character sets (Table B-3).

In Nondocument mode, the status line differs from a document status line as follows:

Status Line Element	Difference
Cursor indicator	Because nondocuments have no pages, the indicator shows only line and column numbers. Line number can be as high as 65,535, and column number can be as high as 999. Mouse click on line number opens Go to Line window.
Auto-Indent	Displayed when Auto Indent is on; ^6 switches it on and off. Press TAB or ENTER to position cursor where the first line is to start. All subsequent lines will begin in that column. This is particularly useful for programming languages where indents are common.

Users of the earlier versions of WordStar will no doubt notice several additions to the status line in version 7.0. And several messages have been removed from the status line and now appear on the title bar. They are listed below.

Title Bar Item	Meaning
File Path/Name	Name and location of the file you're editing.
Command	Any command that is in progress.
Replace Y/N	Appears during find and replace operations when you need to decide whether to replace the word at the cursor.
Wait	Displayed in place of the filename during lengthy operations and when WordStar is accessing the disk. If you type quickly while this message is displayed, you may lose some of the characters you type.
Printing	Appears when you are printing in the background.

Table B-1.   *WordStar Flag Characters (Courtesy WordStar® International, Inc.)*

Flag Character	Meaning
<	This line ends with a hard carriage return.
space	A blank space in the flag column means the line ends with a soft carriage return produced by word wrap within a paragraph.
P	This is a page break; a new page begins below this line.

B

Table B-1.   *WordStar Flag Characters (Courtesy WordStar® International, Inc.)*
            (continued)

Flag Character	Meaning
F	This line ends with a form feed produced by the ^PL command.
C	This is a column break.
^	The file ends on or above this line.
+	Text on this line extends beyond the right edge of the screen.
.	The dot command on this line changes the on-screen format and the printout.
:	The dot command on this line changes only the printout.
|	Printing of this blank line at top of a page has been suppressed.
?	The dot command on this line is not recognized by WordStar.
1	The dot command on this line changes the on-screen format and the printout; it works best if it's placed at the beginning of a page.
–	This line ends with a carriage return but without a line feed (produced by ^P ENTER); it will be overprinted by the next line.
J	This line ends with a line feed but without a carriage return (produced by ^PJ); the next line will print on the line below, but may not begin at the left margin.
W	Second window in Nondocument mode.

Table B-2.   *Status Line Messages*

Status Line Message	Meaning
Column	Indicates Column mode.
ColRepl	Indicates Column mode and that Column Replace is on.
123456789	Numbers displayed show which markers are set. (Move cursor to marker with mouse click.)
\<B>\<K>	A block is marked in the file.
Insert INS-off	Insert mode is on; insert toggles on/off by pressing INS key or using a mouse click.
Protect	This document is protected.
Cursor Position	Shows the page, line, vertical position, column number, and distance of the cursor from the left margin. (Mouse click on page number opens Go to Page window.)
±	Two windows are open and mouse is active. Mouse click on ± increases active window one row.

Table B-3.   *ASCII and Extended Character Sets*

ASCII Value	Character	ASCII Value	Character
0	Null	8	◘
1	☻	9	○
2	☺	10	◙
3	♥	11	♂
4	♦	12	♀
5	♣	13	♪
6	♠	14	♫
7	•	15	☼

B

Table B-3.   *ASCII and Extended Character Sets* (continued)

ASCII Value	Character	ASCII Value	Character
16	▶	48	0
17	◀	49	1
18	↕	50	2
19	‼	51	3
20	¶	52	4
21	§	53	5
22	▬	54	6
23	↨	55	7
24	↑	56	8
25	↓	57	9
26	→	58	:
27	←	59	;
28	∟	60	<
29	↔	61	=
30	▲	62	>
31	▼	63	?
32	Space	64	@
33	!	65	A
34	"	66	B
35	#	67	C
36	$	68	D
37	%	69	E
38	&	70	F
39	'	71	G
40	(	72	H
41	)	73	I
42	*	74	J
43	+	75	K
44	,	76	L
45	-	77	M
46	.	78	N
47	/	79	O

Table B-3.   *ASCII and Extended Character Sets* (continued)

ASCII Value	Character	ASCII Value	Character
80	P	112	p
81	Q	113	q
82	R	114	r
83	S	115	s
84	T	116	t
85	U	117	u
86	V	118	v
87	W	119	w
88	X	120	x
89	Y	121	y
90	Z	122	z
91	[	123	{
92	\	124	|
93	]	125	}
94	^	126	~
95	_	127	⌂
96	'	128	Ç
97	a	129	ü
98	b	130	é
99	c	131	â
100	d	132	ä
101	e	133	à
102	f	134	å
103	g	135	ç
104	h	136	ê
105	i	137	ë
106	j	138	è
107	k	139	ï
108	l	140	î
109	m	141	ì
110	n	142	Ä
111	o	143	Å

Table B-3.   *ASCII and Extended Character Sets* (continued)

ASCII Value	Character	ASCII Value	Character
144	É	176	▒
145	æ	177	▓
146	Æ	178	▓
147	ô	179	│
148	ö	180	┤
149	ò	181	╡
150	û	182	╢
151	ù	183	╖
152	ÿ	184	╕
153	Ö	185	╣
154	Ü	186	║
155	¢	187	╗
156	£	188	╝
157	¥	189	╜
158	Pt	190	╛
159	ƒ	191	┐
160	á	192	└
161	í	193	┴
162	ó	194	┬
163	ú	195	├
164	ñ	196	─
165	Ñ	197	┼
166	ª	198	╞
167	º	199	╟
168	¿	200	╚
169	⌐	201	╔
170	¬	202	╩
171	½	203	╦
172	¼	204	╠
173	¡	205	═
174	<<	206	╬
175	>>	207	╧

Table B-3.   *ASCII and Extended Character Sets* (continued)

ASCII Value	Character	ASCII Value	Character
208	⊫	232	φ
209	⊤	233	θ
210	π	234	Ω
211	⊔	235	δ
212	∟	236	∞
213	⌐	237	ø
214	π	238	∈
215	╫	239	∩
216	╪	240	≡
217	⌐	241	±
218	⌐	242	≥
219	█	243	≤
220	▬	244	⌠
221	▌	245	⌡
222	▐	246	÷
223	▀	247	≈
224	α	248	°
225	β	249	•
226	Γ	250	·
227	π	251	√
228	Σ	252	η
229	σ	253	^{2}
230	μ	254	■
231	τ	255	(blank 'FF")

C

Customizing WordStar

WordStar comes with most of its options set to the most widely useful values, but it is rare that you won't want to change at least one of the default settings. Fortunately, WordStar 7.0 makes it easy to modify the optional settings, with the WSCHANGE program. These settings can be modified as many times as you like, so feel free to experiment—you can always change the settings again.

The changes made with WSCHANGE do not affect your ability to modify an individual file or setting by using dot commands (discussed throughout this book), or your freedom to use paragraph styles (discussed in Chapter 12).

Loading WSCHANGE

To load WSCHANGE, make sure you are in the subdirectory that contains WordStar, usually the WS subdirectory. Then type **WSCHANGE WS** at the DOS prompt, and press ENTER. With **WS.EXE** highlighted, press ENTER twice. This procedure loads the program WSCHANGE, which in turn loads the WS.EXE file that contains WordStar's operating instructions. The program

WS.EXE is the one that is modified during this process. The screen displays the WSCHANGE main menu, shown in Figure C-1.

Prompted Changes to WordStar

You can use WSCHANGE to make two types of changes to WordStar settings: prompted changes and patches. *Prompted changes* provide a question, and you provide a response that may be a simple yes or no, or a more elaborate answer such as defining a new ruler line. We will explore a few examples of prompted changes here; the process is similar for making other prompted changes.

Patches require that you enter changes in hexadecimal code; this technique is primarily intended for users familiar with programming. Be careful—errors in entering patches can have disastrous and far-reaching effects.

On the WSCHANGE main menu displayed in Figure C-1, you can see a great many changes are possible. Experiment with these options; remember,

Figure C-1.   *WSCHANGE main menu*

```
                      WSCHANGE Main Menu

   A  Console......Monitor              Video attributes
                   Monitor patches      Keyboard patches

   B  Printer......Choose a default printer
                   Change printer name   Printer defaults    Printer interface

   C  Computer.....Disk drives          Operating system    Memory usage
                   WordStar files       Directory display   Patches

   D  WordStar.....Page layout          Editing settings    Help level
                   Spelling checks      Nondocument mode    Indexing
                   Macros               Merge print         Miscellaneous

   E  Patching.....General patches      Reset all settings  Auto-patcher

   X  Finished with installation

   Enter your menu selection...      F1 = Help
                                     ^C = Quit and cancel changes
```

you can always change back to the original settings. For now, to see how to make a prompted change, let's modify the page layout.

Modifying Page Layout

If you commonly use paper with a printed letterhead, or a paper size other than 8 1/2 by 11 inches, you may find it helpful to modify WordStar's page layout settings. To explore this area of WSCHANGE, select **D** from the main menu. From the WordStar menu that appears, select **A**, Page Layout, and the screen will look like Figure C-2.

You have seven page layout options; for this exercise we need to use A, Page size and margins. Press **A**, and you will see a screen like the one in Figure C-3.

You can change any of these default values by selecting the letter in the first column and entering a new value for that item. If you don't want to

Figure C-2.   *Page Layout menu*

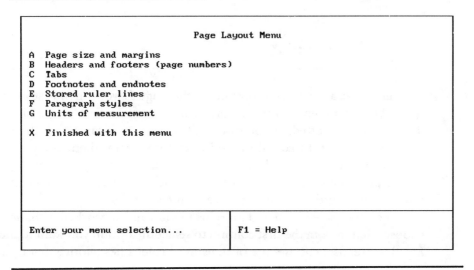

```
                            Page Layout Menu

    A   Page size and margins
    B   Headers and footers (page numbers)
    C   Tabs
    D   Footnotes and endnotes
    E   Stored ruler lines
    F   Paragraph styles
    G   Units of measurement

    X   Finished with this menu




    Enter your menu selection...        F1 = Help
```

Figure C-3.   *Page Sizing and Margins menu*

```
                    Page Sizing and Margins Menu

    A   Page length........................11.00"      INIEDT+18  .pl
    B   Top margin.........................0.50"       INIEDT+14  .mt
    C   Bottom margin......................1.33"       INIEDT+16  .mb
    D   Header margin......................0.33"       INIEDT+1F  .hm
    E   Footer margin......................0.33"       INIEDT+21  .fm
    F   Page offset on even page...........0.80"       INIEDT+24  .poe
    G   Page offset on odd page............0.80"       INIEDT+26  .poo
    H   Left margin........................0.00"       RLRINI     .lm
    I   Right margin.......................6.50"       RLRINI+2   .rm
    J   Paragraph margin (-1 for none).....(none)      RLRINI+4   .pm
    K   Suppress blank lines on/off........OFF         INIEDT+0C  .sb

    X   Finished with this menu




    Enter your menu selection...      |   F1 = Help
```

change a value, press ENTER. Try changing some of these values. When you are through with this section, press **X** to return to the Page Layout menu.

Stored Ruler Lines

Let's look at one more option on the Page Layout menu—stored ruler lines. WordStar comes with ten stored ruler lines. The first four, .rr0 through .rr3, are preformatted, as you saw in Chapter 5. You can set up the last six, .rr4 through .rr9, to contain margins and tabs convenient for your work. Actually, you can modify the first four as well.

To modify any of the ten stored ruler lines, select option E from the Page Layout menu, and you'll see the screen in Figure C-4.

As on the Page Sizing and Margins menu you just worked with, here you choose a letter from the first column to select the option you want to modify. For this exercise, choose one of the stored ruler lines. Notice that option A

Figure C-4.   Stored Ruler Lines menu

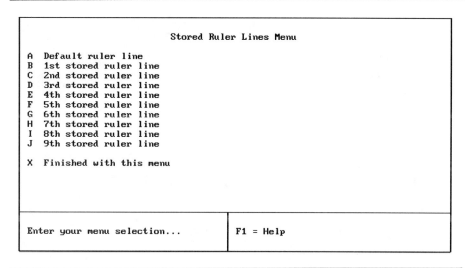

is the default ruler line; if you change this one, all files you open will initially have the margins and tabs you set here.

Once you select a ruler line to modify, your screen will look like Figure C-5. The number of the ruler line you are modifying is shown at the top of the screen.

Initially, ruler lines 4 through 9 (E through J on the Stored Ruler Lines menu) are the same as the default ruler line. To create a ruler line with your own settings, decide on the values you want for each of the items on the menu. Select the key in the first column, and enter the value for that item. You can enter as many regular and decimal tabs as you like. When you have finished making changes, press **X** to retreat through the menus to the main menu. The last question presented will be, "Are you through making changes (Y/N)." Select **Y** to return to DOS.

To see the ruler line you have created, open a file and enter the dot command **.rr#** (where # is the number associated with the ruler line you created).

Figure C-5.   Ruler Line #4 menu

```
                    Ruler Line #4 Menu
A   Left margin.................................0.00"        RLRINI+128
B   Right margin................................6.50"        RLRINI+128+2
C   Paragraph margin (-1 for none)..............(none)       RLRINI+128+4
D   Regular tab stops...........................11           RLRINI+128+8
E   Decimal tab stops...........................0            RLRINI+128+9

X   Finished with this menu




Enter your menu selection...         F1 = Help
```

Automatic File Backup

Unfortunately, power failures do occur, for various reasons. And if this should happen while you are editing a file, all the work you have put into that edit session will be lost, unless the file has been saved to disk. With WSCHANGE, you can set WordStar to save your file automatically whenever the keyboard is inactive for a specific number of seconds that you assign.

To activate this feature, from the WSCHANGE main menu select **D**, for WordStar. At the WordStar menu select **C**, for Other features. From the Other Features menu select **G**, for Miscellaneous. Finally, from the Miscellaneous menu, select **I**, for Auto-backup.

In response to "Enter new value," enter the number of seconds of keyboard inactivity you want WordStar to wait before automatically backing up the file. A reasonable value to enter is 10—you can always change it later if you prefer a longer or shorter time period. Type **10** (or another value) and press ENTER.

Units of Measurement

The default or current measurement setting in WordStar is inches. It is displayed in the status line and in dialog boxes where measurements are set. You can, however, use different measurements for horizontal, vertical, and line height settings, as long as you specify the unit used. WordStar supports page layout measurements in units of inches, columns, centimeters, or points. The symbols used to specify the units are as follows:

Inches	" or **i** or **in**
Columns	**r** (for ruler units)
Line height	**l** (line height and vertical setting)
Centimeters	**c** or **cm**
Points	**p** or **pt** (1 point = 1/72 inch)

Centimeter, column, and point equivalents to an inch are as follows:

1 inch = 2.54 centimeters
1 inch = 72 points
1 inch = 10 columns (default column setting is 1/10 inch)

If you specify in a dialog box a unit of measurement other than the default value, the measurement will automatically convert to the current unit when you press F10. To change the default unit, follow the path through WSCHANGE as explained in the next section.

Path to Additional Default Values

As you have probably concluded, the path through the various WSCHANGE menus to the option you want is not always obvious. The following list gives the path to various default options. Most of these paths lead to options that have no effect on memory. If the option does involve changing a buffer size or adding a new feature, such as definitions, you'll want to be aware of its memory requirements and the memory available for WordStar as well as any memory-resident programs you use.

Here are features you can change, the paths to those features (starting at the WSCHANGE main menu), and the action you take when you arrive at the feature:

Feature	Path	Action
Default Paragraph Style	D/A/F/B	Toggle Yes/No; enter name
Auto Paragraph Align	D/B/C/E	Toggle On/Off
Definitions during Spelling Check	D/C/A/E/D	Toggle On/Off
Font (Alternate)	B/C/H	Type letter to choose a font
Font (Normal)	B/C/G	Type letter to choose a font
Header and Footer Buffer Size	C/C/2/A	Enter value in bytes
Paragraph Styles (Default)	D/A/F/B	Toggle Yes/No; enter name
Personal Dictionary Prompt	D/C/A/E/C	Toggle On/Off
Unerase Buffer Size	C/C/H	Enter value in bytes
Units of Measurement	D/A/G	Select from list
Word Wrap at right margin	D/B/B/A	Toggle On/Off

Return to Default Settings

Feel free to experiment as much as you like with the WSCHANGE program. You can quickly revert to the original default values with these simple steps: From the WSCHANGE main menu, select **E** to see the Patching menu. Press **C** to return all settings to their original values. In response to the next prompt, enter **Y** to confirm your request.

After you have completed a change to WordStar settings, from any point in WSCHANGE you can return to the previous menu by pressing **X**. Continue to press **X** to retrace your path back to the WSCHANGE main menu. At that point you will be asked if you are through making changes. Pressing **Y** for yes returns you to DOS.

D

Essential DOS Commands for WordStar

DOS offers a wide variety of commands; this appendix discusses those that are essential to the efficient use of WordStar. For a complete discussion of DOS, consult your PC-DOS or MS-DOS manual.

Organizing Your Hard Disk

Your hard disk contains 20 or more megabytes of storage space—enough for about 6400 pages of typed material. Because a hard disk has so much storage space, it is useful to divide the disk into smaller units. There are as many ways to organize a hard disk as there are people to do the organizing. What's right is what's convenient and efficient for you. This section points out what you can do and offers a sample layout. You can modify this layout to suit the combination of programs you use and the way you use them.

A hard disk is divided into units called *directories*; you may have as many directories as you like. Directories are further divided into *subdirectories*. The top directory (level 1), from which all other directories branch, is called the *root* directory. Below that, at level 2, are the directories that branch from the root. A diagram of one arrangement is shown here:

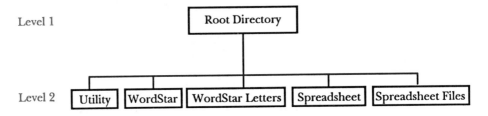

The levels in this diagram can extend downward to include subdirectories branching from subdirectories branching from other subdirectories.

The size of any directory or subdirectory is limited only by the memory on the hard disk. As long as space remains on your disk, new material can be added to any directory.

Naming Directories and Subdirectories

The first step in organizing your disk is to decide on the number and names of your directories and subdirectories. Making a diagram like the one shown earlier is a good idea.

The naming convention for directories and subdirectories is the same as for DOS files: You can use up to eight characters. You can also use three-character extensions, but that is not commonly done. The root directory is designated by the backslash (\) symbol; this name cannot be changed. Using the previous diagram, let's assign some real names:

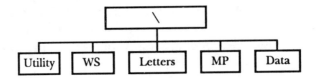

The following is a list of the directories and their contents for this layout:

Directory	Contents
(Root)\	Must contain COMMAND.COM, AUTOEXEC.BAT, and CONFIG.SYS. It will also contain all directories that branch from the root (in our example, all the directories shown).
Utility	All of the DOS commands not in COMMAND.COM and other utilities you may have purchased.
WS	All the WordStar operating programs with the extensions .EXE, .OVR, .DCT, and .SYN.
Letters	WordStar documents you create.
MP	Multiplan operating and data files.
Data	Merge Print master documents and data files.

Creating Directories and Subdirectories (MKDIR or MD)

The command for creating directories and subdirectories is MKDIR or MD (make directory); either form of the command may be used. To make a directory named Letters, at the DOS prompt (C>), type

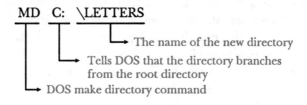

Use the same procedure to create the other directories and subdirectories you have planned.

Changing from One Directory or Subdirectory to Another (CHDIR or CD)

Once you have created your directories and subdirectories, you must be able to move comfortably from one directory to another. The command to do this is CHDIR or CD (change directory); again, either form may be used. You can move directly from any directory or subdirectory at any level to any other directory or subdirectory. To go from a directory at level 2 (the level below the root directory) to the root directory, type **CD**. To move from one directory to another on the same level, type **CD** followed by the name of the directory you are moving to. For example, to move from the Letters directory to the Multiplan directory, type **CD\MP** and press ENTER.

Using Wildcards (* and ?)

Wildcard characters are very useful with WordStar's directory commands. You can filter out groups of files and display only the files you want to work with. Two wildcards are available with DOS: the asterisk (*) and the question mark (?). The ? matches any single character of the filename or extension at the position of the ?. For example, the command DIR WS?.ABC displays all filenames on the current directory that have a three-letter name beginning with WS, have any character in the third position, and have the extension .ABC.

The * matches a group of characters in either the filename or the extension; thus *.* matches all filenames and extensions. For example, WS*.LET matches all filenames starting with WS and ending with the extension .LET; the remaining filename characters (from 0 to 6) could be anything. The command DIR *.BAK would display all files with the extension .BAK, and DIR ???85.* would display all files with any characters in the first three positions followed by 85 and any extension.

Consider how these wildcard characters could be used when you are assigning directory names and filenames. By using the appropriate filters, you can have the directory display only specific groups of files.

Creating a Path for DOS to Follow

Command files are those files on your disk with the extension .COM, .BAT, or .EXE. When you ask your computer to load and execute a command file, it looks for the file on the current directory or subdirectory (the one that you are logged into). If the command file DOS is looking for is not on the current directory, the message "Bad command or file name" will be displayed. The solution to this problem is to build a *path* for DOS to follow that leads it to the command file. To build this path, you use the DOS command, PATH. The PATH command statement is in your AUTOEXEC.BAT file so that it is automatically loaded each time you turn on your computer.

For the hard disk organization diagram shown in this appendix, an appropriate PATH command and path are as follows:

```
PATH=C:\;C:\UTILITY;C:\WS;C:\MP
```

Only directories with command files should be in the path. Also, the Utility directory must be in the path to access FORMAT, BACKUP, or other command files from other directories.

Note the format used by the PATH statement. Each directory name is followed by a semicolon. The drive designation is not essential, but including it is a good habit to get into. With the drive designated, this path will work if you are logged onto the A drive and type **WS** to load WordStar. If the drive is not designated, only the logged drive is searched.

Changing the DOS Prompt

After working with your PC for a while, you will probably accumulate several directories and subdirectories on your hard disk. To make it immediately apparent which directory or subdirectory you are logged into, you can set the DOS prompt by using the DOS PROMPT command.

D

The default DOS prompt is the disk drive letter followed by a > symbol, for example, C>. Using the PROMPT command, you can set the prompt to display the subdirectory you are logged into, as well as the disk drive, for example, C:\>. To accomplish this, first log into the subdirectory that contains the PROMPT command; then type **PROMPT pg** and press ENTER. The **$** symbols are part of the PROMPT command; **p** tells DOS to print the default directory and drive; and **g** tells DOS to print the symbol >. (For a complete discussion of the options available with the PROMPT command, see your DOS manual.)

Tip

The changes to the prompt, as described here, will stay in effect only as long as the computer is turned on. To have this special prompt automatically take effect each time you start the computer, use WordStar in nondocument mode to place the PROMPT command in the AUTOEXEC.BAT file.

This brief discussion of a few DOS commands will be helpful if you are just starting to work with a personal computer. DOS has many other commands, however, that are useful, even essential, in organizing a hard disk for even the most casual user. Read through your DOS manual or one of the secondary source manuals available for DOS—first to get an overview of DOS, and then to learn the specifics of the commands that will be most helpful with your type of work.

Index

389

X